Praise for
THE MARCH ON WASHINGTON

"This book goes beyond Martin Luther King's 'I H~~ave A D~~ ~~m~~'
speech, looking at the role of the l   :s
history. . . . [A] fresh take on ever   n
Washington."   s

"Jones insists that the march was about more than King's famous
speech. . . . [*The March on Washington*] provides an alternative to
the standard account by stressing the part played in the movement by
unions and women's groups."   —Louis Menand, *The New Yorker*

"[A] fresh picture of the movement . . . Jones shows that much we
thought to be intrinsic to the 1960s movement had earlier origins. And
he reminds us that the movement's later victories were not miracles
wrought by King but depended on organizers who had been toiling
locally for decades."   —Benjamin Hedin, *Chicago Tribune*

"Jones thoroughly recovers the radical reality of the events leading up
to the march, as well as the march itself, and exposes the important
question of how such a radical event was so quickly remembered as a
model of moderation."   —Moshe Z. Marvit, *Washington Monthly*

"[A] spellbinding history of the civil rights movement. Characters and
movements come to life with his retelling of this hidden aspect of African American activism. . . . Mr. Jones has done a great public service
making Randolph's story known."
    —Karl Wolff, *New York Journal of Books*

"Jones' work, meticulously researched and eminently fair, does not
paper over the many problems the cause faced. . . . For those familiar

with the broad outlines of the civil rights struggle, Jones' book offers an enlightening and more detailed account. His story illuminates the roles played by Randolph and others."　　　　　　—Jay Strafford,
Richmond Times-Dispatch

"From union leader A. Philip Randolph's initial proposal . . . to how the movement grew in size and political clout during the 1940s, this is a powerful focus that considers individuals and history that few civil rights books cover. The result is a powerful account recommended for any social issues collection."　　　　　　—*Midwest Book Review*

"The main question that arises upon reading this book is, 'Why did it take so long for someone to write it?' Jones has crafted a very readable study of one of the best-known events in US history, the March on Washington."
　　　　—P. B. Levy, *Choice: Current Reviews for Academic Libraries*

"Jones does a remarkable job of canvassing the massive amounts of records . . . and identifying the relationship between labor and social organizations. . . . Anything but a traditional text on the modern civil rights movement."　　　　—Selena Sanderfer, *Park City Daily News*

"At a moment when the March is being widely commemorated, Jones gets past the heroic myths and provides us with the history we need to not just celebrate the march but to *understand* it. This is the single best book on that historic event to date."　　　　　　—Eric Arnesen,
The George Washington University

"A magnificent work of historical reconstruction. . . . Jones provides a rich, robust understanding of the meaning of the March on Washington."
　　　　—Michael Honey, author of *Going Down Jericho Road*

"A masterful history. . . . Will Jones's deeply satisfying book makes the history of the march whole and demonstrates the depth of change its participants embraced."
—Glenda Elizabeth Gilmore,
author of *Defying Dixie*

"One of the great moments in American history becomes fresh again. Peeling away layers of myth, Jones shows the profound radicalism of the March on Washington and its deep roots in a tradition of African American labor struggle."
—Joshua Freeman,
author of *American Empire*

"Finally we have the definitive history of the 1963 March on Washington."
—Judith Stein, author of *Pivotal Decade*

"Jones vividly reassesses the 'forgotten history' of the civil rights movement in this deeply researched investigation. . . . This excellent revisionist account places the march, on its 50th anniversary, in its historical context, while revealing the economic roots of the modern civil rights movement."
—*Library Journal*, starred review

"For those who were there, this is an illuminating book; for those who were not, it will be transporting."
—*Publishers Weekly*

"By refocusing on the jobs agenda of the march, Jones notes that it was relatively easier to allow blacks to have access to seats on buses and at lunch counters than to provide them with access to jobs at restaurants and bus companies. . . . This is an important look at the true significance of the March on Washington."
—*Booklist*

ALSO BY WILLIAM P. JONES

The Tribe of Black Ulysses:
African American Lumber Workers in the Jim Crow South (2005)

THE MARCH
—ON—
WASHINGTON

JOBS, FREEDOM, AND
THE FORGOTTEN HISTORY
OF CIVIL RIGHTS

William P. Jones

W. W. NORTON & COMPANY NEW YORK | LONDON

For Christina

For information about permission to reproduce selections from this book,
write to Permissions, W. W. Norton & Company, Inc.,
500 Fifth Avenue, New York, NY 10110

For information about special discounts for bulk purchases, please contact
W. W. Norton Special Sales at specialsales@wwnorton.com or 800-233-4830

Manufacturing by RR Donnelley, Harrisonburg
Book design by Dana Sloan
Production manager: Devon Zahn

Library of Congress Cataloging-in-Publication Data

Jones, William Powell, 1970–
The March on Washington : jobs, freedom, and the forgotten history of civil
rights / William P. Jones. — First Edition.
pages cm
Includes bibliographical references and index.
ISBN 978-0-393-08285-2 (hardcover)
1. March on Washington for Jobs and Freedom (1963 : Washington, D.C.)
2. African Americans—Civil rights—History—20th century. 3. Civil rights
demonstrations—Washington (D.C.)—History—20th century. 4. Civil rights
movements—United States—History—20th century. I. Title.
F200.J66 2013
323.1196'07309046—dc23
                                2013006173

ISBN 978-0-393-34941-2 pbk.

W. W. Norton & Company, Inc.
500 Fifth Avenue, New York, N.Y. 10110
www.wwnorton.com

W. W. Norton & Company Ltd.
Castle House, 75/76 Wells Street, London W1T 3QT

1 2 3 4 5 6 7 8 9 0

CONTENTS

Illustrations follow page 136

PREFACE

NEARLY EVERY AMERICAN and millions of people around the world are familiar with Martin Luther King's "I Have a Dream" speech, yet most know little about the March on Washington at which it was delivered. The tremendous eloquence and elegant simplicity of the speech meant that many, then and now, came to associate the broader goals of the demonstration with King's compelling vision of interracial harmony—a dream of a nation that would finally live up to its founders' proclamations about the "self-evident" equality of all people, in which children would be judged "by the content of their character" rather than the color of their skin and in which citizens would "be able to work together, to pray together, to struggle together, to go to jail together, to stand up for freedom together, knowing that we will be free one day." Few know that King's was the last of ten speeches, capping more than six hours of performances by well-known musicians, appearances by politicians and movie stars, and statements of solidarity from groups across the nation and around the world—as well as an actual march. Even fewer know that it was a march "For Jobs and Freedom," and that it aimed not just to end racial segregation and discrimination in the Jim Crow South but also to ensure that Americans of all races had access to quality education, affordable housing, and jobs that paid a living wage. We forget that King's task was to uplift the spirits of marchers after a long day in the sun and, for most, a night travelling by bus or train from as far away as New York, Chicago, Atlanta, and even Los Angeles. One reporter observed that while King "ignited the crowd" with his optimistic vision of the future, the other speakers "concentrated on the struggle ahead and spoke in tough, even harsh language." Yet those other speeches have been virtually lost to history.[1]

On August 28, 1963, nearly a quarter-million people descended on the nation's capital to demand "Jobs and Freedom." By "freedom" they meant that every American be guaranteed access to stores, restaurants, hotels, and other "public accommodations," to "decent housing" and "adequate and integrated education," and to the right to vote. They also wanted strict enforcement of those civil rights, including the withholding of federal funds from discriminatory programs and housing developments, the reduction of congressional representation in states where citizens were denied the right to vote, and authorization of the attorney general to bring injunctive suits when "any constitutional right is violated." Some of those demands were addressed by a civil rights bill that President John F. Kennedy had introduced to Congress on June 11, 1963, two months before the demonstration. Marchers wanted to pass that bill, but they believed it was far too limited. In addition to equal access to public accommodations and the right to vote, they demanded a "massive federal program to train and place all unemployed workers—Negro and white—on meaningful and dignified jobs at decent wages." They wanted to raise the minimum wage to a level that would "give all Americans a decent standard of living," and to extend that standard to agricultural workers, domestic servants, and public employees, who were excluded from the federal law that created the minimum wage. For many marchers, the most important objective was the creation of a Fair Employment Practices Committee (FEPC) to prevent private firms, government agencies, and labor unions from discriminating against workers on the basis of race, color, religion, or national origin.[2]

King delivered the finale at the Lincoln Memorial, but the tone for the day was set in an opening address by A. Philip Randolph, the

Randolph's First Speech
spoke of the need for economic
and social justice

seventy-four-year-old trade unionist who was the official leader of the
March on Washington. Randolph agreed with King on the need for
integration and racial equality in the South, but he linked those objectives to a broader national and interracial struggle for economic and
social justice. "We are the advance guard of a massive moral revolution
for jobs and freedom," he told the crowd that stretched out for more
than a mile before him. He declared that the civil rights movement
affected "every city, every town, every village where black men are segregated, oppressed and exploited," but insisted it was "not confined
to the Negroes; nor is it confined to civil rights." It was critical to
end segregation in southern stores and restaurants, the union leader
insisted, "but those accommodations will mean little to those who cannot afford to use them." What good was an FEPC, he asked, if the
rapidly expanding automation of industry was allowed to "destroy the
jobs of millions of workers, black and white?" Whereas King appealed
to the nation's founding principles of equality and freedom, Randolph
insisted that "real freedom will require many changes in the nation's
political and social philosophies and institutions." Ending housing
discrimination, for example, would require Americans to reject the
assumption that a homeowner's "property rights include the right to
humiliate me because of the color of my skin." In the civil rights revolution, he declared, "The sanctity of private property takes second place
to the sanctity of a human personality."[3]

Randolph used language and imagery that reflected a lifetime of
activism in organized labor and the Socialist Party, but his points were
echoed by the younger and, for the most part, more moderate speakers who followed. Roy Wilkins of the National Association for the
Advancement of Colored People (NAACP), the nation's oldest and
largest civil rights organization, charged that President Kennedy's civil
rights proposal amounted to "so moderate an approach that if it is
weakened or eliminated, the remainder will be little more than sugar
water." Emphasizing the need for an FEPC law, the sixty-two-year-old

former journalist stated, "We want employment and with it we want the pride and responsibility and self-respect that goes with equal access to jobs." Walter Reuther, the fifty-five-year-old president of the United Auto Workers union, concurred that "the job question is crucial; because we will not solve education or housing or public accommodations as long as millions of American Negroes are treated as second class economic citizens and denied jobs." According to the *New York Times*, "Harshest of all the speakers was John Lewis," the twenty-three-year-old chairman of the Student Nonviolent Coordinating Committee (SNCC), who currently represents Georgia in the U.S. Congress. Lewis endorsed Kennedy's civil rights bill "with great reservations," pointing out that the proposed legislation did nothing to protect African Americans from police brutality and racist violence, to uphold their right to vote in the South, or to "ensure the equality of a maid who earns $5 a week in the home of a family whose income is $100,000 a year." Urging marchers to seek alternatives to a political system corrupted by power and money, Lewis declared, "Let us not forget that we are involved in a serious social revolution."[4]

In addition to complicating popular memories of the March on Washington, the tenor of those speeches also challenges a common misconception about the broader history of the civil rights movement. Until recently, the most influential accounts presented the 1963 protest as the apex of an exceptional moment when civil rights leaders transcended their ideological and strategic differences by focusing narrowly on "moral imperatives that had garnered support from the nation's moderates—issues such as the right to vote and the right to a decent education." The "classical" phase of the civil rights movement began with the Supreme Court's *Brown* decision in 1954, which struck down the legalized system of segregation in the Jim Crow South, and it ended in the late 1960s, we were told, when the Black Power and New Left movements shifted the focus toward the urban North and to "issues whose moral rightness was not as readily apparent," such as poverty and discrimination in housing and employment. That interpretation was embraced by critics representing a broad spectrum of American political thought. Conservatives praised King and other civil rights leaders for suppressing calls for "radical social, political, and economic changes" while leftists chided those same leaders for failing to "even grapple with [the] social and economic contradictions" of American capitalism.

Historians have complicated the traditional narrative by tracing the "radical roots of civil rights" back into the 1930s and '40s and by demonstrating that civil rights activists of many ideological varieties always insisted that access to jobs, housing, and economic security was as vital to their struggle as voting rights and integration. They also reminded us that the movement faced stiff resistance to those demands in the most moderate regions of the urban North, as well as in the conservative South. With few exceptions, however, scholars simply inverted the older story by allowing the March on Washington to remain a moderate exception to a radical "long civil rights movement." The most influential recent studies still either end the story before 1963 or shift our attention from "leaders on the platform high above the crowd" to local movements and grassroots activists that, scholars contend, more accurately "capture the motivations that led relatively obscure individuals to the March." By relegating well-known leaders and events to the background, historians have reinforced the old thesis that political constraints of the era "kept discussions of broad-based social change, or a linking of race and class, off the agenda" during the classical phase.[5]

Both the power and the limitations of the traditional narrative are evident in the political career of Barack Obama, who became the nation's first black president during the most severe economic crisis since the Great Depression. During his campaign for president in 2008, Obama credited the civil rights movement—often gesturing directly to Congressman John Lewis—with "leading a people out of bondage" and laying the foundation for his own success. When discussing social and economic policy, however, he suggested that the racially egalitarian politics of Lewis' "Moses generation" had lost their effectiveness in an era when poorly funded public services, stagnant wages, and skyrocketing unemployment rates threatened the livelihoods of all Americans, regardless of their race. "Most working- and middle-class white Americans don't feel that they have been particularly privileged by their race," he stated in his campaign's most direct attempt to address the question of racial inequality, suggesting that African Americans could transcend the "racial stalemate" that dominated American politics by "binding our particular grievances—for better health care, and better schools, and better jobs—to the larger aspirations of all Americans." Referring to his own white grandparents, who came of age during the Depression and the Second World War, the candidate suggested that the social-democratic and race-neutral policies of the New Deal era offered a more effective model for social and economic policy in the twenty-first century.[6]

Obama's appeal to the "greatest generation" certainly aided his election in 2008, but when he ran for reelection four years later the lessons to be drawn from their experiences seemed less clear. The president had implemented an ambitious economic recovery program and the most dramatic reform of the nation's health care system since the 1960s, both of which benefited white Americans as much as or more so than nonwhites. Yet the racial polarization of American politics had only increased. Although unemployment rates had fallen at a slightly faster rate for black and Latino workers than for whites, they remained far higher than the national average. Still reluctant to address racial inequality directly, Obama spoke out powerfully against clear cases of discrimination and racist violence but had no narrative to explain the more complex interactions between racial and economic inequality. Meanwhile, polls indicated that white voters were even less likely to support the black candidate than they had been four years earlier.

Rather than transcending racial differences through a color-blind appeal to economic interests, Obama won reelection by uniting a broad coalition of nonwhite workers, women of all races, liberal youth, and a few white men around demands for equality and economic justice.[7]

By tracing the roots of the March on Washington to A. Philip Randolph's demand for fair employment during the Second World War, this book demonstrates that the civil rights movement was always closely linked to the social democratic politics of the New Deal. Randolph initiated the March on Washington before the United States entered the war, but federal investments in weapons, equipment, transportation, and military bases had already begun to lift the nation's economy out of the Great Depression. President Franklin D. Roosevelt sought to strengthen the economic recovery by directing federal spending toward the South and other particularly depressed regions, and by strengthening federal labor laws to protect workers' rights to form unions and bargain collectively for better wages and benefits. While those policies were ostensibly race-neutral, Randolph pointed out that they allowed private employers, unions, and local officials to bar African Americans from jobs that were funded by federal tax dollars and protected by federal laws. He demanded an FEPC law, not just to end discrimination by unions and employers but also to extend to African Americans the promise of economic and social citizenship that Roosevelt had linked to participation in the defense effort.

It was that egalitarian vision of social citizenship, as much as constitutional principles of political equality, that inspired the modern civil rights movement. Like many other labor leaders of his generation, Randolph believed that the most effective path to "first-class citizenship" was to ensure that black men had access to wages and benefits necessary to ensure economic and social security for their families. The March on Washington never became the mass movement that he envisioned in 1941, but its objectives were sustained by a generation of young militants who would play key leadership roles in the "classical" phase of the civil rights movement. Emphasizing the need for sustained grassroots organizing rather than a nationwide mobilization, Pauli Murray, Bayard Rustin, Anna Arnold Hedgeman, and other activists linked the March on Washington Movement to women's organizations, unions, and churches in communities across the country. Inspired by the movement against British imperialism in India, they adopted the nonviolent techniques of civil disobedience that had been developed by independence leader Mohandas Gandhi. They also expanded the agenda of the movement from winning jobs to building unions and, more controversially, to demanding family-supporting jobs for black women as well as for black men. Finally, they pushed for an immediate end to segregation in the armed forces, universities, and other public institutions, which they viewed as inherently discriminatory and incompatible with the democratic rhetoric that Roosevelt used to inspire the defense effort.

The "classical" phase of the civil rights movement emerged in the context of a booming postwar economy, but it displayed important continuities with the March on Washington Movement. While the United States' claim to leadership of "the free world" made it difficult for federal officials to defend the legal system of segregation and discrimination in the Jim Crow South, the democratic rhetoric of the Cold War proved just as empty as Roosevelt's when presidents Eisenhower and Kennedy refused to confront white southerners who defied the Supreme Court's decision that segregation violated the U.S. Constitution. When grassroots activists mobilized to enforce that decision, they drew on networks that had been developed during the Second World War, and they employed the nonviolent strategies pioneered by the March on Washington Movement. They also argued that in addition to violating their constitutional rights, barriers to education and transportation in the South—as well as to unionized jobs and quality schools and housing in the North—prevented them from taking advantage of the unprecedented economic expansion of the postwar era. As

Martin Luther King stated in the often-overlooked opening to his "I Have a Dream" speech, "the Negro lives on a lonely island of poverty in the midst of a vast ocean of material prosperity."[8]

Rather than narrowing their objectives "in the interest of gaining broader support," organizers of the March on Washington united the various strands of black protest around the bold and expansive demand "For Jobs and Freedom." The initial proposal for the 1963 march came from the Negro American Labor Council (NALC), a largely forgotten organization that Randolph and other black trade unionists created to highlight the economic crisis caused by black workers' exclusion from skilled jobs and unions. Anna Arnold Hedgeman pushed the union activists to expand their agenda to include access to public accommodations and voting rights in the South, a move that allowed them to gain support from Martin Luther King's Southern Christian Leadership Conference (SCLC), John Lewis' SNCC, and the Congress of Racial Equality (CORE), a network of nonviolent activists that Bayard Rustin had created during the Second World War. Hedgeman also persuaded them to seek support from the National Council of Negro Women, a network of organizations claiming nearly 800,000 members, although Randolph and other male activists rejected her request to include black women in the official leadership of the march. The most reluctant supporters of the demonstration were Roy Wilkins of the NAACP and labor leader Walter Reuther, who joined the mobilization only after they were convinced that it would occur without them.[9]

The March on Washington focuses primarily on leaders and experienced activists in the civil rights movement, but it also challenges the assumption that their beliefs and concerns differed significantly from those of their followers. While Randolph, King, and other national figures were the official spokesmen for the March on Washington, the primary task of organizing the protest fell to staff and elected officials of local civil rights organizations, unions, churches, and other groups who lived in the same working-class communities that formed the

primary base of support for the movement. Perhaps the most important evidence of agreement between leaders and marchers was simply
the fact that so many people travelled hundreds or even thousands of
miles—most missing a day or more of work and all but a few paying
their own way—to be in Washington that day. Some were students
or full-time activists, but the vast majority consisted of auto workers
and meatpackers, teachers and letter carriers, domestic servants and
sharecroppers who—aside from their membership in unions and civil
rights organizations—had little history of political protest. Journalist
Russell Baker described them as "a gentle army of quiet, middle-class
Americans who came in the spirit of the church outing," suggesting
that they were in Washington for pleasure or out of a sense of religious or patriotic duty. Malcolm X, a black nationalist who accused
Randolph, King, and other leaders of tempering the radicalism of the
protest, argued that the marchers had been "fooled." Given the size
and enthusiasm of the crowd, however, it seems more likely that they
believed deeply in the message that Randolph, King, and others proclaimed from the steps of the Lincoln Memorial that day.[10]

Even on the basis of King's dream of racial equality and integration,
that message was hardly moderate. By 1963, the civil rights movement
had already changed Americans' views about racial equality. Polls
showed that 83 percent of whites believed that "Negroes should have
as good a chance as white people to get any kind of job," for example,
nearly double the percentage that held that same view when A. Philip
Randolph first called for a March on Washington in 1941. Even in
the rigidly segregated South, a majority of whites had no objection to
riding a bus with a black person or to a black family "with the same
income and education" buying a house on their block. Civil rights
leaders faced resistance, however, when they asked the government to
enforce those ideals. Nearly a decade after the *Brown* decision, only
one percent of black students in the South attended school with any
white students. Yet 75 percent of white southerners and 50 percent of

white northerners accused President Kennedy of "pushing integration too fast." Three-quarters of white northerners believed that a property owner had the right to sell or rent a home to a family regardless of their race, but less than half of them thought the government should force them to do so.[11]

The economic policies that marchers demanded were no less controversial. They wanted to raise the minimum wage to $2 an hour, even though Kennedy had struggled to increase it to $1.25 just two years earlier. By 1963, Kennedy had abandoned the "old slogans," like wage increases and public works programs of the New Deal era, in favor of "new tools" for creating economic growth, such as tax cuts and free trade. A. Philip Randolph's FEPC had been defeated in nearly every session of Congress since the Second World War. After watching Bayard Rustin close the March on Washington by reading the full list of demands while "every television camera at the disposal of the networks was upon him," left-wing journalist Murray Kempton remarked: "No expression one-tenth so radical has ever been seen or heard by so many Americans."[12]

Of course the true test of any political movement lies not so much in its goals or objectives as in its ability to achieve them, and in this regard as well, historians have been too eager to dismiss the March on Washington. While some adopted Russell Baker's assertion that marchers were simply affirming the basic principles of "middle-class" America, others agreed with Malcolm X that they were naïve to believe that they could challenge 400 years of white supremacy with a "one day 'integrated' picnic." More recent scholars have acknowledged the radical roots of Randolph, King, and other leaders but—echoing broader trends in the literature—conclude that media coverage "simultaneously blunted the march's broad political demands" and reduced its message to King's optimistic Dream, while continued resistance from Congress "meant that the march yielded no immediate legislative gains." It is true that newspapers and television broadcasts were filled with praise for King's speech, but they also highlighted the other leaders and the full list of the march's demands. It took nearly a year to pass Kennedy's bill, and many supported it to honor the president after his assassination in November of 1963 rather than to respond to the civil rights movement. But the Civil Rights Act that President Lyndon Johnson signed on July 2, 1964, had the marks of the March on Washington all over it. Most importantly, it included the FEPC clause that Randolph had fought for since the 1940s. Unexpectedly, the law also banned employment discrimination based on sex, in addition to race, color, religion, and national origin, thus realizing—through a complicated and often contradictory set of events—Anna Hedgeman's and other black women's efforts to expand the scope of the March on Washington Movement. In addition to supporting the passage of the Civil Rights Act, Johnson pledged to couple it with an "unconditional war on poverty," an idea he adopted from the Kennedy administration but bolstered with measures—such as the minimum wage increase and federal investments in education, housing, and job training—that were demanded by the March on Washington. Those items were scaled back dramatically as the War on Poverty made its way through Congress, and civil rights leaders would soon realize how weak the Civil Rights Act was, but they had won a victory for African Americans and the cause of racial equality that was certainly appropriate for the hundredth anniversary of the Emancipation Proclamation.[13]

Speaking to a conference of black leaders sixteen months after the March on Washington, A. Philip Randolph observed that the "Civil Rights Revolution has been caught up in a crisis of victory." Comparing that crisis to the disillusionment that set in among former slaves and abolitionists in the 1870s and 1880s, when the achievements of emancipation were undermined by the rise of Jim Crow, and to the decline of labor militancy following the upheavals of the 1930s, he warned that many activists were frustrated with the limited nature of the victories they had already achieved, that they had stopped moving forward and were in danger of losing ground. He was responding to divisions that had challenged the movement during preparations for the march and widened during the campaign to pass the Civil Rights Act. They included debates over the utility of mass protest versus legislative lobbying, the relationship between race and sex discrimination, and the possibility of interracial cooperation. In many respects our historical memory of the March on Washington is still caught up in that crisis of victory, in part because those conflicts have not been resolved but also because we still allow them to overshadow the significance of what was actually accomplished by bringing a quarter-million people to the nation's capital on August 28, 1963. This book attempts to lift that veil.[14]

THE MARCH ON WASHINGTON

CHAPTER ONE

THE MOST DANGEROUS NEGRO IN AMERICA

No greater wrong has been committed against the Negro than the denial to him of the right to work.

—A. PHILIP RANDOLPH, 1944[1]

"MR. CHAIRMAN," AN anonymous black woman shouted to A. Philip Randolph from the floor of a mass meeting in Chicago, "we ought to throw 50,000 Negroes around the White House, bring them from all over the country, in jalopies, in trains and any way they can get there . . . and keep them there until we can get some action from the White House." Randolph agreed with "the sister" and pledged the support of his union, the Brotherhood of Sleeping Car Porters, which had nearly 7,000 members in cities across the country. It was January 1941, and the fifty-one-year-old union leader had spent the past six months urging President Franklin D. Roosevelt to stop racial discrimination in the armed forces and by defense contractors during preparations for the Second World War. The previous September, Roosevelt had met with Randolph and leaders of the nation's largest civil rights groups, the NAACP and the National Urban League; but he rejected their proposals. On January 25, Randolph issued a call for

1

10,000 black workers "from various sections of the country, from all trades, professions and callings" to march on the nation's capital under the slogan "We Loyal Negro-American Citizens Demand the Right to Work and Fight for Our Country."[2]

The anger expressed by African Americans in Chicago and across the United States in 1941 stemmed not only from their exclusion from jobs and military service but also from the contradiction between that reality and the rhetoric that President Roosevelt had used to rally Americans behind the defense effort. Elected to a third term on a promise to keep the United States out of the war, the commander in chief argued that the nation still had a special mission to play in defending democratic governments from the rising tide of fascism. In a radio address in late December 1940, he urged Americans to build "the great Arsenal of Democracy" to provide their allies in Europe and Asia with weapons, equipment, and other supplies necessary to win the war. But Roosevelt believed that it was not enough simply to preserve democracy as it currently existed. In his State of the Union address on January 6, 1941, the president urged Congress to expand the very meaning of citizenship. In exchange for their "sacrifices" during the war, he explained, citizens would expect more than the traditional liberties, such as "freedom of speech" and "freedom of worship," which were written into the U.S. Constitution and had been adopted by democratic countries around the world. They would also demand protections such as "freedom from want" and "freedom from fear," which Roosevelt insisted were not extravagant entitlements but rights to "the simple, the basic things," such as "equality of opportunity," jobs for those who could work and "security" for those who could not, and the "preservation of civil liberties for all." When A. Philip Randolph and the others met in Chicago just a few days after Roosevelt's speech to Congress, they understood that exclusion from the defense effort threatened to rob them of those "four essential human freedoms" that Roosevelt promised as a reward for the defense of democracy. "We seek the right to

[handwritten: Calling at FDR on his 4 Freedoms.]

[handwritten: Randolph's background]

play our part in advancing the cause of national defense and national unity," Randolph wrote soon afterward. "But certainly, there can be no true national unity where one-tenth of the population is denied their basic rights as American citizens."[3] *[handwritten: Born in Florida — joined Great Migration to NY 1911]*

A. Philip Randolph called the first March on Washington to address that contradiction between the rhetoric and reality of the "Four Freedoms," but, as he admitted two decades later, the fifty-one-year-old trade unionist had waited all his life for such an opportunity. The child of an itinerant preacher from Jacksonville, Florida, he was instilled from an early age with a sense of justice and a responsibility for leadership. "You have the ability to speak," Randolph's father told him and his brother James. "You have the books here that I've bought for you to read . . . and your school leaders and teachers, they love you and have faith in you, they believe you're unusually gifted chaps." Although Randolph resisted the "great pressure" to adopt his father's profession, he remained deeply committed to the racially egalitarian social gospel of his family's African Methodist Episcopal church. He also embraced his father's appreciation for the power of speech and often recited sermons out loud while imitating the styles of his father and other local ministers. As a teenager he was selected to speak at his graduation from Cookman Institute in Jacksonville, which had been founded to train former slaves to become teachers and other professionals during the effort to rebuild the South following the Civil War. Born three decades after Reconstruction, in 1889, he found it impossible to realize his parents' expectations within the rigid Jim Crow system that settled over the South in the late nineteenth century. One of his earliest memories was of his father and other men standing "all night like sentries" outside the county jail to stop the lynching of a black prisoner. "I'll never forget it," he told an interviewer. "It had a tremendous effect on me."[4]

Randolph found more opportunities in New York City, where he moved in 1911 at the age of twenty-two. Like many early participants in the Great Migration that would bring more than five million black southerners to northern cities over the next half-century, the young man found his expectations of greater freedom and possibility tempered by rigid residential segregation and exclusion from nearly all jobs except low-wage service positions such as waiter, porter, and elevator operator. Even before his arrival he was fired for trying to organize his co-workers to protest "miserable living quarters" on the ship that he hired onto for the trip from Jacksonville. Phil, as friends called him, also embraced the vibrant intellectual and cultural life of Harlem, the multiracial working-class community in northern Manhattan that he would call home until his death in 1979. He attended classes at the City College and joined an amateur Shakespearean theater group where he met his future wife and political collaborator Lucille Campbell Greene. Six years older than Randolph, Greene had moved to Harlem from Washington, D.C., where she had graduated from Howard University (established for African Americans after the Civil War), married, worked as a schoolteacher, and been widowed. Greene opened a beauty salon in Harlem and would continue to be the primary breadwinner of the family after marrying Phil in 1913.[5]

Lucille introduced her husband to Chandler Owen, a North Carolinian who was studying economics at Columbia University and who would remain Randolph's closest political collaborator for the next decade. In 1917 the two men formed a union of elevator and switchboard operators that grew to 600 members in three weeks but collapsed quickly after losing a strike aimed at winning better wages and an eight-hour day. Later that year a union of hotel waiters hired them to edit their journal, the *Hotel Messenger*, but then fired them for commenting on the low wages and poor working conditions of the waiters' assistants. Frustrated by the conservatism of the waiters' union and other affiliates of the American Federation of Labor, Randolph and Owen turned to the political trade unionism promoted by the Socialist Party and the Industrial Workers of the World. With financial backing from Lucille and the left-wing *Jewish Daily Forward*, Randolph and

Owen created *The Messenger*, an independent journal that they called "The Only Radical Negro Magazine in America."[6]

That was an exaggeration, but Randolph and Owen certainly distinguished themselves in the hotbed of radical politics that Harlem became in the years surrounding the First World War. Their primary rivals were "old Negro leaders" who attempted to negotiate within the established political system to win small gains for African Americans. "Now, since almost all Negroes are workers, live on wages and suffer from the high cost of food, clothing and shelter," Randolph wrote in 1919, "it is obvious that the Republican and Democratic Parties are opposed to their interests." He and Owen were more sympathetic to the NAACP, which had been founded by the prominent black scholar W. E. B. Du Bois and several white Socialists to protest racist violence in 1909 and had grown to over 100,000 members in its first decade. They disagreed over strategy, however, and argued that African Americans could fight for equality more effectively by joining with white workers to overthrow capitalism than by trying to demonstrate to white elites that they were morally and intellectually fit for equality. These were serious issues in an era when black workers were not even allowed to join many unions and when white workers seemed far more eager to join a race riot than an interracial revolution; but Randolph and Owen insisted that white capitalists encouraged those conflicts to sustain a system that exploited both groups and that black workers had no choice but to engage the revolution and attempt to push it in a positive direction. "Whatever the condition of the transition, the labor and Socialist movement is making every effort for peace," Owen wrote in a scathing critique of Du Bois' skepticism toward "the class struggle." Writing in 1919, Randolph urged black radicals to "form an alliance with white radicals . . . to build a new society—a society of equals, without class, race, caste or religious distinctions."[7]

While they dismissed the "old Negro" and sparred with the NAACP, Randolph and Owen saved their harshest criticism for Marcus Gar-

[handwritten marginalia: "6 Randolph socialist also until black an white workers to appear" / "Anti- Garvey"]

vey, a Jamaican-born black nationalist whom Randolph met while lecturing from a soapbox on Harlem's Lenox Avenue in 1917. Randolph was impressed by Garvey's description of movements against racism and exploitation in the West Indies and gave him a turn on the soapbox, introducing Garvey as "one of the militant black fighters for social and racial justice." They parted ways, however, as Garvey turned away from labor activism and focused on building a network of black-owned businesses and social associations that he believed could form the basis of racial independence in the United States, the West Indies, and, eventually, Africa. Randolph was not one to dismiss utopian ideas, but he charged that Garvey's plan would "not only not liberate Africa" but also "set back the clock of Negro progress by cutting the Negro workers away from the proletarian liberation movement" in the United States. Launching a vitriolic "Garvey Must Go!" campaign, *The Messenger* carried regular denunciations of Garvey, supported a federal investigation into corruption within his Universal Negro Improvement Association (UNIA), and called for his deportation from the United States, which happened in 1927 after he served three years in prison for mail fraud. Despite these attacks, Garvey's UNIA claimed nearly half a million members in more than forty countries, making it the largest black organization in the Americas before the Second World War. While Randolph expressed sympathy for the sentiments behind Black Nationalism, he maintained that black radicals had to make every effort possible to build common ground between black and white workers.[8]

Randolph's faith in the possibility of interracial solidarity was truly remarkable for a black man living in the early twentieth-century United States, but it was nurtured by the crowd of equally remarkable activists that he met through the Socialist Party. They included Hubert Harrison, a West Indian radical who led a campaign encouraging African Americans to refuse enlistment during the First World War unless they were guaranteed equal treatment. Anticipating Randolph's

Andy of E Dabs

proposal for a March on Washington in 1941, Harrison charged that political leaders who "so loudly proclaimed and formulated the new democratic demands never had the slightest intention of extending the limits of applications of democracy." Randolph also got to know Elizabeth Gurley Flynn and "Big Bill" Heywood, of the Industrial Workers of the World, who risked their lives and went to jail countless times for organizing black, white, Asian, and Mexican American workers in Texas, Colorado, and other places that were hardly known for interracial cooperation. None of those radicals were typical of the Socialist Party, and each quit the party at one point or another out of frustration with a movement that was politically diverse and, contrary to Chandler Owen's response to Du Bois, dominated by activists who were either ambivalent about or outright hostile toward nonwhite workers. Against the background of an expanding labor movement and a growing yet still very small vote for the Socialist Party, however, activists like Harrison, Flynn, and Heywood lent substance to Randolph's belief that it was at least possible for white and black workers to unite around shared economic problems.[9]

For Randolph, the most important source of optimism about socialism was Eugene V. Debs, a seventy-five-year-old former railroad worker who won nearly a million votes as the Socialist Party's presidential candidate in 1920. Both Phil and Lucille Randolph ran for statewide office on the Socialist ticket in New York, along with Chandler Owen and two other black activists. Phil went to jail for sedition along with Debs and other Socialists for opposing U.S. entry into the First World War—although he was released after a few days, while Debs remained in federal prison for over two years. Debs had a complicated record of racial politics, from his alliance with white supremacists who overthrew Reconstruction after the Civil War to his refusal to challenge the violent expulsion of black workers from the AFL's railway brotherhoods in the 1890s; but in the early twentieth century he emerged as a leading voice in an effort to push the Social-

1920
race
nos & anti-slds

ist Party to the forefront of struggles for racial equality. Starting with
his first campaign for president in 1904, Debs refused to speak before
segregated audiences, called for the restoration of black voting rights
in the South, and insisted that "the Socialist Party would be false to its
historic mission, violate the fundamental principles of Socialism, deny
its philosophy and repudiate its own teachings if, on account of race
considerations, it sought to exclude any human being from political
equality and economic freedom." When a handful of white Socialists
helped W. E. B. Du Bois create the NAACP in 1909, Debs wrote, "I
am with you thoroughly"; and when he campaigned for president in
1912, party leaders cancelled tours in several southern states because
he insisted on denouncing segregation. In addition to their shared commitment to interracial solidarity, Debs shared Randolph's roots in the
Christian social gospel. "I had not met a white man with such spiritual
character," Randolph recalled of his first encounter with Eugene Debs.
When the Socialist leader died in 1926, an obituary in *The Messenger*
compared the "Grand Old Man" not to revolutionaries like Karl Marx
or Vladimir Lenin but to "the Carpenter of Nazareth" and the "Bible
preacher in the South."[10]

Randolph's optimism faded in the 1920s, after a wave of racist violence swept through American cities from Chicago in the North to Tulsa,
Oklahoma, in the South and when federal authorities cracked down on
any form of radicalism ranging from the most conservative Socialists in
Milwaukee to Marcus Garvey in Harlem. By 1925 the left-wing movements of the First World War had been replaced by the Ku Klux Klan,
which had nearly three million members and supporters in governors'
mansions and legislatures in twelve states. Rallying white Protestants
against the combined threats of Catholicism, Judaism, Communism,
labor unions, and the Great Migration, the KKK staged mass marches
and cross burnings, encouraged lynching and other forms of racist violence, and made an impressive show of its force by organizing 40,000
members to march down Pennsylvania Avenue in Washington, D.C. In

that context many of Randolph's allies either abandoned their radicalism or moved toward more desperate measures. Lucille Randolph continued to support Phil financially and used her beauty shop to promote his causes but no longer engaged directly with political protest. Chandler Owen packed up for Chicago, where he joined the Republican Party. Others gravitated toward the Communist Party, which had been formed by Socialists who were inspired by the Bolshevik Revolution in Russia. Randolph was also impressed by the Russian Revolution but, like Debs, grew disillusioned by reports of police repression and political purges under Bolshevik rule and frustrated by the increasing reliance of American Communists on political analysis and financial resources from the Soviet Union. He stayed active in the Socialist Party but shifted the focus of *The Messenger* from politics to the literary Renaissance that drew the world's attention to Harlem in the 1920s. With little to show for a decade in publishing and political activism, Randolph accepted a job organizing a union for black men and women who carried luggage, cleaned rooms, and cared for passengers on the luxury railway cars that carried wealthy Americans across the country in the years before air travel.[11]   *1925 — Randolph sees ado la bar again.*

Randolph's new job was daunting. The Brotherhood of Sleeping Car Porters and Maids was created in 1925 by a handful of the 12,000 African Americans employed by the Pullman Company, which was based in Chicago but operated sleeping cars on rail lines across the United States. Established during the Civil War, the Pullman Company enjoyed a reputation for hiring more black workers and treating them better than any other firm in the nation. In the 1890s, when Eugene Debs's Railway Brotherhood was driving black men from most other jobs on the rails, the Pullman Company initiated a "good works" program that donated thousands of dollars to the Chicago Urban League, the Young Men's Christian Association, and other institutions that served black workers in Chicago. Company officials allowed porters to purchase stock in the firm, offered singing lessons so they could increase their tips, and helped form the Pullman Porters Benefit Association to provide insurance and recreation programs for porters. When a few porters formed a Protective Association to push for more control over their jobs during the First World War, managers deflated the conflict by creating an Employee Representation Plan to address grievances about pay and working conditions. The men who hired Randolph called the plan "a contrivance to pacify and fool the porters," but most of their co-workers and African Americans around the country considered Pullman "the greatest benefactor of our race."[12]

While many of his friends withdrew from politics, Randolph returned to the difficult task of organizing black workers into a labor movement that did not seem to want them. With few members to pay dues, he funded the effort with a small grant from a left-wing foundation that had Elizabeth Gurley Flynn and several NAACP leaders on its board. In 1927 the union sought recognition under a new federal law requiring rail companies to negotiate with unions that represented a majority of their employees. It also sought to affiliate with the American Federation of Labor, but the request was blocked by the Hotel Employees and Restaurant Employees union, which claimed jurisdiction over sleeping car porters and maids but made no effort to organize them. After three years of hard work, Randolph had organized 7,300 out of roughly 12,000 porters and maids employed by the Pullman Company. Membership in the South was "negligible," but the union claimed to have signed up 80 percent of eligible members in the North and Midwest and nearly 100 percent in the West. The biggest advantage Randolph had was that union members worked on the rails and thus had daily contact with people in cities and small towns stretching from New York and Chicago to New Orleans and San Francisco. That network of union members would remain Randolph's primary base of political support for the next fifty years.[13]

In addition to building the Brotherhood of Sleeping Car Porters, Randolph encouraged the formation of Colored Women's Economic

Randolph organized
the Sleeping Car Workers Union at a time when
Unions didn't want blacks

Councils, which were headed by wives and female relatives of porters
to support the union and push for economic improvements in their
communities. Significant numbers of maids and other women workers
joined the Brotherhood, but, as the name suggests, they were margin-
alized and often ignored by the male membership. Like most labor
leaders in the early twentieth century, Randolph believed the primary
task of unions was to increase men's wages to the point that they could
support their families without sending their wives and children into
the labor market. He was a strong supporter of political equality for
women and *The Messenger* carried frequent endorsements of women's
suffrage, notices about access to birth control, and positive reports on
the feminist movement in Harlem. When it came to economic justice,
however, he viewed women primarily as consumers rather than pro-
ducers and encouraged them to support the union by boycotting businesses that did not support the union, organizing demonstrations and
fundraising drives in their communities, and encouraging their hus-
bands to join. Women who headed the Economic Councils embraced
the view that the primary goal of the Brotherhood was, as the wife of
one union official stated, to fight for "the very bearing of our men who
are fighting for simple manhood rights, a grander manlier tone."[14]

Despite the rapid expansion of the Brotherhood and the base of
support it established in cities across the country, the union was still
not strong enough to challenge the Pullman Company. In 1928, after
failing to convince a federal mediating board that the Brotherhood
represented a majority of porters and maids, Randolph called a strike
to force their employer into negotiations. Union members voted in
favor of the walkout, but when Pullman began hiring workers to
replace the strikers, and the federal board refused to intervene, Randolph postponed the walkout at the last minute. He insisted the strike
could be renewed at any moment and argued that the "strike maneuver" had forced the company to spend millions of dollars and gained
nationwide attention without compelling the porters to follow through

with their threat. He also pointed to a compromise reached with the American Federation of Labor soon after the strike, which allowed individual locals of the Brotherhood to affiliate directly with the AFL rather than through the Hotel Employees and Restaurant Employees. In 1929 Randolph made the dubious decision to purchase a building on 136th Street in Harlem, stating that nothing would demonstrate the viability of the union better than "buying its own home." Most members of the union and much of the black press accused Randolph of selling out the porters, however; and by the spring of 1929 all but 3,000 porters had left the union, several organizers had been laid off, and Randolph had stopped publishing *The Messenger*. "The failure of the Brotherhood has been laid at Randolph's door," black scholars Sterling Spero and Abram Harris wrote in their influential 1931 study *The Black Worker*. While they remained sympathetic to the cause, the scholars attributed the loss to Randolph's "hunger for publicity," his "undue haste for action," and the hope that federal authorities would step in to protect an "unskilled and easily replaceable" workforce. "The great pity of the virtual collapse of the porters' union lies not merely in its effect upon the porters who have grievances which sorely need correction but in its effect upon Negro labor generally," they concluded. "The hope that this movement would become the center and rallying point of Negro labor as a whole is now dead."[15]

Randolph's miscalculation was exacerbated by the collapse of the New York Stock Exchange, which was just ten miles from the Sleeping Car Porters' headquarters in Harlem. Within two months of "Black Tuesday," on October 29, 1929, the number of unemployed workers in the United States skyrocketed from 500,000 to over four million. By 1933 there were sixteen million Americans—nearly a quarter of the workforce—looking for work. For black workers, the Great Depression only intensified hardships they had been facing for a decade. In the rural South, where most African Americans still lived, the economic crisis had begun before the First World War, when increased production overseas, new parasites, and soil erosion made it nearly impossible to make a profit by growing crops that had been the mainstays of economic growth in the region for centuries. Cotton prices plunged by two-thirds between 1929 and 1932 after declining steadily in the 1920s. Southern cities had been more hospitable to black workers in the 1920s, but that advantage dissipated as whites rushed to fill jobs like domestic service and garbage collection that had previously been reserved for blacks. "No Jobs for Niggers until Every White Man Has a Job!" was the slogan chanted by mobs that marched through Atlanta in 1930. The situation was only slightly better in New York, Chicago, and other northern cities. Traditional "Negro jobs" like porter, waiter, cook, and maid all became harder to find as restaurants and hotels lost customers and middle-class families reduced their domestic staff. "At no time in the history of the Negro since slavery has his economic and social outlooks seemed so discouraging," wrote T. Arnold Hill, of the National Urban League, in 1931.[16]

Black leaders were cautiously optimistic about the election of President Franklin D. Roosevelt, who won a decisive victory in 1932 on a vague promise to stabilize the economy and give a "New Deal" to American voters. Most African Americans were denied the right to vote, but the majority of those who did cast their ballot for the incumbent, Republican Herbert Hoover. In part, this decision reflected a latent loyalty for the party of Lincoln, although the Republicans had done little to challenge segregation or racial discrimination since the end of Reconstruction in 1877. For most, it was driven by black voters' distrust of Roosevelt, who, like most white Democrats in the early 20th century, made it clear that he would never challenge the segregationist wing of the party that had defeated Reconstruction and still ruled over the Jim Crow South. Roosevelt selected a white Texan as his running mate and campaigned hard for the white vote in the South, while going out of his way to avoid any appeal to black voters. Privately, black leaders were dismayed at his victory; but in the press they expressed hope that his economic programs would at least help to alleviate the horrific situation created by the Great Depression. "Almost every reconstructive act of the new administration will have some effect on the status and welfare of the Negro citizens," read a tepid editorial in the *Pittsburgh Courier*, one of the few black newspapers that had backed Roosevelt before the election. "Economic and international issues absorb the nation's attention. So long as the white man's political rights are secure, the Negro may keep howling or go hang," read a more blunt analysis by Kelly Miller, the dean of Howard University, who had remained neutral in the election. Arguing that Roosevelt had appointed southerners to head departments such as Treasury, Navy, and commerce, which had "little or no racial import," he concluded that "all in all the new cabinet promises well for the country at large and gives the Negro contingent no anxious concern."[17]

Kelly Miller had been a frequent target of attacks in *The Messenger*, and if the magazine had still existed it would almost certainly have labeled the professor's assessment of Roosevelt naïve or worse; but A. Philip Randolph also saw potential in the New Deal. In August 1933 Randolph planned a march through Harlem to "emphasize the demand for equal rights for all workers under the industrial recovery act and to protest against all forms of discrimination because of color or race affecting wages, hours and rules governing working conditions by President Roosevelt's new deal." The law he referred to had been implemented a month earlier in an attempt to stabilize economic activity by setting uniform standards for wages and hours as well as prices and production levels in manufacturing. For many labor leaders, the most important part of the law was a section protecting workers' rights to form unions, bargain collectively with employers, and go on strike if necessary to enforce the wage and hour standards. The National Industrial Recovery Act did not discriminate against African Americans directly but, like most New Deal labor laws, it applied only to industrial jobs, where few black workers were employed. That

[handwritten: criticized by many black leaders — few protections for black workers]

restriction followed from the advice of economists who were focused on stabilizing large manufacturing firms that would have a broader impact on the broader economy and could afford to pay higher wages, but it also reflected pressure by southern Democrats to exclude black workers from coverage. Agricultural workers were covered by the Agricultural Adjustment Act, which had passed a month earlier, but Congress had left the collective-bargaining protections out of that law, with the result that workers were powerless to protect their interests when it went into effect. Domestic service workers, public employees, and many service employees of private firms—including Pullman porters—were excluded from the laws completely.[18]

Criticism of the National Industrial Recovery Act was widespread among black leaders and newspapers, but Randolph had a more nuanced response. Some pointed out that Congress had allowed regional differentials that set wage standards lower in the South, which had a disproportionate impact on the significant numbers of black workers in lumber, mining, and other major industries in the region. Others warned that increasing wages would only give employers an incentive to replace black workers with whites, an argument that a study by Howard University professor Ralph Bunche found "in all likelihood much exaggerated." Black newspapers excoriated the National Recovery Administration, which administered the law, calling it the Negro Run Around, the Negro Removal Act, and the Negro Robbed Again; and when the U.S. Supreme Court ruled the law unconstitutional in 1934 no black newspaper editors "mourned its demise." In Randolph's view, the solution was not to get rid of the law but to ensure that black workers could benefit from its provisions. "Because of many conflicting opinions about the status of workers under the recovery act," he told the *Chicago Defender*, the Brotherhood of Sleeping Car Porters wanted to call the attention of black leaders and the public to "the fact that in order for the Race to benefit fundamentally under the act, they must form and join trade and industrial unions to

1935 *wins*
Randolph working for his union. Got recognized by Pullman +
AFL. in 1935

fight to secure effective collective bargaining power." No major civil rights group backed his protest march in Harlem, but he drew a spirited crowd that included members of his union, an Elks lodge, several West Indian benevolent societies, and a surviving chapter of Marcus Garvey's Universal Negro Improvement Association.[19]

Randolph was hardly in a position to launch a broad campaign against the racial limits of the New Deal, but he managed to win a major victory of the porters. Soon after his protest march, the union was evicted for failing to pay the mortgage on its new headquarters and forced to settle in a rented space nearby. Soon after that, Randolph learned that Congress was considering amendments to the Railway Labor Act, a 1926 law that granted collective-bargaining rights to railway workers but excluded service workers such as porters, cooks, and waiters. With support from several AFL unions and Senator Robert F. Wagner of New York, the Sleeping Car Porters lobbied to remove the exclusion. Black newspapers also championed the case as an effort to expand the scope of Roosevelt's recovery program, as indicated in a *Pittsburgh Courier* article titled "Porters Demand Accommodations on 'New Deal Special.' " In a tremendous victory, Congress not only ended the exclusion but also sustained a ban on "company unions" like the Pullman's Employee Representation Plan, and created a mediation board to oversee elections to determine whether a union had support from a majority of the workers. With the ability to win concrete gains for his members, Randolph moved quickly to rebuild membership and prepare for an election, which the Sleeping Car Porters won by a landslide in June 1935. Impressed by the outcome, the American Federation of Labor issued a full charter to the union, making Randolph the only black president of a union affiliated with the largest labor federation in the country. The Pullman Company challenged the Railway Labor Act but relented after the Supreme Court refused to hear the case and, in the fall of 1937, signed a contract with the Brotherhood. The contract created a formal grievance procedure, limited working hours to

Wen a victory for porters 1957
Contract

240 per month with extra pay for overtime, and raised wages by $12 a month—which amounted to more than a million dollars for all the porters combined.[20]

Although it was based on a law specific to the railway industry, Randolph's victory gained broader significance from a law that Senator Robert Wagner drafted soon after he helped Randolph remove the exclusions from the National Railway Act. Designed to preserve and strengthen the collective-bargaining provisions of the National Industrial Recovery Act, which the Supreme Court struck down in 1934, the Wagner Act created the National Labor Relations Board to "encourage collective bargaining" by preventing employers from interfering in efforts to form unions, conducting elections to determine whether workers supported a particular union, and prosecuting "unfair labor practices." The law retained the same exclusions as its predecessor and thus did not apply to the majority of African Americans, who were employed in agriculture, domestic service, or the public sector. Congress also rejected proposals from Randolph and other black activists to withhold the protections of the Wagner Act from unions that segregated or discriminated against workers on the basis of race. It applied to black workers in manufacturing, however, and held out hope that the law could be extended just as the porters had won protections from the railway law. Roosevelt signed the Wagner Act almost immediately after Congress approved it in 1935, but implementation was delayed until the Supreme Court upheld the law in 1937, four months before the Pullman Company signed the contract with the Sleeping Car Porters. Recognizing that Randolph's victory set a precedent for similar protections for other black workers, the *Chicago Defender* applauded the Pullman contract for "the inspiration it will give other Race workers of hand and brain and the Race generally to organize and fight for our rights." Leaders of the NAACP agreed, writing: "As important as is this lucrative contract as a labor victory, it is even more important to the Negro race as a whole, from the point of view of the Negro's up-hill climb for respect, recognition and influence."[21]

Even before he signed the contract with Pullman, Randolph sought to expand his campaign to win protection from New Deal labor laws. In May 1935, as the Sleeping Car Porters were preparing frantically for the election at Pullman, he attended a conference on "The Position of the Negro in Our National Economic Crisis," hosted by Abram Harris, Ralph Bunche, and other young professors at Howard University. The meeting drew a broad range of militants—including W. E. B. Du Bois, a large contingent of Pullman porters, and leaders of the Socialist and Communist Parties—and it led to the formation of the National Negro Congress (NNC) at a much larger meeting in Chicago the following February. Demonstrating the widespread concern about the economic crisis, over 800 elected delegates attended the founding conference, representing nearly 600 civil, religious, and labor organizations in twenty-eight states. Nearly half were from Chicago and the vast majority from the Northeast and Midwest. Only 55 came from the South. Noting that union activists formed a large and vocal minority, one report concluded that the group "represented the northern urban Negro population rather than the entire country and attempted to express the interests of the urban industrial workers."[22]

In addition to emphasizing the concerns of urban industrial workers, leaders of the NNC shared Randolph's view that the most effective way to address the economic problems facing those workers was to improve black men's ability to support their families without sending their wives or children into the labor market. While that priority was held widely among labor activists and social reformers of Randolph's generation, it was linked most directly to the struggle for racial equality by the sociologist E. Franklin Frazier. One of the young faculty members who hosted the meeting at Howard University that inspired the formation of the National Negro Congress, Frazier had written a dissertation at the University of Chicago on the impact of the Great

Migration on the structure and survival of black families in the urban North. Published in 1939 as *The Negro Family in the United States*, Frazier's influential study challenged the commonly held belief that African Americans were culturally or biologically predisposed toward having children out of wedlock, abandoning their families, and other behaviors that many blamed for high rates of poverty and homelessness in their communities. Pointing out that African Americans had developed relatively stable family lives in the rural South, he argued that employment discrimination prevented migrants from adapting the male-as-breadwinner model that was more common in the urban North. "It appears that, as the Negro worker becomes an industrial worker, he assumes responsibility for the support of his family and acquires a new authority in family relations," wrote Frazier, who spoke frequently at National Negro Congress conventions while he was completing his study. "Moreover, as the isolation of the black worker is gradually broken down, his ideal and patterns of family life approximate those of the great body of industrial workers." Not all members of the NNC shared that view, and a few would challenge it vigorously in a few years, but Frazier's influence was evident in the call to the founding convention: "Let us unite the Negro organizations and the friends of Negro freedom on a program for security and manhood for the Negroes in America."[23]

Negotiations with the Pullman Company prevented Randolph from attending the founding convention of the NNC, but even so he was asked to serve as its first president. He laid out the goals for the group in a keynote address that was delivered on his behalf by Charles Wesley Burton, a prominent supporter of the Brotherhood of Sleeping Car Porters who became president of the Chicago chapter of the National Negro Congress. "The issues should be obvious, clear and simple," Randolph wrote, citing reductions in relief payments and public works programs and manufacturing, the repression of "unpopular groups," and the "denial of civil rights to Negroes such as the right to be served in hotels and restaurants, to have access to public utilities, and forms of transportation, such as Pullman cars." He also cited specific causes that won support from black and white leftists in the 1930s, including opposition to Fascist Italy's invasion of Ethiopia, support for unions and strikes, efforts to stop the execution of nine black boys accused of raping two white girls in Scottsboro, Alabama, and "exposing the menace" of conservative groups such as the American Liberty League and the Ku Klux Klan. To address those problems, he recommended six specific tasks for the congress: ending "fascism and war," creating "a powerful Negro civil rights organization," improving conditions for "sharecroppers and tenants," building "mass consumers movements," expanding efforts to bring black workers into organized labor, and developing an "independent working class political party." Acknowledging that this mission was "too big for any single organization," he urged his audience to unite existing organizations of African Americans "into the framework of a united front, together with the white groups of workers, lovers of liberty and those whose liberties are similarly menaced for a common attack upon the forces of reaction, backed by the embattled masses of black and white workers."[24]

Not all black leaders were enthusiastic about Randolph's plan for a "united front." Kelly Miller blasted the National Negro Congress in a weekly column that was picked up widely by the black press. Shortly before the meeting, he warned participants to "steer clear of Communism or any brand of radicalism out of harmony with the spirit and genius of American institutions." He was responding to reports from the "red squad" of the Chicago Police Department, which attempted to stop the congress from meeting in the Windy City on the grounds that it was a "radical organization meeting for the purpose of spreading subversive doctrine"; but Miller continued the attacks after the meeting was finished. Calling it "primarily and fundamentally a leftward movement," he described the NNC as an invention of black activists in the Communist Party and "A. Philip Randolph, sometime editor of the

Communists played [?] role in Unions that broke from AFL CIO.

Messenger, a radical Negro magazine, which heads toward Moscow."
Although Miller mischaracterized Randolph's view of the Soviet Union,
it was true that Communists played an important role in creating the
National Negro Congress. Randolph's use of the term "united front"
echoed a consensus that emerged among leaders of the Communist
and Socialist Parties to put aside their strategic and ideological differences and come together to realize the potential contained in President
Roosevelt's New Deal. This allowed Communists to play a leading role
in the labor uprisings of the early 1930s, particularly those organized
by unions that broke away from the AFL to form the Congress of
Industrial Organizations (CIO). Communists also took leading roles
in fights against racism within unions and the broader society. Only
a small handful of black activists joined the Communist or Socialist
Party, but by the mid 1930s many considered them the most ardent
and effective supporters of their cause.[25]

Even among its allies, the NNC faced skepticism about its ability
to sustain such a "united front." The founding convention drew strong
support from black churches in Chicago, but ministers were angered
that although they were asked to participate in "sectional programs"
and make "invocations" and "benedictions," not one of them had been
asked to give a major speech to the entire gathering. "This prevents
the church which has the largest following of any organized group
among us from having any real part in shaping opinions that may ema-
nate from the Congress," three preachers wrote in a column printed
by the *Chicago Defender*. Two influential black journalists praised the
National Negro Congress for "focusing the attention of the Negro
community on many fundamental social, economic, and political fac-
tors," but criticized its leadership for failing to "set up a concrete program and machinery for the accomplishment of this end." "They told
the Negro what to do," another writer charged, "but not how to do
it." Leaders of the NAACP were so impressed by the congress that they
invited several NCC activists to speak about efforts to organize black

[handwritten margin note: National Negro Congress brought many blacks into unions]

workers into the CIO's United Auto Workers union at the NAACP national convention in Detroit. NAACP leaders also asked delegates to approve a resolution praising the industrial union movement and encouraging black workers to join the CIO. A group of black ministers called for a boycott of the session, however, and convinced delegates to replace the resolution with a statement condemning racial discrimination in organized labor.[26]

[handwritten margin note: Communists opposed Randolph's support of New Deal]

The National Negro Congress helped bring thousands of black workers into unions and built important links between black civil rights and civic groups in Chicago, Detroit, and even a few cities in the South; but the united front broke down in the face of renewed tensions over the Communist Party and its relationship to the struggle for civil rights. Conflicts had rumbled below the surface since the founding convention, but they came into full view as Communists grew increasingly critical of Randolph's position that the New Deal represented an important—if limited—opportunity to address the economic problems facing black and white workers. Differences emerged initially over Randolph's decision to stick with the AFL, rather than bring the Sleeping Car Porters into the new CIO, leading some to charge him with blind loyalty to its racially conservative white leaders. That dispute sharpened when Communists suddenly started calling President Roosevelt a "warmonger" because of his efforts to supply weapons and other equipment to the United Kingdom, France, and other European nations that were trying to stop the expansion of Nazi Germany. This move was confusing for activists who had united a few years earlier around a common commitment to fighting fascism, and some suspected that the shift was caused by an agreement that the Soviet Union reached with Nazi Germany to not attack each other while Germany invaded Poland and the Soviets battled Japan for control of northeast Asia. It also seemed to confirm the charges of Kelly Miller and the "red squad" that many in the Congress were "subversives" who were more loyal to Moscow than to Washington, D.C. While many black activists had grown accustomed to working alongside Communists without looking too deeply into their loyalties and beliefs, the consequences of the party's involvement with the NNC took on increased significance after Texas congressman Martin Dies created the House Committee on Un-American Activities to investigate people or individuals suspected to be subversive or disloyal to the U.S. government.[27]

Having suspended his longtime suspicion of Communists to build the National Negro Congress, Randolph was furious when they pushed hard to pass a series of resolutions that he saw as proof that their loyalties lay primarily with the Soviet Union. He raised that charge initially in a short speech on the opening night of the NNC's third annual convention, on April 26, 1940, which opened with a speech by CIO president John L. Lewis in the Department of Labor's new auditorium in Washington, D.C. Lewis was a hero to everyone in that hall for his leadership of the United Mine Workers, one of the largest, most militant, and most racially diverse unions in the country; but his prominence in the program only fanned the flames of conflict between Randolph and the Communists. A staunch isolationist and longtime Republican, Lewis had delighted Communists in recent months by taking an increasingly hostile stand toward what he viewed as Roosevelt's abandonment of the New Deal to support the war in Europe. Warning voters not to be waylaid by "foreign entanglements and political circuses," he insisted that "if it is our mission to save Western civilization then let us begin by saving it right here in our own country." Randolph did not respond directly to Lewis, whose speech was greeted with "thunderous applause," but after criticizing the Dies committee and calling for stepped-up efforts to bring African Americans into organized labor he suggested that the large presence of white delegates in the audience and the predominance of "Red" motions criticizing Roosevelt's foreign policy on the convention agenda suggested that the NCC was dominated by groups that were "not working for the interest in the American people as a whole or the Negro people in particular."[28]

Randolph stays down from leadership of NCC due to split w/ Communists

Randolph returned to this charge in his closing address to the convention on April 28. "Without the right, freely to express one's opinions, wrong as well as right, a democratic society cannot long endure," he began—referring directly to the Dies committee but also pointing a finger at black Communists who claimed, against all evidence, that citizens of the Soviet Union enjoyed "genuine equal rights and freedom." Astounded that a majority of delegates had adopted the Communists' resolutions, he called it "passing strange" that any black people would "place their fortunes at the feet" of a party that was riven with internal "violence and shakeups," lacked any "stability of purpose," and was beholden to "an alien master." Convinced that the NNC was no longer a united front, Randoph announced that he would not run for reelection as president. Howard University's Ralph Bunche compared the announcement to throwing a "bombshell into the Congress" and predicted that the group would "now be reduced to a Communist cell." The group sustained vibrant chapters in several cities for nearly a decade, but, as one founder observed, Randolph's departure "marked the passing of the Congress from any effective role as coordinating agent serving the Negro population on a national basis."[29]

Randolph's final speech to the National Negro Congress was punctuated by hisses and shouts of "traitor," and two-thirds of his audience stormed out of the hall before he was finished, but it displayed a level of confidence and independence that is rarely seen in political movements of any stripe. Four months before his resignation Randolph joined the national board of the NAACP, a group that he had criticized vehemently for more than two decades. While it would appear on the surface that he was simply shifting his allegiance from radical to moderate strains of black protest, a closer look suggests that he had actually succeeded in pulling the leaders of both major civil rights organizations—the NAACP and the Urban League—closer to him. Despite the infighting that eventually destroyed it, the National Negro Congress brought civil rights and labor leaders into a dialogue that Randolph had struggled to initiate since he started *The Messenger*. Although civil rights leaders continued to criticize discrimination and segregation within organized labor, both the NAACP and Urban League entered into lasting and extremely effective alliances with unions in the following decades. For the NAACP, this evolution created the foundation for its most rapid membership growth ever, mostly among urban industrial workers, during the Second World War. Furthermore, while Randolph and other civil rights leaders grew closer in their views about organized labor, they continued to clash frequently about strategic questions such as the relative effectiveness of demonstrations versus lobbying elected officials, or whether to prioritize economic demands such as jobs or union protections over desegregation or access to higher education.[30]

The clearest evidence that Randolph had not abandoned his radicalism was how quickly he renewed the campaign against discrimination in the New Deal order. In the summer of 1940, President Roosevelt stepped up his efforts to support allies in Europe and Asia, directing billions of dollars into constructing military bases, retooling factories, and improving infrastructure to move raw materials and finished products. As a result, unemployment plummeted to levels not seen since the 1920s while hours and paychecks ballooned for workers in defense plants. Black workers felt those changes but in ways that only sharpened their anger at the racial limitations of Roosevelt's policies. Demand for black farm workers, domestic servants, porters, and janitors increased as whites abandoned those occupations for military service and defense jobs. There were also more opportunities in low-paid southern industries, such as lumber, coal mining, and cigarette manufacturing. "These gains, however, are of little strategic significance," one influential study concluded, pointing out that they offered little opportunity for advancement. In contrast, "data suggest that *during the early stages of the war boom the Negro was virtually excluded from most armament industries*," where demand for labor and unionization had increased pay and benefits dramatically. Although 100,000 Americans

Randolph begins push to end discrimination of federally funded war industry jobs

were employed in aircraft plants in 1940, only 300 of them were black. A survey of employment patterns in twenty defense industries showed that black workers got only 5.4 percent of the jobs created that year and that this figure fell to only 2.5 percent a year later. Employment decisions in the defense industries were determined by private firms but, as A. Philip Randolph pointed out, those jobs were funded by federal taxes that came, in part, out of black workers' wages.[31]

Discrimination in the armed forces

The situation was not much better in the armed forces, where hiring was controlled by government officials. Black men looked to the Army as a place where wages and working conditions were far better than most other jobs available to them and where they had some hope for advancement through education and training. They were restricted to a handful of segregated regiments, however, denied access to the Air Corps, and shut out almost completely from the officer corps. The Navy allowed African Americans to serve only as messmen and other menial tasks, and there were no black Marines. Pointing to this near-complete exclusion of black workers from the economic revival, leaders of the National Urban League charged: "The status of the Negro and of his inalienable rights is the final test of whether we can unflinchingly and conscientiously face the world in our claims to the right to defend true democracy as a living force and the 'American Way.'"[32]

Initially, civil rights leaders hoped they could persuade Roosevelt to address these problems. Despite his ambivalence toward black voters in 1932, and a general disregard of their interests in his first term, he softened slightly after 1935. This shift was in part a response to the rising clout that the Great Migration lent to black voters in the urban North, who showed their approval of New Deal economic policies in a dramatic move to the Democratic Party in 1934 and 1936. Roosevelt was also swayed by his wife, Eleanor, who took an increasingly public role in struggles for racial equality. After black newspapers attacked the president for appointing a white southerner to advise him "on the economic status of Negroes," Roosevelt appointed Mary McLeod

Bethune, of the National Council of Negro Women, and forty-three other African Americans to minor positions in his administration. He still refused to challenge the southern Democrats in Congress, but used his executive power to make substantial changes in the racial policies of the federal government. The percentage of African Americans in the federal workforce doubled during his first two terms, bringing their number to 150,000 by 1941. While the vast majority were employed in menial jobs such as janitors, waiters, and "charwomen," there was a significant increase in professional positions as well. These changes were particularly impressive when considered alongside the records of previous presidents, as well as the expectations black leaders had of Roosevelt when he took office. One indication of that dynamic was the praise they lavished on him for allowing black singer Marian Anderson to perform at the Lincoln Memorial in 1939, after the Daughters of the American Revolution had prevented her from singing in Constitution Hall. It was a small gesture that cost the president nothing, but it led civil rights leaders to believe his heart was in the right place.[33]

A. Philip Randolph, NAACP leader Walter White, and T. Arnold Hill, of the National Urban League, did not retain that belief after meeting with Roosevelt to discuss their proposals for desegregating the armed forces and ending discrimination in the defense industries. In September 1940, Congress approved the first peacetime draft in American history. Roosevelt added a statement banning discrimination in the Selective Service Act, but refused to desegregate regiments or to remove racial barriers to advancement into the officer corps. In 1940 there were only two black combat officers in the Army and none in the Navy. Of 100,000 officers in the Army Reserve, only 500 were black. After newspapers reported that black draftees were being sent to southern bases where they faced violence and intimidation, Roosevelt agreed to discuss the issue with Randolph, Hill, and White. The three men left the meeting feeling they had got their point across but were "inexpressibly shocked" to read newspaper reports that suggested they had reached an agreement with the president that it was not the right time to integrate the military. Pointing out that Roosevelt issued the statement on the same day that Congress rejected a bill to outlaw lynching, a primary goal of the NAACP for over a decade, they called this a "double blow at the patriotism of twelve million Negro citizens." The NAACP sent letters to 600 branches, youth councils, and college chapters asking them to organize demonstrations in their communities, and the Brotherhood of Sleeping Car Porters put up picket lines outside defense plants across the country. Walter White urged NAACP members to increase activities in the leadup to the presidential election that November, in order "to make the protests of Negro Americans most effective."[34]

Roosevelt's efforts to dispel the conflict only made things worse. He sent a letter to White, Randolph, and Hill apologizing for the "misunderstanding" and clarifying that he agreed with the civil rights leaders that African Americans should be admitted into all branches of the military but on a segregated basis. The president ordered the immediate acceptance of black men into aviation training and the officer reserve and promised that "Negroes will be given the same opportunity to quality for officers' commissions as will be given to others." He underlined that commitment just a few days before the election by promoting Benjamin O. Davis to the rank of brigadier general, making him the first black general in the history of the U.S. Army; but he appointed him to lead an all-black division. "Negroes have fought in every war in our history and have been lauded for their bravery by commanding generals from Andrew Jackson to John J. Pershing," Walter White wrote in a scathing article published by the *Saturday Evening Post*. "Despite this record, the United States—in preparation for and the fighting of the next war—hesitates to make use of its reservoir of Negro man-power or has used it as little or as insignificantly as possible." Citing the case of a black man who was turned away from the Air Corps after graduating thirteenth in a class of 300 at

FDR won't integrate armed forces.

the University of Minnesota, only to be accepted into the Canadian army, White suggested that it might take "the national humiliation of military defeat . . . to establish for American Negroes the right to fight for America."[35]

Frustration was not reserved for the president. A. Philip Randolph delivered a harsh rebuke to the American Federation of Labor at its national convention in December. Pointing out that AFL unions shut black workers out of defense jobs even where employers had agreed to hire them, he chided other speakers who "shed crocodile tears" over threats to liberty, freedom, and "this newest one, 'the American way of life.'" While his fellow union leaders sat in stunned silence, Randolph bellowed: "My people want to know whether this convention means what it says about unity, brotherhood, freedom and democracy. What do the delegates say? What word shall I take back to my people?" Recounting the event in his weekly column in the Harlem-based *Amsterdam News*, NAACP leader Roy Wilkins accused the AFL of acting "its usual stupid self" by not supporting the cause of black workers. "Does the A.F. of L. think Negroes are going to continue to swallow that old stuff about 'what hurts labor hurts the Negro'?" he asked.[36]

By December 29, when President Roosevelt went on the radio to call for an "arsenal of Democracy," African Americans were in open revolt. Six days before the president's speech, a young black union activist named Ernest Calloway walked into a selective service office in Chicago and requested that he be exempted from the draft "until such a time that my contribution and participation in the defense of my country can be made on a basis of complete equality." A group called Conscientious Objectors against Jim Crow announced that they had sent letters to thousands of eligible men asking them to make similar statements. "If a few hundred Negro youth have to go to jail to wake America up, what of it?" said St. Clair Drake, a leader of the group, who was a graduate student in sociology at the University of Chicago. "We don't have any martyr complex, we're just a bunch of fellows who have taken the Declaration of Independence seriously, who have got along all right with white people in school, in the neighborhood, and on the job, and don't see the sense in Jim Crow camps." The director of the Illinois selective service responded to Calloway's protest by stating that conscientious objectors would be sent to civilian work camps to work on reforestation and conservation projects, but Drake insisted that "quite a number of young men—some of them white—will flatly refuse to join any national defense program, be it military or civil, so long as discrimination exists." Congratulating the NAACP for providing legal assistance to Calloway and other draft resisters, editors of the *Pittsburgh Courier* declared that Calloway's case "should be a cause *célèbre* calculated to raise the whole issue of democracy and arouse the conscience of white America, if any."[37]

Soon after that Randolph addressed the mass meeting in Chicago where the March on Washington was first proposed. It was the type of mobilization that he had been hoping to build for decades but had never had the following to help him build. It was also far more ambitious than any protest he had ever organized, so he started with the fairly modest goal of 10,000 marchers. In a column printed in the *Pittsburgh Courier* on January 25, 1941, Randolph explained his rationale for the protest. "Negroes are not getting anywhere with the National Defense," he began, pointing out that the armed forces were "virtually controlled by southerners" and that officials from other regions just "wink, connive at and acquiesce in the fact that Negroes are being brutally pushed around." When "responsible committees of Negroes" sought to intervene on behalf of black workers, he recalled, federal officials gave them "polite assurances that Negroes will be given a fair deal" but did nothing to address the problem. "Evidently, the regular, normal and respectable method of conferences and petitions . . . don't do the job." Black leaders were correct to appeal for justice and equality, the union leader maintained; but the "power and pressure" required to win results lay only in "the organized masses, the masses united for a definite purpose." Since the nation's leaders assumed that black workers were too timid and divided to stand up for their rights, he asserted, "Such a pilgrimage of 10,000 Negroes would wake up and shock Official Washington as it has never been shocked before."[38]

Despite his initial enthusiasm for a March on Washington, Randolph moved slowly to put it in motion. His job with the Brotherhood of Sleeping Car Porters was particularly busy in February and March as he negotiated contracts with railroads in the Midwest and the Gulf Coast and initiated an organizing drive in Nebraska. He never mentioned the march when discussing those efforts with reporters or in his newspaper columns on black workers in the AFL and the need to defeat fascism in Europe. Randolph also continued lobbying. In late February he worked with leaders of the NAACP and Urban League to convince Senator Robert Wagner to sponsor a resolution calling for a Senate investigation into discrimination by defense contractors, and in March he joined a group of fifty black civil rights, labor, and religious leaders who "invaded Washington" to discuss discrimination in the defense effort with the secretaries of war, the Navy, labor, and the interior. Randolph also worked with leaders of the NAACP and other groups to win a stay on the execution of Odell Waller, a twenty-three-year-old sharecropper who had been sentenced to death for killing his landlord in self-defense. Black newspapers covered those actions extensively, as did the journals of the NAACP and Urban League. The *Amsterdam News* even mentioned that Randolph was sick in bed one day. Yet not one of those articles mentioned the March on Washington.

In addition to not having time to organize the march, Randolph found that leaders of the black press and civil rights organizations were reluctant to support the protest. The only published reference to the march between January and April was a positive, yet skeptical, editorial in the *Chicago Defender*. "To get 10,000 Negroes assembled in one spot, under one banner with justice, democracy and work as their slogan would be the miracle of the century," the editors wrote on February 8. "However, miracles do happen. We fervently hope this one will happen before the battle of England is over, and in the manner prayed for by Mr. Randolph." The labor leader wrote a few weeks later to thank the newspaper for its endorsement, noting that "if other papers of our group give the proposal support as you have done, we will be able to develop a march of Negroes on Washington which will startle the country and win the respect of the American people."[39]

Ironically, it was a protest initiated by the National Negro Congress, which Randolph had left, that persuaded other black leaders—and perhaps Randolph himself—that a march on Washington was possible. For several years, the NNC and other groups had been protesting the practices of bus companies that made significant profits carrying black workers from Harlem to jobs in lower Manhattan yet hired only a handful of African Americans in low-paid service jobs. Reverend Adam Clayton Powell Jr., a young minister who had recently succeeded his father as pastor to the largest black church in Harlem, saw an opportunity to address the problem when the union representing white bus drivers went on strike in early March, 1941. Approaching leaders of the union, he agreed to support the strike in exchange for their backing in the fight for jobs. With support from the National Negro Congress and other local groups Powell launched a boycott of the bus companies that lasted for nearly a month and ended in an agreement, announced April 17, to hire 100 black workers immediately and thereafter to alternate black and white hires until the workforce matched the racial composition of New York City. Operating out of Powell's Abyssinian Baptist Church, the United Bus Strike Committee maintained picket lines around all bus stops in Harlem, operated soup kitchens for volunteers, and organized an "emergency jitney service" to provide alternative transportation for boycott supporters. Powell recalled a few years later that the boycott succeeded with "no blows, no violence, but the steady unrelenting pressure of an increasing horde of people who knew they were right."[40]

Planning for unemployment March on Washington

A few days before Adam Clayton Powell reached the settlement in Harlem, Randolph announced formal plans for an "all-out march" on Washington. After months of hesitation, the Brotherhood of Sleeping Car Porters moved quickly to build support for the protest. In Harlem, union activists spread news of the protest by holding rallies, putting up posters, and distributing flyers at Lucille Randolph's beauty shop and other businesses. Former National Negro Congress leader Charles Wesley Burton turned the union's Chicago office into a regional hub of organizing by sending news of the march with porters who worked on rail lines stretching far into the central portions of the United States. Edgar D. Nixon started preparing for the march with other members of the NAACP branch that he headed in Montgomery, Alabama. The union's office in Oakland, California, played a similar role in the West, relying on members who worked on lines to Los Angeles, Denver, and New Orleans. Those early organizing efforts confirmed Randolph's contention that the march would tap into the power of working-class communities. In addition to their ability to "touch and arrest the attention of powerful public officials," he explained a few years later, the March on Washington was "a form of struggle for Negro rights in which all Negroes can participate, including the educated and the so-called uneducated, the rich and poor. It is a technique and strategy which the 'little Negro' in the tavern, pool-room, on the streets, jitterbug, store-front preacher, and sharecropper, can use to help free the race."[41]

Along with the bus boycott in Harlem, such activities convinced other black leaders to join the march. On May 11 Randolph convened a meeting to build support for the "unemployment march on Washington" with civil rights leaders and ministers in Harlem. NAACP leader Walter White, Lester Granger of the National Urban League, and two other black leaders agreed to serve as a steering committee for the march. National Negro Congress cofounder Ralph Bunche was there with three other professors from Howard, as was Mary Church Ter-

Mary Church Terrell
78

rell, the seventy-eight-year-old founder of the National Association of Colored Women's Clubs. Within two weeks the steering committee had expanded to include Reverend Adam Clayton Powell Jr. and representatives from the Harlem Labor Center, the American Federation of Teachers, the Laundry Workers union, the Federation of Colored College Students, and the Improved Benevolent Protective Order of Elks of the World. Over 50,000 buttons had been distributed to "young ladies" in Harlem who planned to sell them to help defray expenses. In addition to the New York group, which became the National March on Washington Committee, local organizing committees were formed in Washington, D.C.; Richmond, Virginia; Jersey City and Newark, New Jersey; Jacksonville, Florida; Atlanta, Georgia; and Chicago, Illinois. "It was Randolph's immense prestige among all classes of Negroes that made this idea something more than a pretentious notion," recalled Lester Granger of the National Urban League.

The most notable backer of the March on Washington was the National Council of Negro Women (NCNW), a network of women's clubs and sororities that claimed a total membership of over 800,000. Affiliates of the NCNW had supported Randolph's protest from the start. The Alpha Kappa Alpha sorority, for example, coordinated a campaign that sent "an avalanche of more than 3000 letters, telegrams and long distance telephone calls" to the White House calling for integration of the defense effort and hosted a conference on May 18, 1941, "to discuss ways and means of the mass mobilization of Negro women." NCNW president Mary McLeod Bethune, however, a member of Roosevelt's Black Cabinet, feared that a mass protest would alienate supporters in the administration. "Mrs. Bethune fought me like a dog on the March," recalled E. Pauline Myers, a March on Washington activist who led an NCNW-affiliated YWCA in Richmond, Virginia. Jeanetta Welch, who worked as a lobbyist for Alpha Kappa Alpha in Washington, D.C., convinced Bethune to endorse a second conference on the last weekend of June so that "women from

Call for March which
was scheduled for July 1.

all over America can be here to participate in the A. Philip Randolph march on Washington." The NCNW never issued a formal endorsement of Randolph's demonstration, but, according to the *Chicago Defender*, Welch's maneuver lent tacit approval from "an administrative leader whose prestige and influence among womanhood of America is undisputed."[42]

Let's FDR know about most

On May 31, 1941, Randolph issued a formal call to march on behalf of the National March on Washington Committee. "No other force under the sun can save the Negro today but his mass power, orderly and lawfully used to achieve his liberation from economic, social and political slavery," he declared, calling on local committees to begin staging marches in cities across the country a week before the protest in Washington, which was scheduled for July 1. He expected 50,000 to participate, "10,000 from New York alone, with the rest making the pilgrimages from other cities, hamlets and villages throughout the nation." They would gather for a "mammoth demonstration" at the Capitol and then march to the Lincoln Memorial for a concert with black singers Marian Anderson, Dorothy Maynor, and Roland Hayes. "We must under no circumstances allow the July 1 demonstration to be anything but an overwhelming success," Walter White told a gathering of black ministers in New York; "If we demonstrate to the United States Government and the people of America that we mean business, it will help toward the attainment of a real democracy in the United States while we are fighting for it abroad." The following week Randolph wrote to Roosevelt, informing him that "ten to fifty thousand Negroes" would march on Washington unless the president issued an executive order banning racial discrimination by defense contractors and the armed forces. He invited Roosevelt to address the crowd at the Lincoln Memorial, explaining that they had chosen the site "because of its historical symbolism in relation to the issuance of the Emancipation Proclamation for the liberation of Negroes from chattel slavery." He also requested a meeting in the White House following the march, stat-

Eleanor
tries to persuade Randolph not to march

ing that civil rights leaders wanted "to learn whether or not Democracy is going to be given a place to work here since there is so much talk about spreading it to countries abroad."[43]

Roosevelt did not reply to Randolph's letter, but he dispatched current and former members of his administration to talk the labor leader out of marching. "Think it highly important that you come to Washington for a conference on your project," read a telegram to Randolph from the secretary of the Navy. "I agree with every word you say about the current administration, but don't start this march on Washington. It will do infinitely more harm than good," wrote General Hugh S. Johnson, who had headed the National Recovery Administration in the 1930s. First Lady Eleanor Roosevelt informed Randolph that she had discussed his letter with the president and that she felt it would be a "very grave mistake" to stage a protest that "may engender too much bitterness" and embolden their opponents in Congress. On June 13 she travelled to New York for a meeting with Randolph, Walter White, and New York mayor Fiorello LaGuardia, who served as Roosevelt's director of civil defense. Back in Washington on the same day, Illinois congressman Arthur W. Mitchell issued a scathing denunciation of Randolph during his commencement address at Howard University. The first black Democrat ever elected to the U.S. House of Representatives and a close ally of the president, Mitchell warned graduates of the prestigious black institution to "steer clear" of radicals "who would make tools of educated colored men and women." Speaking at an outdoor ceremony while a thunderstorm loomed, the black congressman branded Randolph "the most dangerous Negro in America."[44]

The efforts of Roosevelt's allies only emboldened the National March on Washington Committee, which resolved to "redouble its determination to make the March on Washington the greatest demonstration of Negro mass power for our economic liberation ever conceived." After the meeting in New York, Randolph and White stated that they appreciated "the fine spirit" of the conversation and considered the First Lady "a real and genuine friend of the race," but were confident that the march would "have a favorable and beneficial effect upon the American people, both black and white, since it will show that Negroes themselves have awakened to a definite sense of their mass power." Soon afterward the National March on Washington Committee released a detailed description of the protest: 100,000 "Negro laborers, domestics, mechanics, professionals" would gather at the Capitol and march down Constitution Avenue past the White House and the War Department to the Lincoln Memorial in "a solemn and determined fight for real democracy." They would be divided into brigades representing every state and headed by veterans of the First World War, high school cadets, and Boy Scouts, and they would carry banners reading "Let American Negroes Help America," "Total Democracy for Total Defense," and "If We Are Fit to Fight, We Are Fit to Work." Veterans would be placed throughout the procession to maintain order and unity. While most marchers would arrive by train at Washington's Union Station, a large delegation planned to travel first to the site of President Lincoln's legendary Gettysburg Address—which had called for a "new birth of freedom" after the Civil War—and to walk silently from there to join the march. "Even if the sponsors of the March on Washington . . . had yielded to the advices from high places to cancel the 'March,' it would have been of little avail," read an editorial in the Urban League's journal, *Opportunity*, "since the Negro is so thoroughly aroused by the flagrant abuse of his citizenship rights that hundreds, if not thousands, would have descended upon the capital in spite of anything that the responsible leadership might say or do."[45]

On June 18 Roosevelt finally agreed to meet with Randolph, White, and two other members of the National March on Washington Committee. The president offered to establish a committee headed by Mayor LaGuardia that would draw up a plan for addressing discrimination in the defense effort, but ordered Randolph to cancel the march so that it would not "be considered as an effort to coerce the government and make it do certain things." Randolph refused. "The public knows that the Negroes have a justification for bringing their grievances to the president and to present them to the American people." He explained that the demonstration was not being "fostered by any irresponsible, wild-eyed crackpots," but had the support and participation of "sane, sober, and responsible Negro citizens," including leaders of the NAACP, the National Urban League, the Elks, Howard University, and major unions, churches, and civic, social, and student groups across the country. The meeting ended with an agreement that LaGuardia's committee would develop a proposal, in consultation with Randolph, for addressing the problem of discrimination in national defense. Upon leaving the White House, Randolph and White clarified that the march would still occur as planned on July 1. Reporting that "the momentum of the march on Washington movement is gaining hourly and that sentiment for it is sweeping the Negroes throughout the country like prairie fire," Randolph declared: "The Negro March on Washington is on."[46]

Then the president backed down. Following the meeting on June 18, the White House went into a panic. Attorney Joseph Rauh, then a young staffer in the Roosevelt administration, remembered his supervisor calling and saying "some guy named Randolph is going to march on Washington unless we put out a fair employment practices order." Asked for clarification, his boss said, "All I know is the President says you gotta stop Randolph from marching." Randolph went to Chicago for a mass meeting about the march and rejected Rauh's first draft upon his return to New York a few days later. On June 25, 1941, less than a week before the March on Washington, Roosevelt issued an executive order instructing all government agencies involved with "vocational and training programs for defense production" to "assure that such programs are administered without discrimination" and to include in all defense contracts "a provision obligating the contractor not to discriminate against any worker." He also created a Fair Employment Practices Committee, chaired by five officials appointed by the President, to enforce the order and recommend any measures "deemed necessary or proper to effectuate" its provisions. Without mentioning Randolph or the March on Washington, Roosevelt stated: "There is evidence available that needed workers have been barred from industries engaged in defense production solely because of considerations of race, creed, color or national origin, to the detriment of workers' morale and of national unity."[47]

Roosevelt's executive order did not address every demand of the March on Washington, but it was sufficient to convince Randolph and other leaders to cancel the demonstration. "This is the first executive order which has been issued by a President of the United States on behalf of Negroes since the immortal Abraham Lincoln issued the Emancipation Proclamation in 1863," Randolph stated in a speech that was broadcast over two nationwide radio networks on June 28. Linking this victory to the social-democratic goals of Roosevelt's Four Freedoms, the union leader predicted that the new policy would bring "thousands of jobs and hundreds of millions of dollars in increased wages" to black communities and result in "higher standards of living, more education and recreation for the children, a greater security and assurance of a more abundant life." He acknowledged that the executive order applied narrowly to defense jobs and urged the president to issue a second order banning discrimination in "all departments of the Federal Government." He also asked local March on Washington committees to "remain intact and watch and check the industries in their communities to determine the extent to which they are observing the executive order of the president." Despite those reservations, Randolph announced, "the march is unnecessary at this time."[48]

Some supporters were disappointed by Randolph's decision to cancel the March on Washington, but few questioned the significance of Roosevelt's executive order. Black newspapers reported widespread "grumbling" among people who had invested their time and money in preparing for the march, stating that "hundreds" were "determined to come to Washington" despite Randolph's reversal. The chairman of a National Negro Congress branch from Minnesota fired off an angry telegram accusing Randolph of having "sold-out" the movement, and the national leadership of that group warned, "the real battle for full citizenship rights still remains to be fought and won." On the other hand, some activists expressed relief at not having to prove that they could mobilize "a sufficiently large number to impress the President." Implying that Randolph never expected many people to show up, some called his standoff with Roosevelt "a magnificent bluff." The *Pittsburgh Courier* questioned whether the March on Washington deserved primary credit for the victory, noting that Roosevelt had been pressured by several black newspapers and many organizations. "Aside from this necessary analysis for the record," however, the newspaper conceded, "there must be a feeling of elation and relief in the breast of every American Negro and of all friends of democracy over this great forward step toward unity." The *Chicago Defender* was more direct in its praise, crediting A. Philip Randolph with having "opened the eyes of the President and at the same time demonstrated to the doubting Thomases among us, that only mass action can pry open the iron doors that have been erected against America's black minority."[49]

CHAPTER TWO

THE MARCH ON WASHINGTON MOVEMENT

D ESPITE THE INITIAL euphoria about Roosevelt's executive order, disillusionment set in quickly. "Recriminations and charges flew thick and fast here over the weekend," one black newspaper reported from Washington, D.C., after a Senate committee cancelled a hearing on employment discrimination that had been scheduled for June 30. Senators attributed their decision to criticism from Walter White of the NAACP, who pointed out that no heads of government agencies or defense contractors had been called to testify at the hearing and dismissed the event as a "smokescreen" designed to draw attention from the March on Washington. Other black leaders saw value in the hearing, however, and lashed out at White for undermining what they viewed as a "real opportunity" to draw attention to the problems facing black workers. On the same day the War Department signed a $166 million contract with Glenn L. Martin Aircraft, which had "refused consistently to even consider hiring Negroes." Stating that the agreement had been "discussed" before Roosevelt issued the executive order on June 25, federal officials argued that the firm was not bound by the fair employment policy. The National Negro Congress, which had been protesting Glenn L. Martin's employment policies for months, pointed out that such a loophole would allow "contracts not yet signed" worth billions of dollars to be finalized without a fair employment provision. "Calling off the March left things flat," wrote a columnist in the *Chicago Defender*, reporting that only 1,000 people showed up for a "victory celebration" that A. Philip Randolph planned at a small theater near the Lincoln Memorial on July 1.[1]

While the leaders were arguing about the value of Roosevelt's executive order, hundreds of black women were forging a plan to make it more effective. "One of the most important conferences held in connection with the Negro's participation in national defense," according to the *Chicago Defender*, was the meeting that Jeanetta Welch of the Alpha Kappa Alpha sorority had organized for the weekend before the March on Washington. Despite the cancellation of the march, leaders of women's clubs, YWCA branches, and church groups from across the country gathered at Howard University to discuss a broad range of topics including health care, recreation, housing, and civil liberties, as well as ways to improve access to training and employment in the defense industries. "Particularly effective" was a panel on "Negro Women and Organized Labor," which was led by an organizer with the CIO Clothing Workers union and E. Pauline Myers, the YWCA activist who headed the March on Washington Committee in Richmond, Virginia. NCNW president Mary McLeod Bethune addressed a mass meeting on Sunday, June 29, along with Mary Church Terrell of the National Association of Colored Women's Clubs and other prominent black women. At the closing session on Monday, Welch announced that AKA and the NCNW were cosponsoring the Negro Women's Committee for Democracy in National Defense to gather information on opportunities for training and employment in the defense industries and to help black workers secure them. The following day, she described the initiative at the victory celebration near the Lincoln Memorial.[2]

Randolph, White, and other speakers at the victory celebration

insisted that "a militant, sustained, organized public opinion is necessary to carry out the order," but only Welch presented a specific model
for building such a movement. The day after the victory celebration, a
heated debate over strategy erupted at a meeting of the National March
on Washington Committee in New York City. Reverend Adam Clayton Powell Jr. and Richard Parrish, who headed the youth division of
the March on Washington, accused Randolph of having cancelled the
March without consulting leaders of local committees and demanded
that he resume plans to stage the demonstration immediately. Dismissing the two as "a handful of Negro youth who apparently were more
interested in the drama and pyrotechnics of the march than the basic
and main issues of putting Negroes to work," Randolph argued that
it would be more effective to mobilize March committees around a
nationwide campaign to enforce the executive order. "Now that the
President has 'spoken out' and will soon appoint the Fair Employment
Practice Committee, it is important that all industries in the defense
setup that have barred Negroes from employment should be tried out
immediately by Race workers," Randolph told a press conference following the New York meeting, adding: "All cases of discrimination will
be presented to this Fair Employment Practice Committee."[3]

Randolph referred to this effort to "fool-proof" the executive order
as the March on Washington Movement, but it relied on a loose network of organizations that often had no direct link to the original demonstration. He appointed Harlem trade unionists Frank Crosswaith
and Layle Lane to a committee, similar to Welch's Negro Women's
Committee, which would act as a "clearing house for data" on training and employment opportunities in defense plants nationwide and
pass that information on to local groups in communities near those
plants. Arguing that the effectiveness of the FEPC would "depend upon
the policing of the order in concrete, individual, and special cases of
discrimination against Negroes," Randolph encouraged individual
workers to apply for those positions and keep detailed records of their

interactions with unions and managers, "especially if they are refused employment, and whatever excuses are given for said refusal." That evidence was to be collected by local March committees or, where none existed, local branches of the NAACP, Urban League, Sleeping Car Porters, YWCA, YMCA, or "any Negro trade union or church." Randolph and other members of the national March committee explained the procedures to groups across the country, including the Brooklyn Women's Voters Council, the Atlanta Civic and Political League, and the Improved Benevolent Protective Order of Elks, which drew over 100,000 members to its national convention in Atlantic City. One of the most effective policing efforts was initiated by the Baltimore chapter of the National Negro Congress, which launched a campaign that resulted in the hiring of 5,000 black workers at Glenn L. Martin Aircraft over the next two years.[4]

That broad base of support became critical in the following weeks and months, as employers and federal officials made it clear that they would not comply willingly with the executive order. Rejecting Randolph's and White's recommendation that he appoint Mayor LaGuardia to chair the FEPC, Roosevelt selected Mark Etheridge, an outspoken liberal who edited the *Louisville Courier-Journal*. Etheridge brought important political connections and public relations expertise to the job, but, like most white southerners, he emphasized interracial cooperation over equality and refused to challenge the southern system of segregation. Moreover, Roosevelt provided the FEPC with only $80,000 in its first year, forcing Etheridge to limit its activities to a few largely symbolic hearings in each region of the country. The first of these was not held until October 1941, and it was scheduled for Los Angeles, where the March on Washington had only a small base of support. Although black newspapers carried detailed reports, white-owned papers either ignored the procedures or reported "without analysis or commentary." Despite the fact that "company after company admitted that it did not employ Negroes, or persons of Oriental background, regardless of their fitness for the jobs," Etheridge ended the hearings without ordering any changes in local employment practices. Randolph and other black activists pointed out that this lack of follow-through left many employers, union leaders, and even government officials oblivious to the goals and workings of the FEPC. Newspaper reports confirmed that result in the fall of 1941. "I can't see that the President's order will have any particular effect on our program," stated an official in charge of recruiting defense workers in New Jersey. "It's not for us to say who shall be hired."[5]

In addition to drawing a broad range of organizations into the effort to strengthen the FEPC, the March on Washington Movement created opportunities for those groups to expand their objectives beyond Randolph's original goal of winning jobs for black men. The National Negro Congress worked closely with the United Auto Workers and United Steel Workers unions in Baltimore, for example, and in addition to fighting employment discrimination against black workers the groups cooperated to organize interracial unions at Glenn L. Martin and a massive steel mill in nearby Sparrows Point. Jeanetta Welch had worked for the United Auto Workers while attending law school in Detroit before the Second World War, and she agreed with NNC activists that no "serious thinking Negro in these days can afford to well deny the close tie-up of labor and the salvation of Negro people." She took a more dramatic departure from Randolph's original objectives, however, as she focused the energies of the Negro Women's Committee on opening jobs in the defense industries to women as well as to men. "Negro women have a right and a duty to see to it that they become a recognized part of this picture, especially during this crucial period," she told a reporter in October 1941. "Thousands of our women stand ready and willing to bring a wide variety of skills and abilities to keep defense industry moving without let up."[6]

Welch's focus on building unions and winning industrial jobs for black women represented a shift for Alpha Kappa Alpha and the

National Council of Negro Women as well as the March on Washington Movement. Founded at Howard University in 1908, AKA was typical of the organizations that college-educated black women founded to cope with segregation, disfranchisement, and racist violence at the turn of the twentieth century. Presenting themselves as advocates, protectors, and role models for poor and working-class women in their communities, founders of black sororities, women's clubs, and church conferences focused their energies on local concerns and traditionally female realms such as nutrition, health care, and education. Mary McLeod Bethune began to expand that focus when she organized the National Council of Negro Women in 1935, basing the group in Washington to take advantage of President Roosevelt's promise of a New Deal. Alpha Kappa Alpha adopted a similar approach in 1938 by creating the National Non-Partisan Lobby on Civil and Democratic Rights, the first African American lobbying organization in the nation's capital.[7]

The shift toward national politics and a broader social and economic agenda was completed by a cohort of young black women like Jeanetta Welch, who was hired as a lobbyist for AKA in 1939. An Alabama native, Welch had joined AKA at Tennessee State College, from which she graduated in 1936 before going on to law school and a stint as a union organizer in Detroit. Moving to Washington at the age of twenty-nine, she became close friends with Dorothy Height, who moved to the capital the same year to direct an African American branch of the YWCA. Born in Virginia the same year as Welch, Height was raised in Pittsburgh before moving to New York City to study education. Graduating in 1932, she went to work at the New York State Emergency Relief Bureau before getting hired as assistant director of the Harlem YWCA. Those career choices were typical of a middle-class black woman at the time, but Height also defied tradition by leading a youth chapter of the National Negro Congress and joining a campaign to improve wages and working conditions for domestic workers. Mary McLeod Bethune was sixty-five years old when Height and Welch moved to Washington, but still ran the National Council of Negro Women without a staff. Spending most of their weekends and evenings at the headquarters of the NCNW, the young women helped revitalize the organization and push it into an alliance with the March on Washington Movement.[8]

Having united a broad coalition of black activists, the March on Washington Movement began to fracture after December 7, 1941, when Japan's surprise attack on the U.S. Navy in Pearl Harbor pulled the United States directly into the Second World War. Like most citizens, African Americans responded with a burst of patriotism and support for the war effort. "The hour calls for a closing of ranks, a joining of hands, not a widening of the racial gap," the *Chicago Defender* declared soon after Roosevelt declared war on Japan, Germany, and Italy. Protests continued against discrimination in the armed forces and the defense industries, but all but a tiny handful of activists felt obliged to emphasize their loyalty to the United States as much or more than their criticism. The *Pittsburgh Courier* struck that balance in its "Double Victory" campaign, which urged African Americans to "fight for the right to fight" and asserted: "The more we put in, the more we have a right to claim." Randolph promoted a similar slogan, albeit with more emphasis on the claims: "Winning democracy for the Negro is winning war for democracy!" Support for the war was so strong that the Federal Reserve Bank ran out of defense savings bonds within days of the Pearl Harbor attack. When supplies were replenished in January 1942, the Brotherhood of Sleeping Car Porters pledged to purchase $25,000 worth. "Declarations of war do not lessen the obligation to preserve and extend civil liberties here," insisted Walter White of the NAACP, although he admitted that "this is not going to be easy to do."[9]

Despite the challenges posed by the declaration of war, black activists were in a strong position when the FEPC opened a second series of hearings in Chicago and New York in January and February 1942. Black attorneys held influential positions in FEPC offices in those cities and worked closely with activists from the Brotherhood of Sleeping Car Porters, the NAACP, and other groups. In both cities, activists formed Metropolitan Fair Employment Practice Councils to help workers document discrimination and bring complaints before the FEPC and push local officials to implement Roosevelt's order. New York governor Herbert Lehman ordered all state agencies to aid the FEPC, and Illinois became the first state to pass a law banning employment discrimination. Even FEPC chair Mark Etheridge was emboldened and, in stark contrast to his performance in Los Angeles, opened the Chicago hearings by declaring an "all-out war" on discrimination and warning that "anything that does not fall in line with that idea is close to treason." After hearing complaints against eleven companies in Chicago and Milwaukee, he ordered all of them to bring their hiring policies into line with Roosevelt's order, give written notification of that change to all employment agencies, and file monthly reports with the FEPC indicating their progress toward fair employment. Black attorney and former union activist Eugene Davidson established an FEPC field office in Manhattan, stating that in addition to implementing Roosevelt's order through education and moral suasion he would urge the president to cancel contracts and withhold payment from companies that persisted in discrimination.[10]

The FEPC did not eliminate employment discrimination in Chicago or New York, but government officials and local activists worked together to enforce the president's order. When federal authorities surveyed nearly 800 large defense contractors in the spring of 1942, they found that most still restricted black workers to unskilled or semiskilled positions or employed them in numbers "so small as to represent token compliance with government nondiscrimination policies." They were encouraged, however, to discover that hundreds of African Americans were employed by companies that had previously barred them from employment and that "significant gains in numerical employment and occupational diversification" had occurred in government agencies, firms with a history of employing black workers, and most plants established since the start of the war. Tens of thousands of black workers were employed in shipbuilding and aircraft plants, despite the objections of many white workers, "the acceptance of this attitude by organized labor, and the hesitancy of management to take the initiative in extending the scope of Negro employment." The most dramatic changes occurred in automobile plants, where black activists and white officials in the CIO autoworkers' union forced a showdown on employment discrimination by threatening to expel white union members who refused to work with African Americans. Arguing that integration into organized labor would allow black workers to defend and extend those gains after the war, black economist Robert C. Weaver contended that "patterns are being established in our country today which will be with us for at least a generation."[11]

Those patterns were harder to establish in the South, where civil rights networks were weaker and where the FEPC faced stiff resistance from local employers and elected officials. The Southern Negro Youth Congress, which was formed by young activists in the National Negro Congress, allied with the CIO United Mine Workers union to support FEPC hearings in Birmingham, Alabama. CIO unions also backed a call by New Mexico senator Dennis Chavez for hearings in El Paso, Texas. The El Paso proceedings were cancelled, however, after the State Department complained that they would "arouse Anti-Americanism" and undermine U.S. efforts to win Mexico's support for the allies in Europe. As one diplomat put it, discussions would inevitably focus on discrimination against Mexicans and Mexican Americans, which would "arouse Anti-Americanism" and "kick a sleeping dog who should . . . be allowed to slumber in peace." FEPC leaders boasted that "the Birmingham hearings were among the most successful and fruitful of all those held so far," but they provoked an angry response from southern political leaders, who charged the Roosevelt administration with placing "the segregation system on trial." In stark contrast to

Governor Lehman's support for the FEPC in New York, Alabama governor Frank Dixon declared, "I will not permit the state of Alabama to be subject to the whims of any federal agency, and I will not permit the employees of the state to be placed in a position where they must abandon the principles of segregation or lose their jobs."[12]

By the summer of 1942, it was clear that Roosevelt's executive order was being implemented only in places where black activists could force local officials into addressing discrimination. To increase pressure, Randolph called for mass rallies in New York, Washington, and Chicago on June 16 and 26, nearly a year after he had called off the March on Washington. The rallies were impressive: 25,000 people packed New York's Madison Square Garden in lower Manhattan, and over 12,000 filled the Chicago Coliseum. "Harlem was like a deserted village," one participant recalled; "Every man, woman and child who had carfare was packed into Madison Square Garden." In New York, the "most militant, fighting speech" was delivered by Adam Clayton Powell Jr., who had been elected the previous November to represent Harlem on the City Council and took the occasion to announce his candidacy for Congress. "To those who say 'The Negro is disloyal,'" he declared, "I say, 'we are the most loyal group in America.' For if we did not love democracy, we would have none of it and we would not be gathered here tonight. We would say, 'to hell with the war.'" A. Philip Randolph entered the Garden flanked by 150 porters and maids in uniform and introduced Annie Waller, the mother of the young sharecropper who had been sentenced to death a few months before the March on Washington was cancelled. The execution had been rescheduled for June 19, 1942, and massive "Save Odell Waller" banners hung around the arena. "Yes, we love peace," Randolph bellowed. "But there can be no peace in America until there is peace for the black man throughout the length and breadth of the nation—peace for every American citizen from the lowliest to the most high." It was nearly midnight when Randolph took the podium, but the crowd burst into applause that continued "fully three minutes, only then ceasing at his plea for the lateness of the hour."[13]

The declaration of war had not prevented black activists from pushing the FEPC to be more effective, but they found it difficult to sustain a more direct confrontation with the Roosevelt administration. Despite the enthusiastic crowds in New York and Chicago, Randolph and the others were forced to cancel the rally in Washington, which they viewed as "the most vital and important" of the three. "We were unable to get people of the stature we wanted for such a meeting," Randolph admitted, explaining that some feared his movement would undermine the war effort. "If Randolph arouses and organizes the discontented, what does he propose to do with them?" asked an editorial in the *Pittsburgh Courier* soon before the New York rally. "Is it going to be made clear to them that the nation's fight is also their fight?" Mary McLeod Bethune left no doubt about her priorities. "We have grown tired of turning the other cheek," she told the crowd in Madison Square Garden. "But regardless of our trials and tribulations at home, we must not for one moment lose sight of the fact that we must give all-out, unreserved effort to winning this war." Declining Randolph's request that she speak at the Washington rally, Bethune wrote: "We are all anxious for the winning of the war and seeing democracy in action here and everywhere."[14]

Ironically, the most steadfast supporters of the war effort were Communists, who had abruptly ended their criticism of Roosevelt's "imperialist war" the previous summer after Germany broke its pact with the Soviet Union and invaded the Communist country. The National Negro Congress helped establish Negro Labor Victory Committees in many cities, often with support from the Roosevelt administration, and accused March on Washington activists of "disrupting the war effort." Ben Davis, Jr., who edited the Communist newspaper *The Daily Worker*, led efforts to counter the March on Washington in Harlem. Calling Randolph's Madison Square Garden meeting "a forum for defeatists," he organized a "Unity for Victory" rally on June 28 featuring himself and other prominent black Communists, the head of Roosevelt's War Manpower Board, and Adam Clayton Powell, Jr., who missed no chance to win votes in his race for Congress. Also on stage was Henrietta Miller, the mother of a black cook who earned a Navy Cross for manning an antiaircraft gun during the Japanese attack on Pearl Harbor. The first African American to earn such an honor, Dorie Miller was held up by both the Roosevelt administration and the Communist Party as a symbol of African Americans' determination to win the war despite the discrimination they faced in the armed forces. Noting that 6,000 people turned out for the rally, the *New York Times* reported that the "keynote of most of the speeches was that 'this is not a white man's war; the fate of the Negroes is at stake too.'" Randolph clashed directly with this "all-out-for-war bloc" when he attended the national convention of the NAACP in Los Angeles in late July. After he told a large rally that it was "fully possible to win the war in Europe and lose it" in Texas, Georgia, Mississippi, Alabama and other states, the president of the local NAACP branch, who was sympathetic to the Communist Party, lashed out at Randolph for using "mass pressure tactics" to undermine the war effort.[15]

In the face of that backlash, Randolph found it difficult to reinvigorate the broad coalition that had backed the March on Washington just a year before. He led a delegation of black leaders to the White House to demand intervention after the governor of Virginia rejected Odell Waller's final appeal and scheduled his execution for July 2, 1942. First Lady Eleanor Roosevelt greeted them, but the president refused to see them or to make a statement on Waller's behalf. "The President and the Government of the United States have failed us," Randolph told Walter White, Mary McLeod Bethune, and others as they left the White House. "Waller's death will 'stab in the back' a group of people who are asked to defend their country, but whom the leaders of their country will not defend." Randolph was scheduled to travel to Los Angeles for the NAACP convention, but he recruited Pauli Murray, a thirty-one-year-old law student who had worked on Waller's defense team, to organize a silent march through midtown Manhattan to protest the execution. Working with friends in unions and women's organizations in New York, Murray built an impressive "block system" and distributed tens of thousands of flyers to build support for the protest. It was a striking scene. Five hundred young women marched "in ominous, grim silence" to the sound of muffled drums, wearing white dresses and black armbands and holding signs reading "Justice and Manhood," "Free the South," and "Democracy Here Is Our First Line of Defense." Adam Clayton Powell's newspaper called it "a non-violent demonstration in answer to violent mob acts of southerners." Few others participated, however, and Murray noted that without backing from major civil rights groups or unions, "it was remarkable that we had any demonstration at all."[16]

Deepening the sense that the movement was losing ground, in August 1942 the White House conceded to pressure from southern Democrats by placing the previously independent FEPC under the control of the War Manpower Commission. Roosevelt insisted the move was intended "to strengthen—not to submerge" the antidiscrimination agency, but the chairman of the War Manpower Commission slashed its budget, denied requests for office space, and refused to aid it in conflicts with discriminatory contractors. Randolph blasted this "shameful surrender," and Walter White accused the president of abandoning the promise he had made when they called off the March on Washington. NAACP branches and Metropolitan FEP Councils flooded the White House with telegrams expressing "country-wide indignation," and 9,000 people turned out to hear Walter White and local activists who "scathingly attacked Jim Crowism, segregation and race prejudice in war industries and in the Army" at a rally organized by the Brotherhood of Sleeping Car Porters in St. Louis. Randolph and White asked the president to meet with them and other members of the March on Washington Committee about continued discrimination by defense contractors, but the White House replied that Roosevelt was under "extreme pressure" to address other issues.[17]

Although Randolph continued to use the term, it was clear by the fall of 1942 that "the March on Washington" represented little more than members of his own union, a few loyal friends like Walter White, and young militants like Pauli Murray. A native of North Carolina, Murray had moved to New York in the 1930s, where she lived at the Harlem YWCA while attending Hunter College. Embracing the radical ferment of the era, she contributed a few poems to the literary renaissance in Harlem and joined a small faction of dissident Communists who broke with the Communist Party over its deference to Soviet dictator Joseph Stalin. The group was led by Jay Lovestone, a prominent figure in the international Communist movement and a leader of the International Ladies Garment Workers Union in New York City. Pauli Murray applied to graduate school at the University of North Carolina in 1938 but was told that "members of your race are not admitted to the university." While pursuing legal action she took a job with the Workers' Defense League, which had been founded in the 1930s by the Socialist Party to defend "poor workers and trade unionists." She met A. Philip Randolph, who cochaired the WDL Labor Committee, and studied the strategies of nonviolent resistance that Mohandas K. Gandhi had developed to fight British imperialism in India. Murray noted the differences between their struggles, but wondered if Gandhi's tactics of mass protest and civil disobedience might be more effective than the "legalistic" approach that she associated with the NAACP. In March 1940, Pauli Murray and a co-worker at the WDL were arrested for refusing to relinquish their seats to a white passenger on a bus, and soon after her release from jail the WDL assigned Murray to handle publicity for the Odell Waller case. She continued to work on the campaign after starting law school at Howard University in 1941, and, having worked closely with Waller's wife and mother for nearly two years, Murray responded enthusiastically to Randolph's proposal to memorialize the sharecropper with a march. Two months later, on September 26, 1942, she travelled to Detroit for a "policy conference" that Randolph called to revive the "March on Washington movement."[18]

Murray attended Randolph's conference along with sixty activists representing local committees in New York, Chicago, Detroit, St. Louis, New Orleans, Tampa, Florida, and Richmond, Virginia. Over the course of two days they debated goals and strategies, elected temporary leaders, and drafted a constitution and bylaws for the March on Washington Movement. Pauli Murray handled publicity for the conference and headed a committee charged with developing "techniques for breaking down discrimination in restaurants, hotels, buses, movies, etc." Being a law student, she advocated utilizing civil rights laws where they applied. Elsewhere, she argued "disciplined and trained leaders, students and young people" would have to "use a carefully planned non-violent technique of refusal to accept such discriminations." E. Pauline Myers, the thirty-three-year-old activist who had spoken at Jeanetta Welch's conference following the cancellation of the March on Washington, was elected executive secretary of the March on Washington Movement. A native of Virginia, Myers had first met Randolph in 1925 when she was sixteen and struck up a conversation with the "distinguished gentleman" in the cafe car of a train. Two years later she headed the Socialist Party's student group, the Student League for Industrial Democracy, at Howard University, where she also read and heard lectures about Gandhian nonviolence. After graduating from Howard in the early 1930s, Myers taught school for a few years before taking a position as the industrial and public affairs secretary of an African American YWCA in Richmond, Virginia. In addition to her regular duties, she helped organize a union for domestic workers and led the local organizing committee for the March on Washington in 1941. Randolph was elected president of the March on Washington

Movement, but because of his responsibilities to the Brotherhood of Sleeping Car Porters, he left the planning to Myers, Murray, and other young women.[19]

While it solidified A. Philip Randolph's status as a mentor to a generation of young radicals, his decision to create a new organization worried his closest allies. "If you can figure out what is happening between the March on Washington group and the NAACP you are better than I am at puzzles," wrote sociologist Horace Cayton, one of the most insightful analysts of the civil rights and labor movements in the 1930s and 1940s. Having been impressed by the cooperation between Randolph and Walter White in the previous year, Cayton noted "a parting of the way" when no NAACP leaders attended the March on Washington Movement conference in Detroit. Cayton attributed that change to a fear that the new organization would compete with the NAACP. He also wondered if it reflected pressure from the Roosevelt administration, which, as Cayton had discovered during a recent trip to Washington, was "frankly antagonistic or else scared to death that Randolph was going to throw this country into a series of race riots." Whatever the source of Walter White's eagerness to "drop that 'hot potato,'" Cayton observed, Randolph was now "on his own."[20]

In addition to the NAACP, Randolph faced resistance from within the Brotherhood of Sleeping Car Porters. "We are paying Randolph to negotiate and sign contracts, not to run around like a West Indian Communist agitator or dreamer," wrote one particularly agitated porter. Milton Webster, who headed the union's offices in Chicago, complained that young supporters of the March on Washington Movement seemed unaware that the Brotherhood had "furnished a couple of thousands of dollars to put this mass meeting over." Echoing members' concern that Randolph's activism was taking him away from duties at the union, Webster wondered "whether or not it is worth our while to create a lot of bitterness among our people when it is really doubtful whether we can save the race and maybe it would be better if we just saved the Brotherhood." Revealing a less noble source of his frustration, the fifty-five-year-old porter added: "There are too many women mixed up in this thing, anyhow . . . I don't intend for these women to be pushing us around, because I know, and they ought to have sense enough to know, that if it was not for the Brotherhood there would not be any March on Washington Movement now."[21]

Beyond its potential to compete with existing groups, attract suspicion from the government, and challenge traditional gender hierarchies, the March on Washington Movement came under fire for limiting its membership to African Americans. Whites had been excluded from the 1941 march, but that decision was not controversial at the time. Horace Cayton speculated that NAACP leaders were actually "embarrassed by the fact" that a "purely Negro" effort had challenged their interracial organization's claim to leadership in the civil rights movement. After the attack on Pearl Harbor and in the context of building a formal organization, however, some accused the March on Washington Movement of "flaunting its racial chauvinism by barring white citizens from membership." Those concerns were heightened by well-publicized raids in September 1942 on black nationalist organizations in New York and Chicago, which the Federal Bureau of Investigation linked to a "Japanese-inspired race-hatred and disobedience campaign on a nation-wide scale." Randolph denounced the groups as "pure fanatics," but the arrests made it even harder to assert racial pride and independence without appearing to undermine national unity. "You won't find many Negroes or Negro organizations preaching isolation and Jim Crow like that," wrote one black columnist, accusing Randolph of adopting the same "race conscious" approach that he had lambasted Marcus Garvey for two decades earlier. Randolph responded that "Negroes must develop the spirit of self-reliance, and take the initiative and assume responsibility for the solution of their problem, but collaborate with their natural allies such as the trade union movement and other oppressed minorities, including the Jews and Catholics, and

those liberal forces that seek to extend the frontiers of true democracy."
But the March on Washington was unable to shake the perception that
it had abandoned the cause of interracial cooperation.[22]

Such criticism limited its size and immediate impact, but the March
on Washington Movement still took up Pauli Murray's proposal to
train leadership for the battle against Jim Crow. Many black activists had admired the Indian independence movement for decades, and
they paid closer attention after August 1942, when Gandhi and other
leaders launched a wave of mass marches, consumer boycotts, and
resistance to taxes and the draft to demand that Britain "Quit India"
immediately. "Negro people of America, the West Indies and Africa
should support this grim, determined and courageous battle for freedom of the Indian people under the gallant, wise and dauntless leadership of Mohandas K. Ghandi [sic]," Randolph wrote on behalf of the
March on Washington Movement on August 20, "for they constitute
one of the great oppressed and exploited sections of the darker races of
the world, seeking their liberation from ruthless British imperialism."
Responding to the British government's contention that the independence movement was undermining its ability to fight fascism in Europe,
Randolph added: "The freedom of the people of India is intimately tied
up with the freedom of the Negro people of America and the victory of
the United Nations and the destruction of Axis slavery."[23]

Inspired by the "Quit India" movement, March on Washington
Movement activists stepped up their challenges to legal segregation in
the South. Returning to law school at Howard, Murray helped establish a chapter of the group in Washington and served as an advisor to
the campus chapter of the NAACP. She taught a class on nonviolence,
helped set up a civil rights committee to lobby Congress to ban segregation of restaurants and other public accommodations in the District of
Columbia, and led a sit-in movement that succeeded in desegregating
four restaurants in the city. Despite the complaints from Milton Webster and other porters, Randolph sent a staffer from the Sleeping Car

Porters to expand the March on Washington in the South. By the end of October 1942, chapters had been established in Mobile and Montgomery, Alabama, with assistance from E. D. Nixon, the porter who had distributed literature about the 1941 March on Washington while working on the train from Montgomery to Chicago. Recently elected president of the local branch of the NAACP, Nixon started organizing large groups of African Americans to march en masse to the Montgomery city hall and ask to register to vote. They were met with violence or arrest, but Nixon repeated similar actions for over a decade.[24]

Adopting the legal analysis that Pauli Murray had presented in Chicago, leaders of the March on Washington argued that it was just as important to confront segregation where it was not legally mandated as it was to do so in the Jim Crow South. "Jim crow is integrated so closely to the present social system of the South that it is not surprising that the [Supreme Court], even in its liberal phase, has not ventured to disturb it. But it will be quite a different thing to sanction the practice when it is applied by the federal government itself on a national scale to an army drawn mostly from areas where legalized Jim crow has never existed," read a pamphlet published by the March on Washington Movement. An opportunity to challenge federal policy arose in December 1942, when Winfred Lynn, a landscaper from Long Island, sued the U.S. Army for forcing him to serve in a segregated unit. Lynn had defied a draft notice since the previous June with assistance from his brother Conrad, who was an attorney with the Workers Defense League, but the American Civil Liberties Union persuaded him to accept induction so that it could use his case to test the constitutionality of segregation in the armed forces. By arguing that segregation was itself an act of discrimination, the ACLU hoped to challenge the Supreme Court's ruling, in the 1895 case *Plessy v. Ferguson*, that segregation was legal so long as the state provided equal services to all citizens. The ACLU, NAACP, and other groups had been challenging the legal basis of segregation in the South for years, but, according to the March on Washington Movement, the "novelty of the Lynn case is that it brings up to the court for the first time the question of segregation practiced not by Southern states but by the federal government itself."[25]

Despite mounting opposition from the black press and civil rights groups, the March on Washington Movement succeeded in building a broad base of support for Winfred Lynn. The *Chicago Defender* did not treat Lynn as a "cause *célèbre*," as it had dubbed draft resisters Ernest Calloway and St. Clair Drake two years earlier; but it and other black newspapers carried regular reports on the case. Lynn's attorney with the ACLU was Arthur Garfield Hayes, an ardent civil libertarian who had defended a long list of outcasts ranging from the anarchists Sacco and Vanzetti to the Scottsboro Boys, and he worked closely with Conrad Lynn and other attorneys from the Workers Defense League. Dwight MacDonald, a prominent left-wing journalist, publicized the case in *The Nation* and in a fifteen-page pamphlet that he coauthored with his wife, Nancy. The NAACP helped defray the publication costs of the pamphlet by purchasing a full-page advertisement on the back cover. In February 1943 Randolph sought assistance from his old friend A. J. Muste, who ran a school for labor organizers in upstate New York and headed the Fellowship of Reconciliation, which had promoted pacifist solutions to social conflict since the First World War. Muste put Randolph in touch with Bayard Rustin and James Farmer, two young staff members at the Fellowship of Reconciliation who had created the Congress of Racial Equality in the spring of 1942 to promote nonviolent resistance to segregation.[26]

Having travelled to Puerto Rico just before Randolph cancelled the March on Washington in the summer of 1941, Bayard Rustin was thrilled by the opportunity to work with the union leader in 1942. Raised by his grandparents in the Quaker community of West Chester, Pennsylvania, Rustin had moved to Harlem in 1937 after dropping out of college at the age of twenty-five. A brilliant student, Rustin wanted the freedom to explore his sexual attraction to men, which he did while working for a New Deal public works program and starting a singing career in the cafés of Greenwich Village. Rustin joined the Young Communist League but drifted toward anti-Stalinist radicals. He became friends with Pauli Murray, who shared his frustration with the gender norms of their heterosexual society, and helped organize the March on Washington in 1941. After joining a Quaker peace delegation to Puerto Rico, he took a job at A. J. Muste's Fellowship of Reconciliation, where he met James Farmer, a twenty-one-year-old seminary student who ran the Fellowship of Reconciliation's office in Chicago. The two of them founded the Congress of Racial Equality in April 1942 and, with support from Muste, had established chapters in Chicago, New York, and San Francisco by the time Randolph contacted them. While Farmer feared that such efforts might detract from efforts to establish CORE, Rustin saw an opportunity to spread their ideas about nonviolence among the labor activists, left-wing radicals, and ministers who supported Randolph's March on Washington Movement. "That work was one of the most important things that I ever did," Rustin recalled many years later.[27]

The March on Washington Movement was not the only organization reinvigorated by young black radicals in the fall and winter of 1942. In 1940 Walter White hired Pauli Murray's friend Ella Baker to work as a field secretary for the NAACP in the South. Seven years older than Murray, Baker had attended college in North Carolina before moving to Harlem in 1927, where she lived at the YWCA and worked as a maid and factory worker before getting hired to direct the New Deal work program where Pauli Murray went to work in 1936. Baker also joined Jay Lovestone's Communist Party (Opposition). Attracted to the radical egalitarianism of Communism but frustrated by its hierarchical structure, Baker devoted the rest of her life to building grassroots movements aimed at empowering poor and oppressed peoples to fight for their own liberation. She saw the NAACP as an ideal place to start that career and, after two years of rejected applications, jumped at Walter White's offer to pay her to strengthen and expand the association in the South. Working with activists from a broad range of ideological and partisan affiliations, she knit the NAACP into a dense and inter-racial network of civic societies, unions, churches, student groups, and radical organizations that would support its activities in the region for decades. In 1943 White promoted Baker to be the national director of branches, making her the highest-ranked woman in the NAACP and putting her in charge of the association's work with local groups across the country. One measure of Baker's influence on the association was an unprecedented proliferation of local branches during the Second World War, from fewer than 400 to over 1,000. In those same years, the association's membership grew from 50,000 to nearly half a million.[28]

Young black radicals also had an important impact on the union movement, particularly the rapidly expanding industrial unions associ-ated with the Congress of Industrial Organizations. Ernest Calloway, the conscientious objector whose arrest had helped inspire the March on Washington in 1941, had been involved in the union movement since 1925, when he joined the United Mine Workers union after going to work in a Kentucky coal mine at the age of sixteen. Tiring of the job and seeking adventure, he moved to Harlem in the 1930s, where he wrote for the Urban League's journal, *Opportunity*, won a scholarship to A. J. Muste's labor college, and joined the Lovestonites. There is no evidence that Calloway met Bayard Rustin, Pauli Murray, or Ella Baker, but he did meet A. Philip Randolph after moving to Chicago in 1937. Arriving in the Windy City just before the Sleeping Car Porters won their first contract with the Pullman Company, Calloway found a job organizing porters at Union Station and pushed successfully to extend the Railway Labor Act to cover service workers in stations as well as on trains. That victory established Calloway's union as a leading force in the broader effort to bring black workers into organized labor, and within a few years it represented thousands of mostly African Ameri-can service workers in stations across the country. In 1942 the United

Transport Service Employees affiliated with the Congress of Industrial Organizations, making its president, Willard Townsend, the first African American in the national leadership of the CIO. Later that year the CIO adopted a resolution, drafted by Ernest Calloway, to create a Committee to Abolish Racial Discrimination to do "missionary work" on race relations both inside affiliated unions and "among the general public outside organized labor." Noting that A. Philip Randolph had no such influence within the AFL, the *Chicago Defender* wrote in November 1942: "The widespread interest in this move by the Townsend forces, the cooperation he is getting from CIO leaders indicate that Townsend is fast becoming the most powerful Negro labor leader in the country."[29]

Pauli Murray, Ella Baker, and Ernest Calloway worked for different organizations in disparate regions of the country, but they represented a broad and deeply interconnected web of young black radicals who rose to positions of prominence in the civil rights and labor movements during the Second World War. Starting in December 1942, Pauline Myers proposed to knit those various movements into "one great mass of pressure for freedom and democracy in America by 1945." On January 7, 1943, Randolph announced plans for a week-long campaign modeled on the "technique of non-violent civil disobedience popularized and used effectively by Mahatma Gandhi in India." The specific nature of the campaign would be hashed out at a conference sponsored by the March on Washington in Chicago that May, but he suggested it would include mass marches in cities across the country, a letter-writing campaign aimed at federal officials, and civil disobedience against segregation of trains and stations in the South. Referring to the fascist leaders of Germany, Italy, and Japan, Myers announced that the slogan for "I Am an American, Too" week would be "Defeat Hitler, Mussolini and Hirohito by enforcing and observing the Constitution and abolishing Jim Crow."[30]

Despite its popularity among young radicals, Randolph's proposal for a nationwide civil disobedience campaign was greeted with vigorous opposition by more established black leaders. Pointing out that Gandhi's strategy had been developed to challenge a British minority in India, editors of the *Atlanta Daily World* warned that it would only undermine the progress that racial minorities had already made toward equality in the United States. The *Pittsburgh Courier* proclaimed Randolph "guilty of the most dangerous demagoguery on record," charging that civil disobedience had "not only ended in bloodshed and imprisonment of tens of thousands of Indians but has failed to win Indian independence." When an activist with Randolph's union defended the plan at a public forum in Harlem, a white journalist who was writing a book on race relations in the South predicted that it would result in "the wholesale slaughter of Negroes by hoodlums and mobsters who would perhaps be supported by state troopers." W. E. B. Du Bois, who had founded the NAACP four decades earlier out of frustration with the slow pace of change, charged the March on Washington Movement with moving too fast. Randolph's "program is naturally acceptable to all Negroes," wrote the seventy-five-year-old civil rights leader, but the movement erred in demanding immediately "what every Negro knows cannot be accomplished in a single generation."[31]

Randolph and Myers responded to the backlash by reiterating that civil disobedience was one of several options to be discussed at the Chicago conference, and by moving the conference back to June, but concerns only increased in the following months. In April some expressed fears that a "race riot" would erupt in Washington, D.C. Early that month, Pauli Murray and other students launched a series of sit-ins aimed at integrating local restaurants. Tensions rose when nine black soldiers joined one protest and military police showed up and escorted them out. Soon afterward a restaurant owner agreed to serve the students but then barred other black customers after the protest had ended. When the students moved to renew the sit-in, the president of Howard University ordered them to call it off because he feared that Congress would cut off funding for the school. Two weeks later a coalition of groups including the NAACP, the National Negro Congress, and several unions staged a week-long series of demonstrations to protest employment discrimination by the company that operated buses and streetcars in the nation's capital. The FEPC had ordered the firm to start hiring black drivers nearly ten months earlier, yet no changes had occurred. On the morning of May 15, when organizers expected over 800 people to show up for a mass rally, Mississippi congressman John Rankin lashed out at the protesters for stirring up conflict while "our good white boys of the South are fighting and dying on every battlefield of the world." Learning that groups of white soldiers were gathering at local taverns and drinking heavily while pledging to "clean out" the area, authorities stationed over 100 local and military police to maintain order. Angry whites showed up to shout at the protesters, and a "bag pipe and drum band" played so loudly that some assumed it was "deliberately trying to drown out the proceedings." "Nothing marred events except a sprinkling of rain," and an equally loud "colored Elks band took care" of the musical interference, leading one relieved black journalist to proclaim, "Democracy wins a round." While the conflict was dispelled, the company still refused to hire any black workers.[32]

And that was just the first round. Less than ten days later, on May 24, 1943, thousands of white men and women rampaged through a shipyard in Mobile, Alabama, swinging pipes and wrenches and hurling bricks in an effort to "get every one of them Niggers off" a dry dock where ships were being constructed for the U.S. Navy. The Alabama Dry Dock and Shipbuilding Company had employed an interracial workforce of 30,000 since early in the war, but came under scrutiny during the Birmingham FEPC hearings for restricting black workers to unskilled positions. After delaying for months while encouraging white workers to protest the investigation, the company relented abruptly and upgraded twelve black men into skilled welding jobs. Seven black workers were hospitalized after the riot, along with a white worker who attempted to defend black workers from company security guards who joined the melee, and the fighting continued until U.S. troops and state police arrived from nearby bases. In what the NAACP denounced as an "unsound, unwise and unfair" concession to white supremacists, the FEPC agreed to a "Jim Crow set up" whereby skilled black workers returned to work only in all-black crews. Officials of the company, unions, and state and federal government traded accusations of blame for the violence, but all agreed that it represented a major setback for the president's policy of fair employment.[33]

Detroit exploded next. Racial tensions had escalated in the Motor City since February 1942, when a white mob attacked a group of black families who attempted to move into a federal housing project. The families moved in a few months later under protection from the Michigan National Guard, but, as one local newspaper reported, there was still "a growing subterranean race war going on in the City of Detroit which can have no other ultimate result than an explosion of violence, unless something is done to stop it." Conflict spiked again on June 3, 1943, a week after the Mobile riot, when 25,000 white workers walked out of the Packard Motor Car Company because three black workers had been upgraded into skilled positions at a plant that was manufacturing P-51 Mustang fighter planes for the Air Corps. Managers and union officials fired the strike leaders and coaxed most white workers back to work, but a full-scale riot broke out in Detroit a few days later. After a series of clashes erupted between black and white youth at a crowded amusement park on June 20, rumors of a black "invasion" of white communities led to several days of unchecked violence. White mobs roamed the city looting black-owned homes and businesses and dragging African Americans out of cars and trolleys and beating them in broad daylight. Local police joined the violence on the side of the whites, and peace was restored only after Roosevelt sent federal troops to impose martial law. Thirty-four people were killed, 25 of them black, and more than 500 were injured. Congressman Dies' House Un-American Activities Committee investigated rumors that the riots had been instigated by the Ku Klux Klan, and leaders of the group boasted that they "had enrolled many members in the Detroit area." Mississippi congressman John Rankin laid blame for the violence on "the crazy policies of the so-called fair employment practices committee in an attempt to mix the races in all kinds of employment," however, gloating, "the chickens are coming home to roost."[34]

Occurring in the midst of preparations for Randolph's civil disobedience campaign, the riots in Mobile and Detroit dealt a fatal blow to the March on Washington Movement. The union leader remained defiant following the Alabama incident, urging black workers to return to their jobs at the shipyard and calling on President Roosevelt to send U.S. troops and federal investigators to protect them. Only 300 of an original 2,000 black workers returned to work at Alabama Dry Dock, however; and despite the presence of over 600 U.S. soldiers, according to the *Chicago Defender*, "the general impression in alert Negro circles is that trouble is still brewing in the ranks of disgruntled whites." Facing increased pressure from branch leaders who feared further violence, particularly in the South, leaders of the NAACP and Urban League refused to send representatives to the "We Are Americans, Too" conference in Chicago, which after several postponements was finally held on July 4. "Conscious of deep feeling running among Negroes following the recent riots in Detroit, but uncertain as to its intensity, officials and civic leaders of both races had been watching 'the march on Washington' convention with apprehension," the *New York Times* reported from Chicago. Such concerns limited participation in the conference to 500 delegates from local chapters of the March on Washington Movement. Beyond Randolph and members of the executive committee, speakers included only relatively obscure radicals such as Socialist Party leader Norman Thomas and Eric Williams, a young West Indian independence leader who was teaching sociology at Howard University. Randolph was reelected president of the March on Washington Movement, but E. Pauline Myers and other young women were replaced by staff members of the Brotherhood of Sleeping Car Porters. Delegates reaffirmed their commitment to building an all-black organization—defeating a small minority that advocated opening membership to whites—but rejected Randolph's plan for a civil disobedience campaign. According to the *New York Times*, "Race tension in Chicago was believed to have been relieved considerably" by that decision."[35]

While liberals expressed relief at the demise of the March on Washington Movement, conservatives stepped up their efforts to destroy the FEPC. In September 1943 the FEPC opened hearings on discrimination in the rail industry, which had been postponed following protests from southern politicians the previous January. Twenty-two railroads participated in the hearings but, rather than deny charges that black workers were shut out of all but the most menial jobs, employers contended that any changes in employment practices would violate union contracts that the federal government had approved several months before President Roosevelt created the FEPC. Meanwhile the segregated railway brotherhoods refused to appear at the hearings and, despite opposition from Randolph and a few white union leaders, persuaded the executive committee of the AFL to pass a resolution condemning "this or any other policy interfering with self-government of labor unions." The FEPC carried through with the hearings and ordered both railroads and unions to bring their hiring practices into line with President Roosevelt's executive order, but the railway companies responded that the FEPC lacked the "constitutional and legal jurisdiction and power" to issue such a directive. Pleased by resistance from discriminatory employers and unions, congressional conservatives linked opposition to the FEPC with a broader campaign to undermine the Roosevelt administration. Noting the Communist Party's support for Roosevelt's fair-employment policy, Congressman Dies' Un-American Activities Committee accused the FEPC of adopting the "Communist party practice of inciting Negroes to unrest."[36]

The backlash of 1943 destroyed the March on Washington Movement but not the movement to strengthen the FEPC. When Roosevelt issued the executive order in 1941, he stipulated that it would last only as long as the war. With the possibility of peace developing in the summer of 1943, journalist Horace Cayton and the Chicago Urban League invited other groups to join them in a national campaign to "extend and maintain" the gains that black workers had made during the war. Mary McLeod Bethune accepted their invitation and authorized Jeanetta Welch, who had recently joined the staff of the National Council of Negro Women, to attend a meeting of the Chicago Charter Committee on Employment. On July 15, Welch announced that she would lead a nationwide "Hold Your Job" campaign, which would culminate with a major conference in Washington, D.C., during the week of September 12.[37]

As she had with the initial effort to police the FEPC, Welch expanded the campaign to include organizing unions and winning jobs for both men and women. Whereas the Chicago Charter Committee set out to "impress upon Negro workers themselves the need for efficient performance on the job as a necessary qualification for postwar retention," Welch shifted tone and focus by encouraging black Americans to "protect their rights as workers and continually improve their working conditions through an alliance with organized labor." She also emphasized the "new responsibilities and new opportunities" that black women had gained through wartime employment.

Arguing that women needed access to job training, government services for their families and communities, and equal wages with men, she insisted that they "also must become closely allied with organized labor so that they may learn how to protect their rights as workers and continually improve their working conditions." By September 10, with the campaign under the direction of the NCNW's National Committee on Employment, the goal was to "help Negro women 'hold their jobs' now, and after the emergency period." The campaign retained the Urban League's emphasis on personal behavior, encouraging "girls" to "bathe frequently and insure against body odors," to "be kind and not 'catty,'" and not to "loaf on the job," but it coupled that advice with the order to "join a union, and protect your rights as a worker."[38]

By changing the tone and expanding the focus of the "Hold Your Job" campaign, Jeanetta Welch won support from a broad range of civil rights and labor organizations. The emphasis on unions won pledges of support from the AFL and the CIO, as well as the National Urban League, the NAACP, and several black newspapers. Willard Townsend, the president of Ernest Calloway's United Transport Services Employees union and the only black trade unionist on the executive committee of the CIO, joined the national committee of the campaign. In the fall of 1943, Welch pushed hard to win support from the Ladies Auxiliary of the Brotherhood of Sleeping Car Porters, which had been founded in 1938 through a merger of the Colored Women's Economic Councils that Randolph had created to support his union in the 1920s. Members of the auxiliary voted to affiliate with the National Council of Negro Women at their national convention in 1942, but, after attending an NCNW convention, its leadership expressed concern at the lack of attention paid to "unskilled and unorganized men and women of the race who are badly in need of the advantages and the protection which accrue from labor organizations." The affiliation was still not approved in September 1943, when the recently married Jeanetta Welch Brown invited the auxiliary to join the "Hold Your Job" campaign. Citing her own experience as a union activist in Detroit, and challenging the auxiliary's claim to "represent the unskilled and unorganized women," Brown asked: "Have you ever stopped to think that if your organization represents a certain group of people, that the group of people will be kept out as long as you, yourself, keep them out?" The auxiliary backed the campaign, although it withdrew from the National Council of Negro Women after only one year.[39]

Jeanetta Welch Brown got an important opportunity to expand her base of support when the CIO Political Action Committee invited her to address a conference in New York City on January 21 and 22, 1944. Initiated at the CIO's national convention the previous November, where unions pledged $700,000 to support pro-labor candidates in the 1944 elections, the conference was designed to chart a plan for sustaining the economic growth and low unemployment rates that had been created by the war. Prominent speakers included Mayor LaGuardia, CIO president Philip Murray, and Vice-President Henry Wallace, a strong supporter of the civil rights and labor movements whom Roosevelt had chosen as his running mate to counter left-wing criticism of his defense policies in 1940. A. Philip Randolph addressed a session on "Full Employment and the Negro Worker," along with Willard Townsend of the Transport Service Employees and Ferdinand Smith, a prominent black Communist who was second-in-command of the CIO's National Maritime Union. George L. P. Weaver, a Transport Service Employees activist who headed the CIO's Committee to Abolish Racial Discrimination, took responsibility for building support "among Negro workers and among Negro communities" for any initiatives adopted by the conference.[40]

The respect that Jeanetta Welch Brown had gained from union activists in the past year was indicated by the fact that she was asked to help lead a discussion on "Full Employment for Women Workers." Her co-panelists were Dorothy Bellanca, a fifty-year-old cofounder of the CIO Clothing Workers union and an advisor to the U.S. secretary of labor; and Ruth Young, a twenty-eight-year-old former factory worker who was second-in-command of a CIO United Electrical Workers' district representing over 10,000 workers—a majority of them women—in New York and New Jersey. Both were prominent figures in an interracial "labor feminist" movement that pushed unions to support, as Young stated at a union meeting later that year, "the right of all women to work," "equal pay and the opportunity to advance," and the "government's responsibility for accommodating maternity and child rearing." Bellanca opened the discussion by pointing out that women had "entered every industry in support of the war effort," including thousands of jobs maintaining rail lines and 30–40 percent of all jobs in aircraft factories. "Labor cannot afford to overlook this important factor at this time," she stated, urging men and women in the audience to reject "the outworn idea that women are on the labor scene as temporary employees and that they really belong to the home and will go back there some day." Welch Brown argued that Bellanca's point was particularly important for black women, pointing out that black men had rarely earned enough to support their families alone and that black women took on additional duties as a result of the death and injury of men during the war. "The employment of Negro women is not a social experiment but an economic necessity," she declared, insisting that labor "can and labor must plan and work for fair employment policies and equal opportunities for the advancement of Negro women."[41]

There is no record of how many male labor leaders attended the panel on women workers, or what they thought of its message; but the arguments made by Welch Brown, Young, and Bellanca had a profound impact on the civil rights and labor movements during the Second World War. By the end of 1944, Ruth Young had become the first woman elected to the executive board of the United Electrical Workers, other labor feminists had risen to positions of influence in the Auto, Garment, Packinghouse, and Clothing Workers unions, and the CIO had included demands for maternity leave, state-funded child care, and equalization of men's and women's wages in its legislative agenda. Soon after the CIO conference, A. Philip Randolph recruited a "young feminist" to head the National Council for a Permanent FEPC, which he created to continue the work of the March on Washington Movement. Randolph had created the group the previous November, but it produced only a few press releases protesting the continued weakening of the FEPC, a small "Save the FEPC" rally in New York City, and a plan for a "Back FEPC" conference that never occurred. In January 1944, he asked Anna Arnold Hedgeman to take over.[42]

Randolph first met Anna Arnold in the 1920s, when she invited him to speak at the Harlem branch of the YWCA, and they had collaborated ever since. Ten years younger than Randolph, Arnold had grown up in the only black household in a tiny town in Minnesota. She went to college in St. Paul and took a teaching job in Mississippi in 1922 but found life under Jim Crow so repulsive that she "decided I must return north and organize the Midwest to help eliminate the cruelty of the southern part of my country." After running YWCA branches in Ohio and New Jersey, she was hired at the Harlem Y. In addition to organizing speeches by Randolph, W. E. B. Du Bois, Walter White, and Mary McLeod Bethune, she developed friendships with Pauli Murray and Ella Baker. In 1933 she was the only woman invited to a retreat for young black activists sponsored by the NAACP, where Abram Harris and Ralph Bunche first proposed the labor-oriented movement that became the National Negro Congress. In the same year she married a professional concert singer named Merrit Hedgeman, and the following year she took a job at the New York State Emergency Relief Bureau, where she met Dorothy Height. Anna Hedgeman and Dorothy Height joined the National Negro Congress together, and Hedgeman left her job at the Relief Bureau after supervisors refused to investigate the wages of domestic workers, which—as she pointed out—were so low that the city was supplementing their wages through welfare. In 1937 the YWCA hired her to direct a program for young black women in Brooklyn, which Hedgeman described as "a real opportunity for a new kind of community approach" to social change. She spent much of her time organizing protests against local businesses that refused to hire the women, and the following year a journalist described her as a "young feminist" because she told a group of black college students that "all women have serious employment programs" and that "Negro women carry the additional handicap of color." Hired by the Civilian Defense program during the war, she continued organizing protests and was "eager to join" the March on Washington in 1941. Hedgeman accompanied Randolph to the White House to plead for Odell Waller's life in 1942, and helped Pauli Murray organize the silent parade after President Roosevelt refused to block the execution.[43]

Randolph was more interested in Hedgeman's organizing experience than in her feminism, but it helped that she had connections to young women across the country. On February 4 she kicked off the National Council for a Permanent FEPC with a rally in midtown Manhattan, where she announced that two U.S. congressmen and a senator had agreed to sponsor a bill banning employment discrimination and creating a permanent FEPC. Soon after that she moved to Washington and set up a temporary office in space borrowed from the Workers Defense League. Unable to pay professional lobbyists, Hedgeman hired an all-female staff that included two stenographers, the former secretary of the Boston YWCA, a Socialist Party activist, and the former publicist for the Cooperative League, a group that Ella Baker had led in New York City early in the 1930s. To help with publicity and fundraising, Hedgeman hired college students to set up FEPC Councils in cities and towns across the nation. Drawing on her contacts with YWCA activists across the country, she instructed them to "pull the whole community together" and "lean on the women."[44]

In addition to her staff, Hedgeman relied heavily on the National Council of Negro Women, which, with the exception of the National Negro Congress, was the only black civil rights organization headquartered in the nation's capital. The only fulltime black lobbyist in town was Thomasina T. Johnson, a former colleague of Jeanetta Welch Brown's at the Alpha Kappa Alpha sorority. One of three women who joined the nineteen-member Executive Committee of the National Council for a Permanent FEPC, Johnson provided "invaluable" assistance to the FEPC campaign. "Some of the younger women who are on the firing line have made interesting comments which indicate the trend in Negro communities," Hedgeman wrote after attending a conference on "The Negro Woman in the Postwar World" at the NCNW headquarters on April 1, 1944. Among others, she cited an activist from the Washington Urban League who argued that wartime employment had made women "fuller citizens and workers." Hedgeman was also impressed by Jeanetta Welch Brown's contention that "Prejudice based on sex has no place in the present scheme of social activity—where it is accentuated by the factor of color—doubly affirmative steps must be taken to eliminate both." It is not clear how much Hedgeman agreed with those activists, but she relied heavily on their militancy as she lobbied for the FEPC.[45]

"In our ignorance the staff had decided that a bill which called for equal opportunity of access to employment ought to be simple of passage," Hedgeman recalled. "We soon discovered our innocence." Despite a "clear and impressive" message, a "roster of prominent citizens" asking for a vote on the bill, and ample evidence "that too many citizens of the United States (Indian, Spanish, Oriental, Negro, and other ethnics) had been discriminated against on the basis of race, creed, color, or national origin," conservatives kept various versions of the bill mired in committee for two years. Hedgeman responded to the delay by asking FEPC Councils to promote fair employment policies in state and local governments. FEPC laws were introduced in nearly every northern state and adopted in New York, New Jersey, and Massachusetts by the end of 1946. Soon after passage of the New York law on March 12, 1945, First Lady Eleanor Roosevelt arranged a conference with FEPC supporters at the White House. The president refused to see them, however, and remained silent on the law. After Roosevelt's death on April 12, 1945, Harry Truman spoke in favor of the bill and asked his secretary of labor to assist in lobbying, but the bill was still languishing on August 14, when the surrender of Japan brought the Second World War to an end. "V-J Day has come," Hedgeman wrote to the FEPC Councils on August 29. "It is imperative, therefore, that the bill for a permanent FEPC be passed as soon after Congress reconvenes as possible." Congress provided some additional funding but ordered the FEPC to cease all operations by June 30, 1946.[46]

The *Chicago Defender* credited A. Philip Randolph with pushing ahead on a bill that most black leaders saw as a "pipe dream," but noted that "semi-mystic that he is, St. Phil has left the hard work" to the "tireless crusading Anne Hedgeman" and her staff. Randolph's union contributed $7,500 to the campaign and the Garment Workers gave $17,000; but the NAACP gave only $2,100 and the combined contributions from all other unions amounted to less than $5,000. Similarly small donations came from the American Jewish Committee and the Anti-Defamation League of B'nai B'rith. FEPC councils raised nearly $65,000 at dances, dinners, and other fundraising events. In all, however, the National Council for a Permanent FEPC received less than one-third of the $500,000 that Randolph had estimated to be necessary for a successful campaign. In February 1946 the *Atlanta Daily World* praised Hedgeman's staff for volunteering to work without pay until more funds arrived. When Hedgeman learned of their offer, she "sat at her desk and cried."[47]

The final straw for Hedgeman came later that month, when Randolph planned a major initiative without securing additional funding. An FEPC bill had finally made it to the Senate floor and, after conservatives filibustered a vote for nearly a month, Randolph called for mass rallies in cities across the country during the week of February 15. "The average citizen in each community must become fully aware of the dangers facing the passing of the Federal Fair Employment Practice Law or all the efforts put forth to win the war against the forces of fascism will have been in vain," he told a rally sponsored by the Brooklyn FEPC Council. Knowing that Hedgeman and her staff could not afford to leave Washington, Randolph convinced the Garment Workers Union to release Maida Springer, who had helped Pauli Murray organize the Odell Waller parade in 1942, to devote two weeks of her time with the union to organizing a capstone rally in Madison Square Garden. The event was a tremendous success, drawing nearly 20,000 people to hear Eleanor Roosevelt, actor Orson Welles, and other luminaries emphasize the importance of the bill. In recognition of Springer's work on the rally and other causes, the National Council of Negro Women named her one of twelve Outstanding Women of the Year, along with Pauli Murray and Congresswoman Helen Gahagan Douglas. By that point, however, conservatives had used a parliamentary procedure to kill the FEPC bill in the Senate. On July 15, 1946, Hedgeman offered her resignation to the Executive Committee, and, after she rejected a request to rephrase the letter "in a way that would not damage the image of the FEPC movement," the larger National Board of Directors accepted her resignation at its next meeting, on August 2, in New York City.[48]

The effort to pass a permanent FEPC law continued after Hedgeman's resignation, but on a very different basis from the grassroots campaign that she had begun two years earlier. At the August 2 meeting, A. Philip Randolph announced plans to move the National Council for a Permanent FEPC to New York, reorganize the staff under the control of a policy committee composed of representatives from major civil rights groups and unions, and create a fundraising committee led by publishing magnate Henry Luce and several other wealthy donors. A public relations committee was also headed by the former editor of *Fortune* magazine and other "outstanding personalities in the profession." Some objected that the plan was developed in New York without input from Thomasina T. Johnson and others in Washington and that the August 2 meeting had been called too quickly for many out-of-towners to attend. By that point, however, the NAACP, CIO, and AFL had each agreed to give $2,000–$5,000 immediately, with more to follow; and Walter White, CIO leader George L. P. Weaver, AFL leader Boris Shishkin, and Lester Granger of the National Urban League had agreed to serve on the policy committee with A. Philip Randolph and three others. That group formed the basis for a new Leadership Conference on Civil Rights, which was formally created in

1953 and would lead efforts to pass the FEPC bill and other civil rights initiatives for several decades.[49]

The creation of the Leadership Conference on Civil Rights marked the end of the grassroots movement that A. Philip Randolph sought to build when he called for the March on Washington in 1941. Randolph withdrew from the new group shortly before its official founding and attempted to sustain the National Council for a Permanent FEPC as the "definitive organization in the fight" for the FEPC, but by that point his group had ceased to function. The creation of the Leadership Conference also left Hedgeman and other women wondering why a similar effort had not been made to support the FEPC campaign that they initiated in 1944. Convinced that she could exert greater influence outside the civil rights movement, Hedgeman took a job with the campaign to reelect President Truman and, after a brief stint at the federal Health, Education and Welfare agency, became the first black woman appointed to a cabinet position by the mayor of New York City. Jeanetta Welch Brown remained active in the National Council of Negro Women but focused her energies on creating a national organization for black women in the fashion industry. The same year that Hedgeman resigned from the National Council for a Permanent FEPC, Ella Baker left the NAACP under similar circumstances. E. Pauline Myers took a job lobbying for the Fraternal Council of Negro Churches, while Pauli Murray graduated first in her class at Howard and continued her studies at the University of California, Berkeley—after Harvard University refused to lift a ban on women in its law school. The bitterness that many black women felt toward the civil rights movement at the close of the 1940s was expressed profoundly by a former member of Hedgeman's staff after discovering that two male publicists were employed at high salaries while she and the others were still waiting to be paid for work they had done more than a year earlier. "And this is the group which is working for a law to promote fair employment practices?" Ms. Sidney Wilkinson wrote in 1947. "Don't make me laugh."[50]

CHAPTER THREE

ROCKING THE CRADLE

THE LEADERSHIP CONFERENCE on Civil Rights was extremely effective in the early 1950s, but the limits of its success were apparent from the start. Seven states adopted FEPC laws between 1946 and 1954, but all but one had small populations and nearly no African Americans. The impact of those victories was also overshadowed by the rejection of similar laws in states with much larger black populations and more vibrant civil rights movements. The most devastating defeat came in November 1946, when voters in California rejected a proposition to create an FEPC law by a margin of more than two to one, an outcome that conservatives would cite for over a decade as evidence that "the people of this state want no action forcing Negroes upon them." NAACP leader Roy Wilkins attempted to counter that perception by mobilizing sixty supportive organizations for a massive lobbying conference in Washington on January 15–17, 1950; but only 4,000 people showed up, and black newspapers accused the association of turning away some of its own members because they were suspected to be Communists. In fact the NAACP was more open to Communists than any of A. Philip Randolph's organizations had been in the 1940s, and moved to prevent them from holding leadership positions in local branches only after conflicts broke out at the 1950 mobilization; but the controversy helped to compound the perception that Wilkins and other civil rights leaders were more interested in winning favor with white liberals than with mobilizing their own base of support.[1]

Dismissing his critics as "naïve and confused," Wilkins used the 1950 mobilization to formally launch the Leadership Conference on Civil Rights. Having joined Walter White's staff in 1931 at the age of thirty, with a degree from the University of Minnesota and eight years of experience in journalism, Roy Wilkins had always insisted that educated and responsible black leadership could achieve more than radical protests and mass mobilizations. At the NAACP conference in 1933, where Harris and Bunche formulated the idea for the National Negro Congress, Wilkins called for "a Negro bloc of informed, influential leaders, highly organized, national in scope, and with a franchise to tackle all the problems of Negroes—not just civil rights." After editing the NAACP journal, *The Crisis*, for much of the 1940s, Wilkins saw an opportunity for greater influence in the association when White took a leave of absence to deal with health and marital problems in 1950. Working closely with United Auto Workers president Walter Reuther, who was elected president of the CIO in 1952, Wilkins built a broad coalition of civil rights and labor leaders to pressure the Senate to change the voting rule that had allowed conservatives to filibuster the FEPC law and countless pieces of liberal legislation over the previous two decades. The campaign failed, but it established the Leadership Conference as a powerful lobby funded by regular dues from over fifty organizations. Wilkins saw an even bigger chance to make an impact on June 9, 1952, when the U.S. Supreme Court agreed to hear arguments in a cluster of cases that NAACP attorneys had filed on the premise that the system of segregated schools in the South violated the constitutional rights of black students and their families. Having built the cases slowly over the previous decade, the NAACP rallied the Leadership Conference on Civil Rights to make the argument that segregation was not only harmful and unjust to African Americans but also threatening to the United States' leadership in the mounting Cold War with the Soviet Union. The central premise was the same as in the Winfred Lynn case during the Second World War, that it was inherently discriminatory for the government to provide segregated facilities to citizens on the basis of their race. The NAACP's lead attorney in the case, Thurgood Marshall, stated that he relied heavily on Pauli Murray's 1951 book *State's Laws on Race and Color*.[2]

Wilkins' approach won a stunning victory on May 17, 1954, when the Supreme Court accepted the NAACP's argument in the case *Brown v. Board of Education* and ruled that segregation of public schools was, in fact, unconstitutional—but the Court undermined that victory nearly a year later when it refused to set a firm timeline for desegregation. Rejecting the NAACP's request that the ruling be implemented immediately, the Court stated on May 31, 1955, that local authorities could proceed at the painfully vague pace of "all deliberate speed." Segregationists took this as an invitation to ignore the *Brown* decision completely. President Dwight Eisenhower, a Republican who had defeated a moderate Democrat in 1952 with nominal support from black voters, went out of his way to assure the white South that it would be able to "order and control its own domestic institutions." Eisenhower insisted that racism was "un-American and a danger to the Republic" but, much like Roosevelt in his first term, refused to impose that opinion on elected officials in the South. "These are not bad people," he told Chief Justice Earl Warren during deliberations on the *Brown* case. "All they are concerned about is to see that their sweet little girls are not required to sit in school alongside some big overgrown Negroes." Refusing to take sides on the issue, he insisted that civil rights policies must have "the support of the law, but should not be so punitive as to get anyone upset."[3]

By giving local authorities control over the pace of integration, federal authorities set the stage for a series of confrontations between supporters and opponents of Jim Crow in communities across the South.

Two months after the first *Brown* decision, on July 11, 1954, three white men in Indianola, Mississippi, formed a Citizens' Council "to counteract that NAACP and the other left-wing organizations" that had "contributed to the Black Monday decision." By the end of the year the Association of Citizens' Councils in Mississippi claimed 300 branches and 80,000 members. That grassroots response was encouraged by elected officials. "If we can organize the Southern States for massive resistance to this order, I think that in time the rest of the country will realize that racial integration is not going to be accepted in the South," Virginia Senator Harry Byrd declared on March 12, 1956, as he and 101 other senators and congressmen signed a Southern Manifesto pledging to defy the *Brown* decision. Local officials followed with a wave of repression against the NAACP and other civil rights groups. By the end of 1956, laws or court injunctions had banned the NAACP from operating in Louisiana, Alabama, Virginia, and Texas. Florida had launched a $50,000 investigation into communist activities in the NAACP and South Carolina had barred teachers from joining the group. As a result, from 1955 through 1957 the NAACP lost 226 branches and nearly half its membership in the South and was forced to spend thousands of dollars in legal fees just to survive.[4]

Ironically, the backlash against the NAACP facilitated the emergence of grassroots movements that would ultimately succeed in implementing the *Brown* decision. While leadership of those movements emerged from long-established civil rights oganizations, they mobilized through local churches, unions, women's clubs, and other local groups that could operate outside the bureaucratic structures of the NAACP. The most successful of those grassroots insurgencies erupted in Montgomery, Alabama, where Edgar D. Nixon, the Pullman porter, had built support for the March on Washington back in 1941. Born in rural Alabama in 1899, Nixon had moved to Montgomery at the age of fourteen and got a job carrying luggage at the train station. That job led to one as a porter, and he joined A. Philip Randolph's union shortly after it was formed in 1925. In 1938 he was elected president of the union's local chapter and, like Randolph, utilized the position to fight for racial equality and social justice as well as for better wages and working conditions on the job. Soon after forming the local chapter of the March on Washington Movement, Nixon established the Montgomery Voters League to challenge literacy tests and poll taxes that had prevented nearly all black Alabamans from voting since the 1880s. In 1946 he represented the Montgomery branch of the NAACP at a regional organizing meeting that Ella Baker planned in Atlanta, and soon afterward he was elected president of the Alabama State Conference of NAACP Branches. All through those years he continued working on trains between Alabama and Chicago, building relationships with labor and civil rights activists in the North while relying on the union to shield him from railroad managers who attempted repeatedly to fire him for his activism. By 1955 Nixon and his allies had registered enough black voters to swing a close election in Montgomery. One of Nixon's only white allies was Virginia Durr, a left-wing activist who had moved to Montgomery in 1951. "He probably had more support on a national basis than any man in Montgomery," she wrote about Nixon in February 1955, "and is more effective politically than any other Negro here."[5]

In addition to his national network, Nixon helped nurture a remarkable network of black activists in Montgomery. Chief among them was Rosa Parks, a seamstress who served as secretary of the Montgomery NAACP for most of the 1940s and 1950s. Forty-two years old in 1955, Parks had moved to Montgomery at the age of eleven. She went originally to attend school but, after the school closed in 1928, found work in a garment factory and then as a housekeeper and seamstress for a local tailor. She married Raymond Parks, a barber and NAACP member, in 1931, and the two of them helped raise money to support the nine black boys who were arrested and sentenced to death that year in Scottsboro, Alabama. In 1943, they joined E. D. Nixon's Voters League, and the following year Nixon asked Rosa to investigate the rape of a young black woman in nearby Abbeyville, where Parks had lived briefly as a girl. Gaining support from the Southern Negro Youth Congress, which was affiliated with the National Negro Congress, Parks built a nationwide campaign to demand that the rapists be brought to trial. The National Council of Negro Women, NAACP, YWCA, Adam Clayton Powell, and Ben Davis, the black Communist who was elected to the New York City Council that year, all joined the Committee for Equal Justice for Mrs. Recy Taylor. After two trials and a confession from one of the rapists, however, not one of them was convicted. In 1946 Parks accompanied Nixon to the NAACP meeting in Atlanta, where Ella Baker had a "profound effect" on her. Two years later Parks was elected secretary of the Alabama State Conference of NAACP Branches, and she served as advisor to the Youth Council of the Montgomery branch through the 1950s.[6]

While Nixon and Parks held leadership positions in the NAACP, they relied increasingly on local organizations as the national leadership of the association shifted its emphasis from grassroots mobilization to legal activism in the 1950s. The most important of those local allies was the Women's Political Council, a local group of black schoolteachers, college professors, social workers, and other "professional women" who came together to register voters, push elected officials to address the concerns of African Americans, and end the constant barrage of verbal and physical abuse that African Americans faced at the hands of police, bus drivers, and other white authority figures in Montgomery. The council was founded in 1946 by professors at Alabama State College. Mary Fair Burks, the first president of the group, explained that she and the others believed they could not challenge segregation directly and thus focused on improving conditions for African Americans within the Jim Crow system. Burks stepped down in 1953, although she remained active in the council, and was succeeded by her colleague Jo Anne Robinson, who led it for the rest of the decade. In 1953 Montgomery officials agreed to discuss modest changes with Burks, Nixon, and other black leaders, but police and bus drivers continued to accost, beat, and even shoot African Americans with impunity.[7]

Failing to make progress through negotiation, activists in Montgomery and other southern cities began experimenting with more militant tactics. In February 1953 black ministers and NAACP leaders in Baton Rouge, Louisiana, convinced the city council to allow riders to take seats on city buses on a first-come-first-served basis, so long as blacks started from the back of the bus and whites from the front. This was a significant change from the common policy of reserving an entire section of seats for whites, who used public transportation in smaller numbers than blacks, with the result that black riders were often left standing in the back of the bus while seats remained empty in the front. When the new policy was implemented on March 19, however, it was opposed by the bus drivers—all of whom were white. The city council held firm, but on June 15 the drivers went on strike. Four days later the Louisiana attorney general ruled that the new revision violated a state law mandating segregation on public transportation, and the drivers restored service under the old system. On June 18 black riders responded with a week-long boycott of city buses. The NAACP refused to back the protest because its demands were too moderate—it wanted a complete elimination of segregation rather than a small adjustment—but Baptist minister Theodore Jemison sustained morale by holding mass meetings in his church and organizing a new group called the United Defense League to spread word of the boycott and coordinate a carpool to get participants to work. The action ended in a compromise in which two rows of seats were reserved for whites in the front of each bus, two rows for blacks in the back, with the rest available to anyone so long as black riders filled them from the back forward and did not sit in the same row as a white rider. News of the victory spread quickly among Baptist ministers in the South.[8]

Inspired by the victory in Baton Rouge, the Women's Political Council considered launching a boycott in Montgomery. Jo Anne Robinson started recording cases in which black riders were insulted or physically abused by bus drivers and demanding that the city council take action. On May 21, 1954, four days after the *Brown* decision, she sent the mayor a letter explaining that increasing numbers of African Americans were avoiding the bus and that over twenty-five black organizations were prepared to launch a boycott if conditions did not improve. The situation reached a breaking point in March 1955 when Claudette Colvin, an "intelligent, pretty, and deeply religious" student at Booker T. Washington High School, was insulted, beaten, and then arrested for refusing to give up her seat on a city bus. After Colvin was found guilty not only of violating segregation laws but also of assault and battery against a police officer, the Women's Political Council began planning for a boycott of Montgomery's bus system.[9]

Despite years of preparation, E. D. Nixon opposed the boycott. With a local election coming, he feared that a public protest would galvanize conservatives who were moving to challenge the few moderates remaining on the City Council. When Colvin's attorney appealed her conviction to a circuit court, the state pursued only the assault and battery charges so that her case could not be used to test the constitutionality of segregation. In addition to those legal and political complications, Nixon also discovered that the unmarried young woman was pregnant. "You've got to think about the newspapers, you got to think about public opinion, you got to think policies and so forth, and intimidation," Nixon recalled in reference to his decision not to make Colvin the center of a protest. Rosa Parks agreed, pointing out that white reporters would have had "a field day" with the news of her pregnancy and that "her case wouldn't have a chance" in the court of public opinion. Nixon was also keenly aware of the violent backlash that was rolling across the South in the wake of the *Brown* decision. Citizens' Councils were spreading quickly from Mississippi into

Alabama and other southern states, pressuring local businessmen to deny jobs and credit to anyone—black or white—who dared to criticize segregation. Black activists faced more violent reprisals from the Ku Klux Klan. As Nixon had predicted, conservatives took control of Montgomery's City Council by attacking white moderates who had been willing to negotiate with black leaders during Claudette Colvin's trial. He and his allies passed up three other chances to build protests around discrimination on buses in the summer and fall of 1955.[10]

As Pauli Murray had at the founding conference of the March on Washington Movement in 1942, E. D. Nixon argued that a successful civil disobedience movement required careful planning and a well-trained and disciplined core of leadership. In the summer of 1955 he arranged for several black activists to attend training sessions at the Highlander Folk School in the Appalachian mountains of Tennessee 250 miles north of Montgomery. Highlander had been founded in 1932 by Myles Horton, who grew up in a working-class family in Tennessee but left in 1929 to study under Reinhold Neibuhr, the influential Christian socialist at Union Theological Seminary in New York City. After travelling to Europe, he returned to Tennessee and established Highlander with financial assistance from Neibuhr and the Socialist Party. Inspired by Neibuhr's theological criticism of capitalism, as well as by Danish folk schools that aimed to defend working-class traditions against commercialization, Horton explained that the school was designed to teach working-class people of both races how to organize and address injustices themselves, rather than waiting "for some government edict or some Messiah" to improve their lives. While he focused primarily on mostly white textile and mine workers in the mountains, Horton reached out to E. D. Nixon and others who were organizing black workers in the 1940s. After the boycott in Baton Rouge, and as tensions rose in the wake of the *Brown* decision, he shifted the school's focus completely to the struggle against segregation. Convinced that most white southerners would never abandon the

Jim Crow system voluntarily, he argued that "black people are going to have to force the white people to respect them." Rosa Parks spent two weeks at Highlander in July 1955, with financial support from Virginia Durr and her husband, Clifford, an attorney who had quit a prominent position in Washington to protest the repression of leftists in the federal workforce. Parks left Highlander feeling that black people were too "timid" and divided to challenge whites in Montgomery, but she was impressed by the dedication of Horton and his staff and given "strength to persevere in my work for freedom."[11]

Soon after Parks returned from Highlander, the virulence of white supremacy in the South was illustrated graphically by the brutal murder of Emmett Till, a fourteen-year-old boy from Chicago who was kidnapped by two white men on August 28, 1955, while he was visiting relatives in the small town of Money, Mississippi. After Till's mutilated body was found in a nearby river, his mother demanded that it be returned to Chicago for a full investigation and a proper funeral. Mamie Till-Bradley also insisted on an open-casket viewing to "let the people see what they have done to my boy!" Tens of thousands of people "from every walk of life" filed through a Chicago church before the burial on September 6 in what became a spontaneous protest against the brutality of the Jim Crow system. Larger protests erupted in cities across the country after September 23, when an all-white jury acquitted the murderers after deliberating for less than an hour. Fifty thousand people packed an eight-block radius surrounding a Detroit church, and 10,000 attended the "largest and most enthusiastic civil rights mass meeting ever sponsored by the NAACP in Chicago." Fifteen thousand "irate Negroes" huddled around loudspeakers outside a packed church in Harlem to hear speeches by Mamie Till-Bradley, A. Philip Randolph, and Earl Brown, a black journalist who had defeated the Communist Ben Davis in 1949 to represent Harlem on the New York City Council. Calling Till's murder "an exhibition of human bestiality, brutality and barbarism," Randolph insisted that "only the righteous revolt" of citizens in the North and the South could end "this wave of terrorism." Councilman Brown called for a "Refugee Committee" to organize a mass exodus from Mississippi, and the minister of the church called for a "March on Washington" to protest President Eisenhower's failure to protect black citizens in the South. On October 11 an interracial crowd of 20,000 packed a "Garment Center Labor Rally" in midtown Manhattan, listening to angry speeches by Adam Clayton Powell, Roy Wilkins, and a white minister who declared it "essential that the people of Mississippi feel the sense of shame and moral outrage of the American people." Powell called for a nationwide boycott of goods produced in Mississippi, and March on Washington Committees formed in Chicago, Detroit, New York, and other cities. "Not since the March on Washington days has there been such a sight in New York," the *Chicago Defender* reported.[12]

While Emmett Till's murder sparked mass protests across the country, its impact was particularly resonant in Montgomery. In November 1955, Adam Clayton Powell went on a nationwide tour to promote the boycott of Mississippi and stayed with E. D. Nixon during his stop in Montgomery. The two stayed up talking the night before his speech, and both must have recalled the bus boycott that Powell had led in Harlem fourteen years earlier when the congressman told activists in Montgomery that the power of white supremacists could "be counter met with our own economic pressure." It is likely that Rosa Parks heard that speech, but when she boarded a bus on December 1, after a long day at work, she was still unconvinced that a similar protest would work in Montgomery. She found a seat in the first row of the "Negro" section and watched as additional black passengers boarded and found places to stand at the back of the bus. There were open seats in the first ten rows, but local law reserved them for white passengers. As in Louisiana, state law prohibited blacks and whites from sitting in the same row. When the remaining seats in the "White" section filled up, the driver ordered Parks and three other black riders to vacate the first "Negro" row so that two white riders could sit. The other black riders complied with the driver's request, but Parks slid to the window seat—leaving an empty seat and the aisle between herself and the two whites. The driver told her again to move, and when she refused he got off the bus and called the police. "Why didn't you stand up?" a police officer asked when she recounted the incident, to which Parks replied: "Why do you push us around?" Parks recalled later that she was no more tired or sore than on any other evening after work. "I had felt for a long time," she told an interviewer, "that if I was ever told to get up so a white person could sit, that I would refuse to do so." She added later, "I thought of Emmett Till" when deciding not to move.[13]

Whatever Parks's intentions, E. D. Nixon and his allies moved quickly after learning of her arrest. Knowing that Fred Gray, the black lawyer who had represented Claudette Colvin, was out of town, Nixon contacted Clifford and Virginia Durr and arranged to travel with them to the courthouse. After posting bail, the four activists returned to Parks's home to discuss the incident with her husband, Raymond. "This is the case," Nixon declared. "We can boycott the bus lines with this and at the same time go to the Supreme Court." Clifford Durr pointed out that local law did not actually require Parks to leave her seat unless there was another one available in the "Negro" section, an amendment that had been included in response to a black boycott of streetcar lines when the law had originally been passed in 1900. Parks was not optimistic that her case could be the catalyst for a similar challenge, and Raymond, who had grown weary of political activism, feared for her life. She trusted Nixon's judgment, however, saying, "If you think it is all right, I'll go along with you."[14]

Meanwhile Fred Gray returned home and, upon learning of the arrest, contacted Jo Anne Robinson of the Women's Political Council. Using the mimeograph machine at Alabama State College, Robinson produced over 50,000 copies of a flyer calling for a one-day boycott the following Monday. "Another Negro woman has been arrested and thrown into jail because she refused to get up out of her seat on a bus for a white person to sit down," she wrote, warning that "the next time it may be you, or your daughter, or mother." Pointing out that three-quarters of the city's bus riders were black, she asserted that the bus system "could not operate" without their fares. The next morning, Robinson and other members of the council distributed copies of the flyer to their students, who passed them out in black communities across the city. "Leaflets were also dropped off at business places, storefronts, beauty parlors, beer halls, factories, barber shops, and every other available place," Robinson recalled, stating that "workers would pass along notices both to other employees as well as to customers."[15]

Despite this impressive start, Nixon knew that the boycott could not be sustained without support from a broader range of black leaders in Montgomery. The morning after Rosa Parks's arrest he called Reverend Ralph D. Abernathy, a militant young minister who taught math at Alabama State College. A twenty-nine-year-old from rural Alabama, Abernathy had moved to Montgomery in 1945 after serving in the Army. Using his veterans' benefits to enroll at Alabama State, he got involved in protests over poor food and living conditions in the dormitories and was ordained by the Baptist church in 1948. He moved to Atlanta in 1950 to start a graduate degree in sociology but returned to Montgomery two years later to accept a pastorship at the First Baptist Church. When Nixon called him the morning of December 2, Abernathy agreed to support the protest and call a meeting of the Baptist Ministers Alliance, of which he was an officer. Because First Baptist was on the edge of town, he suggested that Nixon call Martin Luther King, the minister at the more centrally located Dexter Avenue Baptist Church. King was three years younger than Abernathy, and the two had become close friends since King moved to Montgomery in 1954. Meanwhile Abernathy started calling the other ministers.[16]

When Martin Luther King got a call from E. D. Nixon, his first inclination was not to get involved in the protest. The eldest son of one of the most prominent black ministers in Atlanta, King had been raised with a strong sense of responsibility for informed and responsible leadership. In 1944, at the age of fifteen, he carried that mission with him across town to Morehouse, the prestigious college for black men where his father had attended seminary in 1926. The younger King believed at the time that a career in law or medicine would allow him to make a "meaningful contribution to society," but listened attentively to weekly addresses by Morehouse president Dr. Benjamin Mays, a Baptist preacher who had worked as a Pullman porter while studying at the University of Chicago in the 1920s, met Mohandas Gandhi during a trip to India in the 1930s, and was currently a leading force in building alliances between black and white liberals in the South. King may also have heard A. Philip Randolph, who was the commencement speaker at Morehouse at the end of his freshman year in 1945. "Education places upon you the responsibility of courageous leadership," the leader of National Council for a Permanent FEPC had insisted, urging graduates to prepare for a "25-year plan" to achieve "economic security, full and first class and equal citizenship status and education and culture."[17]

Despite his distinguished background, King could not help but be caught up in the radicalism of the 1940s. While Randolph emphasized their responsibility for leadership he also urged the "Morehouse men" to throw in their lot with the masses. "There resides the power," he insisted. "They may be poor in property, but they are rich in spirit." Randolph urged them to look not only to working people in their own country but also to "the ringing challenge of India for freedom" and to an Africa that was "seething with unrest." By the time he graduated from Morehouse in 1948, King had decided to enter the ministry and was accepted at Crozer Theological Seminary near Philadelphia. His father was alarmed to see him reading the *Communist Manifesto* during Christmas break in 1949. King was also impressed by a "profound and electrifying" lecture that Howard University Professor Mordecai

Johnson gave in Philadelphia following a trip to India in 1950. King was not attracted to Gandhi's nonviolence, remarking later that "when I was in theological school I thought the only way we could solve our problem of segregation was an armed revolt." Rather, it was Gandhi's willingness to abandon personal wealth and social status and throw in his lot with the poor that impressed the young Reverend King. A fellow student at Crozer recalled that King had a "pretty serious argument" with A. J. Muste, the Christian socialist who had introduced Bayard Rustin to nonviolence during the Second World War. "King sure as hell wasn't any pacifist then," he claimed.[18]

Graduating at the top of his class from Crozer, after a mediocre record at Morehouse, King won a scholarship to graduate school at several other leading schools of theology. He chose Boston University, where he studied the works of Myles Horton's mentor, Reinhold Neibuhr, and other Christian socialists of the early twentieth century. He also started dating Coretta Scott, a music student from rural Alabama, whom he married in 1953. Coretta was not eager to return to the South, but she relented when he was offered the position at Dexter Avenue Baptist in Montgomery. "He had a strong feeling for the masses," she recalled, and told her, "I'm going to live in the South because that's where I'm needed." Dexter was a "big-shots' church" that had fired its previous preacher for his outspoken views, but King believed that he could be more effective. Taking over on May 14, 1954, three days before the *Brown* decision, he renewed the church's ties to the NAACP and insisted that every member of his congregation try to register to vote. He was elected to the executive committee of the local NAACP and asked to run for president, but he still had a dissertation to finish and a congregation to meet. He finished the dissertation in June 1955. Five months later, on November 17, Coretta gave birth to their first child. When E. D. Nixon asked him on December 2 to host a meeting of Montgomery's black leaders, the tension between radicalism and responsibility shaped his response: he said no.[19]

King changed his mind when Ralph Abernathy called and, after emphasizing the importance of the Parks case, promised that he could host the meeting without taking any responsibility for leading the boycott. Nixon faced similar resistance from other black leaders. The president of Alabama State College was furious to learn that Jo Anne Robinson had used the college's copier to publicize the boycott. He allowed her to continue her work on the condition that she reimburse the college for copying the flyers, not publicize her connection to the college, and not neglect any of her teaching duties. Local leaders of the NAACP insisted on getting permission from Roy Wilkins before endorsing the boycott. "I said, 'man, we ain't got time for that,' " Nixon recalled. With each leader Nixon argued that Parks was the ideal fig- ure around whom to build a mass protest. "I knew she'd stand on her feet," he recalled later, pointing to their long history of collaboration. "She was honest, she was clean, she had integrity. The press couldn't go out and dig up something she did last year, or last month, or five years ago." By the end of the day he had convinced over 100 black min- isters, educators, and civic leaders to discuss the boycott in the base- ment of King's church. Other ministers started walking out after one of them went on for thirty minutes about how he should be in charge of strategy. King stated, "I would like to go too, but it's in my church." Abernathy salvaged the meeting by interrupting the talkative minister and supporting a motion, made by Jo Anne Robinson, to endorse the boycott on Monday and to call a mass meeting for Monday evening to discuss future actions.[20]

Preparations for the boycott continued through the weekend with no centralized leadership. A transportation committee, formed by vol- unteers at the Friday evening meeting, recruited people to drive boy- cotters to work and convinced black-owned taxi firms to reduce their rates to the standard bus fare. Additional copies of Robinson's flyer were produced, and King and Abernathy headed a group that handed them out at nightclubs on Saturday night. E. D. Nixon left town on Friday evening to work on the overnight train to Chicago but leaked news of the protest to a local reporter before he departed. Copies of Robinson's flyer were also passed to white authorities by bus drivers and a black domestic worker who either could not read it or, in Robinson's view, felt more loyalty to her white employer than to "her people." Robinson was alarmed to see the boycott featured prominently in local newspapers and in television and radio news on Saturday and Sunday, stating that she and others had hoped "the whole affair would come as a complete surprise to whites," but she realized later that the publicity actually increased participation in the protest. The *Montgomery Advertiser* reported that police were increasing patrols in response to rumors that "Negro goon squads" planned to intimidate black riders who did not participate. Activists knew the story was inaccurate but, according to Robinson, observed that the threat of violence served to dissuade "any timid souls who would have ridden the bus despite the boycott."[21]

The one-day boycott on December 5 was a tremendous success, although it failed to protect Rosa Parks from prosecution. Martin Luther King rose early Monday morning and was drinking coffee in the kitchen when Coretta called him to the front of the house to watch an empty bus drive by. Their house was on one of the busiest lines in town, and they stood and watched as two others passed carrying only a few white passengers. King drove around to inspect other major lines and counted only eight black riders. "During the rush hours the sidewalks were crowded with laborers and domestic workers, many of them well past middle age, trudging patiently to their jobs and home again," King wrote a few years later, noting that "there was nothing more majestic than the determined courage of individuals willing to suffer and sacrifice for their freedom and dignity." King then joined E. D. Nixon, Ralph Abernathy, and Reverend Edgar N. French at the city courthouse, where several hundred people had gathered in a spontaneous demonstration of support for Parks, who went to trial that morning represented by Fred Gray. Anticipating the challenge that Clifford Durr had proposed to the local segregation law, city attorneys replaced the original charge with one prosecuting Parks for violating a state law giving bus drivers unlimited power to enforce segregation. The judge convicted her after only five minutes of testimony and sought to end the matter by imposing a symbolic ten-dollar fine, but Gray appealed the conviction while Nixon and other black leaders urged protesters to regroup at the mass meeting later that evening.[22]

Despite the near-unanimous participation of black passengers in the bus boycott, some black leaders still doubted the effectiveness of mass mobilization. Nixon, Abernathy, and French attended a meeting of ministers following Parks's trial, where they proposed to continue the protests until the bus company agreed to seat all passengers on a first-come-first-served basis, discipline drivers who insulted or abused black riders, and employ black drivers on "buses running into pre-dominantly Negro sections." While those present agreed to coordinate future protests through a new organization called the Montgomery Improvement Association, some argued that it would be more effective to end the boycott and enter into negotiations with the threat of renew-ing it if their demands were not met. Others refused to identify them-selves publicly with the protest, out of fear for retaliation. Nixon was outraged at their reticence, declaring: "somebody has got to get hurt in this thing and if you preachers are not the leaders, then we have to pray that God will send us some more leaders." Impressed by Nixon's "courageous affirmation," King agreed to serve as president of the new group. The others agreed to put the decision on whether to continue the boycott to a vote at the mass meeting later that evening.[23]

For King, the question of whether to continue the boycott was resolved by the size and enthusiasm of the crowd that turned out for the meeting that evening at Holt Street Baptist Church. Arriving thirty minutes early, he and Abernathy were surprised to find the streets lined with cars and the sidewalks packed by "approximately seven thousand people all trying to get in a church that will accommodate less than a thousand." Identifying themselves, the two ministers were ushered into the church with "cheering and hand-clapping" while "those inside applauded for at least ten minutes." Other speakers had to push their way through the crowd, delaying the meeting for thirty minutes, and then the chorus encouraged the "mammoth audience" to stand and join them in singing "Onward Christian Soldiers." After an opening prayer and reading of scripture, King delivered one of the rousing speeches that would win him international acclaim in the coming decade.[24]

No longer in doubt about the militancy of his audience, King devoted most of his speech to keeping "this fervor within controllable and Christian bounds." Countering local newspapers that compared the boycott to economic sanctions employed by the Citizens' Councils and the Ku Klux Klan, he stated: "in our protest there will be no cross burnings" nor "threats and intimidation." King had not yet come to see Gandhian nonviolence as a model for Montgomery, but instead rooted his appeal in a Christian message of forgiveness. "Love must be our regulating ideal," he insisted, urging protesters to "hear the words of Jesus echoing across the centuries: 'Love your enemies, bless them that curse you, and pray for them that despitefully use you.'" Asserting a significance for the one-day-old boycott that must have sounded inspiring to some but naïve to others, he promised the crowd that if they "protest courageously, and yet with dignity and Christian love, when the history books are written in future generations, the historians will have to pause and say, 'There lived a great people—a black people—who injected new meaning and dignity into the veins of civilization.'"[25]

Jo Anne Robinson recalled that while King and other ministers worked to "keep down violence" and "make the movement more Christian-like," daily operations of the boycott remained under the control of experienced activists like herself, who could "speak out without fear and speak with authority as representatives of the black protesters." The morning after the first mass meeting King began assembling committees to coordinate transportation for boycotters, raise and manage funds, and make strategic decisions related to the protest. Concluding that "a strategy committee was essential," he recruited Robinson, Ralph Abernathy, Fred Gray, "the indispensable E. D. Nixon," and eight other men and women "who had already provided strong leadership in the early days of the protest, and whose clear thinking and courageous guidance were to be of inestimable help in the difficult decisions that still lay ahead." Not all of King's strategic advisors held official leadership positions in the Montgomery Improvement Association, but King recalled that they "were the people with whom, from the beginning, I worked most closely."[26]

Given the militancy of King's advisors, as well as the historic significance that he attributed to the movement, it is remarkable how moderate their demands were. "We are not asking an end to segregation," King told officials from the bus company who agreed to meet with him and other protest leaders three days into the boycott, explaining that they simply wanted to stop bus drivers from abusing black riders and forcing them to give their seats to whites. That moderation led Roy Wilkins and others at the NAACP's national headquarters to reject requests for assistance from Montgomery, saying they were already engaged in a lawsuit challenging bus segregation in Columbia, South Carolina. "Obviously, when our national program calls for abolishing segregation, and our lawyers are fighting on that basis in South Carolina, we could not enter an Alabama case asking merely for a more polite segregation," Wilkins wrote to leaders of the Montgomery NAACP. Employment of black bus drivers was a more substantive objective, because local statutes gave bus drivers the power to arrest passengers—black or white—who violated the segregation law. That demand would be largely forgotten by the time the boycott was over.[27]

Despite its moderate beginnings, the Montgomery movement was radicalized by the refusal of white officials to concede to even its most basic objectives. Three days after the first mass meeting, King and Fred Gray met with Mayor W. A. Gayle, several city commissioners, and a manager and attorney from the bus company. After King read the three demands of the movement, bus company attorney Jack Crenshaw denied that black passengers had been abused, rejected outright the possibility of hiring black drivers, and declared that state law prohibited the bus company from altering its system of segregation. Gray responded that state and city laws required segregation but did not prescribe any specific arrangement, and that bus companies in other cities had adopted policies similar to the one they proposed without violating state law. While one city commissioner agreed that the movement's proposal could work "within our segregation laws," the others agreed with Crenshaw that any reform required legislative action. A larger group of black leaders met with city officials twice in the following week, but found them no more willing to compromise. Within a few weeks, some leaders of the boycott concluded "that further negotiations would be fruitless and were beginning to discuss the possibility of a federal court suit to have bus segregation declared unconstitutional."[28]

The sources of white resistance were more political than legal. As a Harvard-trained lawyer and a staunch supporter of segregation, Jack Crenshaw must have realized that a slight modification of the seating system would have ended the conflict without a major challenge to the Jim Crow system. With the Supreme Court having rejected the constitutionality of segregation in the *Brown* decision, however, many whites were convinced that any concession to black demands would have culminated in a total collapse of the social order. "If we granted Negroes these demands," Crenshaw stated during the meeting with King and Gray, "they would go about boasting of a victory that they had won over the white people, and this we will not stand for." Police commissioner Clyde Sellers displayed a similar resolve when he announced his membership in the local Citizens' Council during a rally of 1,200 segregationists at the Montgomery city auditorium a few weeks later. Mayor Gayle and several other city officials joined the organization soon afterward.[29]

In addition to radicalizing the movement, white resistance forced leaders of the boycott to strengthen their organization. At the first meeting between white officials and black activists, Commissioner Clyde Sellers mentioned that a city ordinance prohibited taxi drivers from charging less than a minimum fare. Recognizing an implicit threat to black cabbies who had been supporting the boycott by charging the regular bus fare, King contacted Baton Rouge minister Theodore Jemison to inquire about the carpool that he and others had created during their own bus boycott two years earlier. At a mass meeting that evening more than 150 people volunteered to transport boycotters, and ministers recruited an equal number the following Sunday. Following Jemison's advice, boycott leaders established a dispatch system and pickup stations to coordinate transportation across the city. By the time Sellers followed through with his threat, according to King, the movement had solved "a transportation problem that the bus company had grappled with for many years."[30]

As the new year began, with the boycott entering its second month and the bus company losing an estimated $3,000 a week, segregationists stepped up their efforts to destroy the protest. The first victim of the backlash was Rosa Parks, who was fired from her job at Montgomery Fair and threatened with eviction from her home. Vandals attacked the car of one of the few white supporters of the protest. City officials met with black ministers who were not involved in the boycott and announced to the press that they had reached an agreement with "prominent Negro ministers" to end the boycott. King was informed of the report before it appeared in newspapers, and he and other ministers countered the misrepresentation in their Sunday sermons; but Mayor Gayle followed quickly with a second blow. Blaming racial tensions in the city on "a group of Negro radicals who have split asunder a fine relationship," the mayor declared that "we have pussyfooted around on this boycott long enough." The following day city police began following carpool drivers, pulling them over for the smallest, often unstated, infractions, and dispersing groups of boycotters who were waiting on street corners for rides. Later that week, Martin Luther King was jailed for driving five miles an hour over the speed limit.[31]

By the end of January 1956, the city of Montgomery was literally on the brink of war. One evening while King was speaking at a mass meeting a bomb exploded on his front porch, nearly killing Coretta and their ten-week-old baby, Yolanda. A second bomb exploded in E. D. Nixon's front yard two days later, while he was working on the train to Chicago. Rosa Parks reported that "strange men have been coming in my neighborhood inquiring about the woman who caused all of this trouble," stating that she was "not worried about myself, but it does upset my mother quite a bit." Mayor Gayle and Police Commissioner Sellers condemned the attacks and offered a reward for information leading to an arrest, but that same week both gave defiant speeches to 10,000 "stamping, cheering Alabamans" who packed the State Coliseum in Montgomery for the largest rally ever sponsored by a Citizens' Council in the state. While Gayle offered a plea to those who "want to maintain peace and harmony" while defending "our way of life," Sellers whipped up the crowd by warning that anyone who wanted integration should move to where it was legal. "Let him go, let him go," the crowd chanted as the police commissioner bellowed, "Let our battle cry be states' rights and white supremacy!" The following week a grand jury ordered the arrest of 115 members of the Montgomery Improvement Association, including King, Nixon, Fred Gray, and Jo Anne Robinson, under a state law that had been passed to stop strikes in the 1920s. "In this state we are committed to segregation by custom and law," the jury stated in its indictment. "We intend to maintain it."[32]

The outburst of violence had two important effects on the Montgomery movement. The first was media attention, which transformed a largely local conflict into a national and even international event. While the boycott had been front-page news in black newspapers since its beginning, white-owned papers had either ignored the story or buried brief and sporadic coverage in its back pages. On February 11 the *New York Times* mentioned the bombings in a front-page story about the White Citizens' Council, claiming erroneously that it had targeted "the homes of NAACP leaders," but the boycott itself became and remained front-page news only after King was indicted on February 25. King's speech at the mass rally following the indictments was covered by the national press, the first for a minister who would soon become a fixture on the evening news. ABC radio commentator Edward P. Morgan compared the actions of city officials to the British government's brutal campaign to wipe out Gandhi's "Quit India" movement during the Second World War, pointing out that repression only inspired a larger revolt that led to independence after the war. "What they've done, rather pathetically in fact," he stated in a nationwide broadcast, "is to reveal the transparency of the sincere but mistaken claims of white supremacy."[33]

Perhaps more important than the media attention created by the backlash was that it pushed leaders of the boycott to accept advice and assistance from supporters outside Montgomery. Nixon and other leaders had been fiercely independent since the start, even refusing to expand their demands to win support from the NAACP. They began to reconsider that position after white officials refused to entertain their more moderate demands, and late in January Fred Gray travelled to New York City to discuss legal strategy with NAACP head attorney Thurgood Marshall. The day after E. D. Nixon's house was bombed, leaders of the Montgomery Improvement Association met with NAACP southern regional secretary Ruby Hurley and leaders of the local branch of the NAACP, and agreed to file a suit in federal court charging that Alabama's segregation laws violated the U.S.

Constitution. Some expressed concern that the Montgomery Improvement Association could not sustain the boycott while also funding a legal challenge, but 4,000 participants in a mass meeting voted nearly unanimously to pursue both strategies simultaneously. "Keep on with the mass meetings," Hurley advised the local leadership. "They will aid psychologically, educationally, and financially."[34]

Having resolved to combine mass mobilization with legal action, leaders of the protest faced the more daunting challenge of protecting themselves and their supporters from violence. "I never will forget those threatening telephone calls and letters of intimidation," Ralph Abernathy wrote two years later, "threatening with such violent statements as 'we would not live until morning'; that 'they were on their way to get us'; that 'they were going to kill us and members of our families.'" The Montgomery Improvement Association posted armed guards at the homes of King, Abernathy, Rosa Parks, and other leaders, and King and Abernathy requested permits to carry pistols from the county sheriff. When their request was denied they appealed to Alabama governor James E. Folsom, who had denounced the bombings but refused to intervene. In the meantime, supporters of the movement donated guns and ammunition to the leadership, and rumors spread that an "arsenal" was being "smuggled by ministers and porters" into Montgomery. A researcher from Fisk University gained a glimpse into the rising tensions when she interviewed a supporter of the boycott two days after King's first arrest. Claiming that whites would "have a war if they" continued attacking King, one boycotter stated that she and others "don't mind dying," but would be sure to take "a white bastard with 'em" to the grave. Abernathy recalled that he and other leaders of the movement were troubled by this rapid trend toward "counter violence," resolving that it was "incompatible with Christian doctrine." Even if they were willing to "employ forces of violence," he observed, protesters lacked the organization and "experience in tactical military campaigns" to engage white supremacists in armed conflict.[35]

The escalation of violence caught the attention of A. Philip Randolph, who received regular reports on the boycott from E. D. Nixon, and soon after the bombings a small group of civil rights and labor leaders assembled to discuss the problem in New York City. They included Bayard Rustin, who was working for the War Resisters' League, which had been founded by Socialists who opposed the First World War; and Ella Baker, who had just completed an unsuccessful campaign for a seat on the New York City Council. Attorney Stanley Levison represented the American Jewish Congress, which had been founded to fight anti-Semitism during the First World War and remained one of the largest civil rights organizations in the country. A wealthy former Communist, after 1955 Levison dedicated himself almost completely to supporting the civil rights movement. Finally, there were two union leaders. Jerry Wurf was president of the New York district of the American Federation of State, County and Municipal Employees, which had recently hired James Farmer and other CORE activists to organize mostly black and Puerto Rican service workers in city hospitals. The second was Cleveland Robinson, the secretary-treasurer of District 65, a large union of retail, wholesale, and department store workers in New York City. Calling themselves "In Friendship," the group set out to draw publicity to civil rights battles and raise funds to support "race terror victims" in the South.[36]

Fearing that open warfare would bring a wave of repression far greater than they had seen already, Randolph and the others resolved to send Bayard Rustin to hold a series of workshops on Gandhian nonviolence in Montgomery. Rustin arrived in Montgomery on February 21, 1956, the day that the grand jury issued its indictments, and set out immediately to try to dispel the threat of violence. A hotel worker told him to bolt the windows in his room and not to walk the streets alone after dark. "This is like war," a local activist warned. "You can't trust anyone, black or white, unless you know him." Rustin met with Abernathy, whose home was guarded by men carrying shotguns and pistols, and then with E. D. Nixon, who expected that his house would be bombed again but stated: "They can bomb us out and they can kill us, but we are not going to give in." At a meeting of the Montgomery Improvement Association's strategy committee later that evening, Rustin convinced them to refer to their movement as a *"non-violent protest* rather than a boycott in order to keep its fundamental character uppermost," to encourage displays of solidarity by asking supporters to wear a pin, and to use the slogan "Victory without Violence," which CORE had promoted during the Second World War. He also suggested that those who were indicted surrender rather than wait to be arrested. Led by Nixon, they showed up at the police station in their Sunday best and entered one by one as hundreds of supporters gathered outside to cheer them on. "This procedure had a startling effect in both the Negro and the White communities," Rustin wrote a few months later. "White community leaders, politicians, and police were flabbergasted. Negroes were thrilled to see their leaders surrender without being hunted down."[37]

King was out of town when Rustin arrived, but both were eager to meet. Since the bombing, King's father had been trying to persuade him to leave Montgomery and move his family to Atlanta, and he recruited Morehouse University president Benjamin Mays and other prominent figures to make that plea to King when the young minister stopped in Atlanta on his way home from a speaking engagement. Both Mays and "Daddy" King were won over by Martin, who pointed out that "it would be the height of cowardice for me to stay away" and stated that he "would rather go back and spend ten years in jail than desert my people now." Still, they insisted on calling Thurgood Marshall to ensure that the NAACP would oversee King's defense on the boycotting charge. Returning to Montgomery, King surrendered himself to local authorities and posted a bond before inviting Rustin to accompany him to a mass meeting and several conferences with his advisors. The two "hit it off immediately" when they finally found time for an extended conversation over coffee in the Kings' kitchen, discovering that Rustin and Coretta had met years earlier when he lectured at her high school in rural Alabama and again at her alma mater, Antioch College. Turning to the topic of protest tactics, Rustin asked whether the bombings and intimidation would lead some supporters of the protest to "return violence with violence." King replied that he "felt the behavior of the White Citizens Council could very easily lead to serious violence and that the results might be catastrophic," but expressed confidence that six weeks of training would be enough to ensure that "the spirit of non-violence may so have permeated our community by that time that the whole Negro community will react non-violently."[38]

Despite King's emphasis on nonviolence and his familiarity with Gandhi, Rustin found that the minister had "very limited notions about how a nonviolent protest should be carried out." In addition to finding the homes of King and other leaders under armed guard, he discovered several guns lying around King's house. Rustin told King that during his travels to India he had learned that "the great masses of Indians who were followers of Gandhi did not believe in non-violence," but came to accept it as a tactic because it was effective. For that reason, he explained, it was particularly important "that the leadership must be dedicated to it in principle" since "if, in the flow and the heat of battle, a leader's house is bombed, and he shoots back, that is an encouragement to his followers to pick up guns." Writing about his experiences in Montgomery several years later, Rustin recalled, "I do not believe that one does honor to Dr. King by assuming that, somehow, he had been prepared for his job . . . The glorious thing is that he came to a profoundly deep understanding of nonviolence through the struggle itself, and through reading and discussions which he had in the process of carrying on the protest."[39]

In contrast to the close friendship that Rustin forged with King, other leaders of the movement were not enthusiastic about his presence. Upon his arrival, Rustin was warned not to carry anything with him that identified him "as an outsider" because, as a hotel worker told him, "They are trying to make out that Communist agitators and New Yorkers are running our protest." The fact that Rustin actually was a New Yorker and a former Communist made him particularly dangerous. In Montgomery a white journalist from a northern newspaper informed Rustin that a local reporter was spreading rumors that he was a "communist NAACP organizer" who hoped to foment a "violent uprising," and a few days later E. D. Nixon called A. Philip Randolph to check the rumors out. Randolph defended Rustin but called a meeting to discuss the matter with other leaders of In Friendship. "Phil Randolph indicated that the Montgomery leaders had managed thus far more successfully than any 'of our so-called non-violence experts' a mass resistance campaign and we should learn from them rather than assume that we knew it all," recalled one New Yorker. Others in the group were concerned that leaders of the boycott had not been informed of Rustin's homosexuality. In 1953 he had been arrested for having sex with two men while on a speaking tour in California; the incident got him fired from A. J. Muste's Fellowship of Reconciliation and received widespread publicity on the West Coast. Randolph called Rustin the following day and asked him to move to Birmingham, a larger city 100 miles north of Montgomery.[40]

Rustin's departure insulated the boycott from charges of outside influence but did not end his influence on the movement. Randolph put him in touch with black union activists in Birmingham, who helped raise funds to send to Montgomery. King travelled to meet him in Birmingham, discussing ways to sustain the morale of protesters while educating them about nonviolence and generate support for the movement in other parts of the country. "Bayard has had a very good influence on King," one activist reported, stating that Rustin had written the "much quoted speech" that King gave after the indictments and "was in on all the strategy" decisions made by the movement. In addition to deepening King's understanding of nonviolence, Rustin encouraged him to view the boycott in broader terms than the struggle against segregation in Montgomery. "The basic conflict is not really over the buses," Rustin wrote in an article that was published under King's name, contending that the protest had initiated a broader struggle for black political and economic power in the South. King echoed that sentiment in a speech to a mass meeting in Montgomery, declaring that the movement was "bigger than Montgomery" and involved more than integration. "We must oppose all exploitation," he declared. "We want no classes and castes . . . We want to see everybody free."[41]

The need for political power was emphasized by a series of legal developments that spring, in which white authorities made it clear that the conflict in Montgomery would not be resolved through the courts. On March 22, 1956, a grand jury convicted King of violating the anti-boycott law and held the charges against other protesters in abeyance while his case went through an appeals process that could take over a year. A few weeks later the U.S. Supreme Court upheld the NAACP's challenge to bus segregation in Columbia, South Carolina. The Montgomery City Lines ordered its employees to follow the precedent, but an Alabama judge issued a restraining order allowing for the arrest of any driver who did not enforce the local segregation law. Local authorities also appealed a federal circuit court decision affirming Fred Gray's contention that Alabama's segregation law violated the U.S. Constitution. President Eisenhower responded to rising tensions in the South by proposing a civil rights law authorizing federal investigations into civil rights violations, but he did little to promote the bill in Congress. With Democrats divided between segregationists such as Georgia senator Richard Russell, who denounced the proposal as a "campaign to vilify the South," and Harlem congressman Adam Clayton Powell, who dismissed it as "mere buck-passing," the bill died in committee a few months later. "We've got to get political power and economic power for our race," King told a mass meeting after city officials defied the Supreme Court ruling. Pointing out that the boycott was likely to drag on through the summer, King urged other leaders of the Montgomery Improvement Association to focus on registering black voters and building up independent sources of economic power.[42]

Meanwhile A. Philip Randolph sought to solidify support for the nonviolent movement among civil rights and labor activists in the North. On February 28, 1956, he called the first public meeting of In Friendship, which established a temporary headquarters at Stanley Levison's office in midtown Manhattan. Randolph was the chairman and in addition to Jerry Wurf and Cleveland Robinson, sponsors included the Workers Defense League and several prominent Catholic, Jewish, and Protestant leaders in New York City. The president of the Garment Workers union pledged the "fullest financial support," but contributions came almost exclusively from black-led local unions in New York and other cities. On April 11, black leaders of the Auto and Packinghouse unions raised $2,500 at a mass rally in the Chicago Coliseum. They also organized a letter-writing campaign to pressure the National City Lines, a Chicago-based company that owned the bus system in Montgomery, to negotiate with the Montgomery Improvement Association. Black activists in the United Auto Workers initiated similar efforts in Detroit. Speaking to the annual convention of the Garment Workers on May 14, Randolph announced that George Meany, Walter Reuther, and other labor leaders had pledged $2 million to a "war chest" aimed at supporting the boycott in Montgomery, the NAACP's legal team, and black sharecroppers who faced eviction for their attempts to vote in the South. Thanking the Garment Workers for donating $10,000, Randolph stated that 12,000 members of his own union had pledged one hour's pay—an average of $1.50 each—to the fund.[43]

In Friendship's most successful event was organized by Maida Springer, the Garment Workers activist who had organized the rally at Madison Square Garden for the National Council for a Permanent FEPC in 1946. Born in Panama, Springer had moved to Harlem with her parents in 1917, when she was seven. Her parents were followers of Marcus Garvey, but Maida gravitated toward socialism. She became close friends with Pauli Murray and the other young radicals who gathered at the Harlem YWCA and joined the International Ladies Garment Workers Union after going to work in a garment factory during the Great Depression. She also developed a close alliance with Jay Lovestone, the leader of Pauli Murray and Ella Baker's Communist Party (Opposition), who was also a prominent figure in her union. Springer helped Pauli Murray organize the Odell Waller parade in 1942 and the following year was hired to direct education programs for her union local. Two years after she organized the FEPC rally for A. Philip Randolph and Anna Hedgeman, she was promoted to enforce contacts and handle grievances for 2,000 union members in more than sixty factories across New York City. "Trying to settle petty disputes between workers and employers who screamed at one another over the noise of throbbing machines was a contentious job," Pauli Murray recalled, "but Maida's gracious manner and sense of proportion made her a remarkably effective union representative." In 1945 Springer was one of two women selected to represent the AFL on a diplomatic mission to England. She went to Sweden with a delegation of labor feminists in 1951 and to Ghana in 1955 as an AFL observer to a conference of African labor leaders.[44]

On May 31, 1956, Springer raised $8,000 for In Friendship's "war chest" by organizing a massive "Salute and Support the Heroes of the South" in Madison Square Garden. Sixteen thousand people bought tickets to hear speeches by Martin Luther King, Rosa Parks, Eleanor Roosevelt, Adam Clayton Powell, Roy Wilkins, and Autherine Lucy, who had won a lawsuit forcing the University of Alabama to admit her to graduate school only to be expelled because authorities said they could not protect her from white students. Entertainment was provided by bandleader Cab Calloway, singer Sammy Davis Jr., movie star Tallulah Bankhead, and Josh White, a blues musician with whom

Bayard Rustin had performed in the 1930s. King had to cancel at the last minute, so E. D. Nixon took his spot. It was nearly midnight by the time the Pullman porter came to the stage, but he recalled that "people just fell out" with laughter when he boasted that "fifty thousand people rose up and caught hold to the Cradle of the Confederacy and began to rock it 'till the 'Jim Crow' rockers began to reel and the segregation slats began to fall out."[45]

In addition to sustaining the bus boycott, moral and financial support from In Friendship was critical to expanding the movement beyond Montgomery. On May 28, 1956, a group of black college students started a bus boycott in Tallahassee, Florida. "I don't know what would have happened in Tallahassee had we not had the background of this philosophy of love and nonviolence actually demonstrated in Montgomery," said C. K. Steele, a Baptist minister and NAACP leader who supported the protest. On June 1, the day after the rally in New York, a judged banned the NAACP from operating in the state of Alabama. The Alabama State Conference of NAACP Branches, which Ella Baker had helped establish over a decade earlier, had fifty branches and over 14,000 members. The southern regional office of the NAACP was also headquartered in Birmingham. While branches across the state stopped holding meetings and the regional offices moved to Atlanta, the minister of Birmingham's Bethel Baptist Church and a former membership chairman of the city's NAACP branch called a mass meeting to form an alternative organization. Having been in Montgomery on the first night of the boycott and watched the Tallahassee movement closely as it developed, Reverend Fred Shuttlesworth adopted the Montgomery Improvement Association's model of recruiting black ministers for official leadership positions and making decisions at weekly mass meetings that rotated among the city's black churches. On June 3, 1956, he called a mass meeting to form the Alabama Christian Movement for Human Rights. While most of the funding for movements in Birmingham and Montgomery continued to come from local participants, outside funding allowed grassroots activists to operate independently from the NAACP.[46]

By the end of 1956, King, Shuttlesworth, and other ministers had started to knit their local movements into a regional network. On December 3 the Montgomery Improvement Association hosted a week-long "Institute on Nonviolence and Social Change," which was designed to prepare for an expected Supreme Court decision on Montgomery's segregation law but also strengthen ties to movements in Birmingham, Tallahassee, Baton Rouge, and other cities. On December 17 the Supreme Court rejected the City of Montgomery's appeal and ordered integration of buses to proceed three days later. Montgomery's buses operated on an integrated basis without conflict for three days, but in the middle of the night of December 23 a shotgun blast tore through the front door of King's house. A bomb exploded in Shuttlesworth's home on Christmas night, and he and twenty other protesters were arrested when they attempted to desegregate buses in Birmingham the next day. Two days later, snipers began shooting at buses in Montgomery, injuring a black passenger and leading Police Commissioner Sellers to halt service for one day and then allow service during daylight hours only. On New Year's Day, King and Shuttlesworth sent 100 invitations to black ministers, educators, labor leaders, and business owners in nearly a dozen states, asking them to attend a "Southern Leadership Conference on Transportation and Nonviolent Integration," to be held at Martin Luther King Sr.'s church in Atlanta on January 10.[47]

The original purpose of the Southern Leadership Conference was not to create a new civil rights organization but, rather, to strengthen ties among the various local movements that had developed in the South during the previous year. King and Abernathy initiated that process on the state level in the summer of 1956, meeting regularly with Shuttlesworth and Reverend Joseph Lowery, who headed the Interdenominational Ministerial Alliance in Mobile, Alabama, to coordinate statewide activities as it became clear that the NAACP could no longer play that role. They expanded those discussions in the fall to include Theodore Jemison in Baton Rouge, C. K. Steele in Tallahassee, and Reverend A. L. Davis, who led a series of mass protests against bus segregation in New Orleans. Meanwhile Rustin and Randolph met with Ella Baker, Stanley Levison, and other supporters of In Friendship to discuss ways to support and strengthen connections among southern movements. The largest contributions came from the United Packinghouse Workers, which had a large and militant black membership in Chicago. While King and others made it clear that they did not intend to compete with the NAACP for resources or members, they believed that mass mobilizations could complement the legalistic approach that had been so successful in the first half of the decade. "Historically, the major emphasis in our struggle to obtain civil rights has been legal and legislative," Rustin wrote in a series of working papers designed to frame discussion at the conference: "The center of gravity has shifted from the courts to community action." Ella Baker, who ten years earlier had resigned from the NAACP out of frustration with the lack of support that Wilkins and other officers gave to her efforts to organize in the South, recalled that she and others viewed the southern movement as "a mass force that would somewhat become a counterbalance, let's call it, to the NAACP."[48]

Despite serious obstacles, the Southern Leadership Conference got off to a promising start. King and Abernathy had to leave Atlanta the morning of the January 10 meeting after bombs ripped through First Baptist and five other churches in Montgomery. Fred Shuttlesworth and Coretta King took over, and after the others returned they held a press conference announcing that the group would expand nonviolent civil disobedience to enforce the *Brown* decision and protect black southerners from racist violence. Nearly 100 people attended a second meeting in New Orleans on February 14, when they elected an executive board that included King and leaders from Tallahassee, Baton

Rouge, Birmingham, and Jackson, Mississippi. Dominated by ministers but also including educators, businessmen, and union leaders, the
group invited northern civil rights groups to join them on a "Prayer
Pilgrimage" to the Lincoln Memorial on May 17, 1957, the third anniversary of the *Brown* decision. A. Philip Randolph lent enthusiastic
support, comparing the mobilization to the 1941 March on Washington and helping to recruit black trade unionists in New York, Chicago,
and other northern cities. Roy Wilkins opposed any use of "the particular form of direct action used in Montgomery," but agreed that "a
dignified massive public expression of our determination" could make
a difference. Harlem minister Thomas Kilgore took a six-week leave to
direct the organizing effort out of the NAACP's headquarters in New
York City, assisted by Rustin, Baker, and NAACP field officers working
out of four regional offices. Speaking at large rallies in New York, Chicago, and other northern cities, King, Randolph, and Wilkins predicted
that between 50,000 and 100,000 people would show up to "renew
our strength, communicate our unity and rededicate our efforts to the
attainment of freedom."[49]

Fewer than 30,000 people participated in the Prayer Pilgrimage,
drawing positive reporting from both black and white newspapers but
also revealing that King and other black leaders had overestimated
their influence. The *Amsterdam News* charged Wilkins, Randolph, and
other northern leaders with "dragging their feet in the March on Washington" out of fear that King was overshadowing their leadership.
NAACP attorney Thurgood Marshall, who was even more skeptical of
mass marches than Roy Wilkins, did not even show up for the Prayer
Pilgrimage that was designed, in part, to celebrate his victory in the
Brown decision. "I was invited to be a speaker, but I didn't feel there
was any use in my speaking," he explained to a reporter, stating that
he was "up to my neck in work" and missed the last flight from New
York to Washington. The Prayer Pilgrimage also revealed an expanding
divide between King and other leaders of the Montgomery movement.

E. D. Nixon supported King's efforts to build on the momentum created by the boycott, but wanted to focus on winning political power rather than appealing to the hearts and minds of northern whites. "He does not go all out for the nonviolence creed, and while he certainly does not want violence he thinks the Negroes should make it clear that they are going to depend on the Courts and on political action to back them as well as God," Virginia Durr wrote about the Pullman porter in 1957. Nixon and others were also offended that King seemed to have forgotten that they selected and trained him for leadership in the movement. Durr wrote that Rosa Parks was "very, very disgruntled with MLK and really quite bitter" at being denied a staff position at the Leadership Conference after having lost her job as a result of her role in the boycott. Parks travelled to Washington for the Prayer Pilgrimage, but was not recognized by organizers until a friend saw her and "rescued" the initiator of the Montgomery bus boycott from the crowd. Three months later, Parks left Montgomery to find work in Detroit, telling a group of local activists that "they could never win unless they fought for the right of everyone to have opportunities, and not just themselves."[50]

By the end of 1957, the movement that had begun in Montgomery less than two years earlier had stalled. Attention shifted to Little Rock, Arkansas, where the local school board was starting to implement a desegregation program that it had adopted soon after the *Brown* decision. Local NAACP leader Daisy Bates organized nine black students to enter the all-white Central High School but retreated after the Citizens' Councils organized thousands of angry white supremacists to surround the school and terrorize the black students when they tried to enter. A standoff ensued when the governor of Arkansas defied a federal court order and sent the state's national guard to block the desegregation plan. President Eisenhower tried to stay out of the conflict but finally federalized the guard and ordered them to escort black students into the school and stay with them for months to protect them from abuse. It was the first time since Reconstruction that a president had used armed troops to protect black citizens in the South, but the Little Rock crisis also illustrated how effectively "massive resistance" had paralyzed the process of desegregation. Congress also passed the first Civil Rights Act since Reconstruction in 1957, just after the Little Rock conflict began, but it was so weak that a congressman from Georgia claimed it invalidated the *Brown* decision. In 1958 voters in Little Rock voted by more than a two-to-one margin to close four high schools in the city rather than proceed with desegregation. The schools reopened in 1959, but a year later only five black students were enrolled at Central High.[51]

As Randolph and the other founders of In Friendship had predicted, the failure of nonviolent civil disobedience led black southerners to seek other methods for achieving justice. In May 1959 a wave of outrage swept through black communities following the lynching of a young black man in Mississippi—the first since Emmett Till—and the rape of a black college student by four white men in Tallahassee, Florida. On May 5, a jury of twelve white men in North Carolina acquitted a white man who admitted to having beaten and attempted to rape a black woman but pleaded that he was not guilty because he was "drunk and having a little fun." After the trial, the forty-three-year-old president of the local NAACP branch turned to a group of reporters and stated that it was time for black southerners to "meet violence with violence." Answering the same question that Bayard Rustin had posed at Martin and Coretta King's kitchen table three years earlier, Robert F. Williams declared, "We must be willing to kill if necessary. We cannot take these people who do us injustice to the court and it becomes necessary to punish them ourselves. In the future we are going to have to try and convict these people on the spot."[52]

Recognizing the serious threat that such a statement posed to their efforts to rebuild the southern movement, civil rights activists put aside their differences and lined up to denounce Robert Williams. Pauli Murray, who was working for a law firm in New York City, represented Williams at an NAACP board meeting in early July. "I would recommend that the NAACP not condone violence," she stated, although she urged board members not to punish him for an angry outburst made in a context in which "violence was the order of the day." Daisy Bates, who boasted of stockpiling weapons and posting armed guards at her home during the Little Rock crisis, drew a distinction between self-defense and retaliation. That position was affirmed by Martin Luther King, Bayard Rustin, and the aging pacifist A. J. Muste, each of whom debated Williams in journals and public forums that summer. One of his few defenders was Conrad Lynn, the attorney who had defended his brother Winfred Lynn before the March on Washington Movement took up the case in 1942. Seventeen years later he urged the NAACP to "reaffirm the right and duty of Negroes in those areas of the South where no law protects them to defend themselves." A nearly identical statement was adopted by delegates to the NAACP convention, although they also voted nearly unanimously to uphold Roy Wilkins' decision to remove Williams from leadership in the association.[53]

While civil rights leaders lined up to condemn Robert Williams' call to arms, none of them worked harder to create a nonviolent alternative than Ella Baker. Martin Luther King sought to institutionalize the newly renamed Southern Christian Leadership Conference by establishing an office in Atlanta and securing an $11,000 donation from the Packinghouse Workers in Chicago, but turned the campaign over to Baker while he completed a book, accepted speaking engagements across the country, and, after recovering from a near-fatal stabbing, departed for a two-month tour of Europe, India, and the Middle East in the spring of 1959. Building on contacts from her work with the NAACP in the 1940s, Baker helped to expand grassroots movements that had emerged in Georgia, Alabama, Mississippi, and other states during the Montgomery boycott. She helped organize an SCLC meeting soon after the rape in Tallahassee and was impressed when over 1,000 students joined a protest to demand justice for the victim. She must have been pleased when Edward Edmonds, an SCLC founder and veteran of the March on Washington Movement, revitalized an NAACP youth group in Greensboro, North Carolina, by leading protests to demand integration of public schools and swimming pools during the summer of 1959. And she certainly made an impression on a group of black college students from Nashville, Tennessee, whom SCLC activists brought to Atlanta that summer for an "Institute on Nonviolent Resistance to Segregation." Ella Baker was not surprised—as most observers were— when members of Edward Edmonds' youth group launched a sit-in at a segregated lunch counter in Greensboro on February 1, 1960; but she was startled by the speed with which their movement spread to Nashville, Tallahassee, and more than 100 other southern cities by the end of April. Seeing an opportunity to revive the grassroots movement that had begun in Montgomery five years earlier, she invited leaders of those protests to attend a Southwide Student Leadership Conference on Nonviolent Resistance to Segregation at her alma mater in Raleigh, North Carolina. Before the conference ended on April 18, they had decided to create the Student Nonviolent Coordinating Committee.[54]

The founders of SNCC must have reminded Ella Baker of Dorothy Height and her youth chapter of the National Negro Congress in the 1930s, or of Pauli Murray and the other young activists who built the March on Washington Movement in the 1940s; but she would have recognized important differences. John Lewis, a twenty-year-old seminary student from Nashville who had seen Baker speak in Atlanta a year earlier, was typical of the large majority of SNCC members who attended segregated colleges and high schools in the South. The child of a sharecropper and a domestic worker from Alabama, Lewis had gone to American Baptist Theological Seminary in Nashville because his parents could not afford the tuition at Morehouse, where he aspired to go after hearing Martin Luther King on the radio when he was fifteen. In contrast to Baker and her friends from the 1930s, who had grown up in middle-class households where young people were expected to go to college, Lewis and other SNCC activists were products of an expanding postwar economy that allowed millions of working-class families to purchase their first homes, visit doctors on a regular basis, and send their children to colleges that they had never dreamed of attending. Many of the white students at Baker's conference belonged to Students for a Democratic Society, which was created the same year by members of the Student League for Industrial Democracy, the Socialist group that E. Pauline Myers had led at Howard in the 1920s. Also mostly from working-class families, SDS members described themselves as "bred in affluence, housed now in universities, looking uncomfortably to the world we inherit." What made them most uncomfortable was not poverty or war—although they opposed both—but the racial barriers that still determined who benefited the most from their "affluent society." John Lewis expressed a similar frustration when describing his realization, in the fall of 1955, that he would begin the school year "by climbing onto the same beat-up school bus and making the same twenty-mile trip to the same segregated high school I'd attended the year before. *Brown v. The Board of Education* notwithstanding, nothing in my life had changed."[55]

CHAPTER FOUR

JIM CROW UNIONS

A T THE "SALUTE and Support the Heroes of the South" rally in Madison Square Garden on May 31, 1956, Eleanor Roosevelt and several other speakers emphasized that "everything isn't sweetness and light in the North insofar as the Negro is concerned," and that discrimination existed in New York as well as in Montgomery. Earl Brown, the city councilman who had urged a mass exodus from Mississippi following Emmett Till's lynching, disagreed. "By no means should we overlook or cover up racial ills existing North of the Mason-Dixon line. But conditions are far different below it than above," wrote the black journalist and politician. Pointing out that racism was more firmly planted in southern "law, public opinion and practices," Brown insisted: "we cannot solve our problems in the North until we at least make some appreciable headway toward solving them in the South." For that reason, he applauded A. Philip Randolph for initiating the "truly mammoth" event. In addition to letting "the enemy know we are coming," the councilman wrote, it was significant that the rally was sponsored by a black trade unionist who had succeeded in convincing white union leaders that "their welfare is tied up in civil rights as well as the Negro's."[1]

Earl Brown overestimated the support that Randolph received from white union leaders, but it was true that Randolph and other black trade unionists played key roles in drawing attention to and raising funds for the grassroots movements that erupted in the South following the *Brown* decision. The massive rallies following Emmett Till's murder in August 1955 had been initiated by Willoughby Abner, a leader of the United Auto Workers in Chicago. That September, activists from the Chicago district of the United Packinghouse Workers had accompanied Emmett Till's mother to Harlem, where Mamie Till-Bradley spoke at a rally sponsored by the Brotherhood of Sleeping Car Porters. Cleveland Robinson and other black leaders of the Retail Workers District 65 organized the "Garment Center Labor Rally" on October 11 in New York, and the Madison Square Garden rally was organized primarily by Maida Springer, of the Garment Workers.[2]

While black trade unionists agreed with Councilman Brown that segregation and discrimination were more deeply rooted in the laws and customs of the South, however, they were equally committed to eliminating them in the North. Willoughby Abner had been born in Chicago in 1920 and joined the union while working night shifts at a Studebaker factory to pay his way through college and law school during the Second World War. Hired onto the staff of the union after completing his degrees, he rose through the ranks by organizing thousands of black and white workers in factories on the South Side of Chicago after the war. By the 1950s Abner was director of education and political action for 50,000 UAW members in Chicago. Willoughby Abner's closest ally in Chicago was Charles Hayes, a black leader of the United Packinghouse Workers. Formed during the Great Depression by Communists and Socialists who believed that fighting racism was essential to building unions, by the Second World War the Packinghouse Workers had become one of the most racially diverse and egalitarian unions in the United States. Hayes and other black workers pushed it to expand that commitment by supporting a permanent Fair Employment Practices Act and by mobilizing its members to confront discrimination in employment and housing after the war. In 1954 he was elected director of the union's largest district, which encompassed all its locals in Chicago. The same year, Willoughby Abner was elected chairman of the executive committee of the Chicago NAACP, and the two threw their unions behind efforts to integrate public housing projects in Chicago, open white-collar jobs to black workers in meatpacking and other industries, and elect black workers to leadership in unions, civil rights groups, and city government.[3]

Noting the influence that Abner, Hayes, and other black trade unionists had gained in Chicago's labor movement by 1954, the *Chicago Defender* reported that "these men exemplify the New Negro labor leadership" that served as leaders of local unions and district councils, organizers and business representatives, and representatives to joint boards and municipal labor federations in cities across the United States. In contrast to the 1920s, when A. Philip Randolph had organized a separate union for black workers who were excluded from the AFL railway brotherhoods, this younger generation gained leadership primarily in CIO Packinghouse, Auto, and Clothing unions in which the majority of members were white. "So when a Negro in these interracial unions is elected district leader the fact is not only a salute to his character," observed the *Defender*, "but a tribute to the ability of the labor movement to overcome prejudice."[4]

The New Negroes were not just men. One of Charles Hayes's closest collaborators was Addie Wyatt, who had joined the Packinghouse Workers in 1942 after union leaders prevented management from replacing her with a less experienced white woman and firing her when she took leave to have a baby. Having taken a job in a packinghouse at the age of seventeen, with the hope of getting a job in the office, the Mississippi native was elected president of her union in the late 1940s and hired as an organizer in 1954. Maida Springer worked closely with Dorothy Lowther Robinson (no relation to Cleveland), the education director for a CIO union that represented 20,000 laundry workers in

New York City. A North Carolinian, "Dolly" Lowther had moved to Brooklyn with her mother in 1930 when she was thirteen. She worked in an industrial laundry while attending high school and college and helped create her union in 1937 by leading a strike to win better wages and working conditions for her mostly black co-workers, who earned $6.00 for a 72-hour week. She met Maida Springer through the Women's Trade Union League, an interracial group of labor feminists, and helped her organize the Odell Waller march in 1942 and the FEPC rally in 1946. A close ally of Adam Clayton Powell and a prominent figure in the Democratic Party, Dorothy L. Robinson was appointed secretary of labor for New York State in 1955.[5]

Having risen to power in unions across the country, black trade unionists moved to assert their influence at the national level in the early 1950s, when leaders of the AFL and CIO began to merge the federations after nearly two decades of competition. Over half a million black workers joined unions during the Second World War and by 1955 their numbers had ballooned to three times that number. Reporting that the "astounding success" of CIO unions in meatpacking, auto, clothing, and other industries had forced "more conservative AFL" unions to reach out to black workers, the *Chicago Defender* observed: "the few unions that continue to discriminate are trying to buck a strong anti-discrimination tide that is mounting public pressure against Jim Crow in industry." Having entered the union movement when the tide was moving in the opposite direction, A. Philip Randolph used his leadership position in the AFL to place the issue of employment discrimination on the table during the merger. On October 27, 1955, just weeks after Emmett Till's murder, Randolph introduced a resolution to a joint meeting of the executive committees from both federations that would have barred the merged AFL-CIO from issuing a charter to any union that discriminated against workers on the basis of race or that allowed "any racist" to serve in its national leadership.[6]

Randolph was particularly adamant about excluding the AFL railway brotherhoods that still maintained the bar on nonwhite member-ship that had forced the Pullman porters to create their own union three decades earlier; but he also pointed to the hypocrisy of white union leaders who denied charters to unions that were led by Com-munists or gangsters but gave free rein to those led by members of the Ku Klux Klan or the Citizens' Councils. Like the leaders of most AFL unions, Randolph had never allowed Communists to hold leadership positions in the Brotherhood of Sleeping Car Porters. As a result of his conflict with Communists in the National Negro Congress, he was an enthusiastic supporter of CIO leaders who expelled nine unions because their leaders refused to sign pledges stating they were not Communists. He and other anti-Communists agreed that the oaths infringed civil liberties and that they were designed primarily to dis-credit and divide organized labor, but he saw the refusal to sign the cards as further evidence that Communists and their supporters had placed the interests of the Soviet Union above those of the workers they represented. Applying the same standard to union leaders who excluded black workers and reinforced racial divisions among work-ers, he insisted that racists and segregationists had no place in the leadership of organized labor. In November 1955 Randolph hosted a two-day conference in New York, where 250 black trade unionists called on President Eisenhower to convene a special session of Con-gress to pass civil rights legislation and demanded that organized labor take "bold and forthright action in the protection of civil rights." The *Chicago Defender* reported that "rumbles of dissatisfaction in labor were growing louder and louder," noting that the "angriest voice being raised is that of A. Philip Randolph."[7]

Black trade unionists considered Randolph to be the "dean of Negro labor leaders," but most viewed their conflict with the AFL-CIO through the perspective of a generation that came of age in the Second World War rather than the First. While Maida Springer was old enough to have got caught up in the left-wing factionalism of the 1930s, Dorothy Lowther and Addie Wyatt expressed their political beliefs through their union or the Democratic Party. Cleveland Robinson was only four years younger than Springer when he migrated from Jamaica to New York City in 1944, but he had avoided the battles between Communists and Socialists that tore his union apart after the war. He allied with Communists who quit the CIO to protest anti-Communism in 1948 and was elected to office in the National Negro Labor Council, which black activists from the expelled unions created to protect themselves from anti-Communism in 1950. When Socialists regained control of District 65 in 1953, however, Robinson helped them steer the union back into the CIO. Willoughby Abner allied with Walter Reuther and other anti-Communists who drove Communists from the United Auto Workers after the war, but also formed close alliances with Charles Hayes and other black trade unionists who sided with Communists in the Packinghouse Workers. In contrast to Springer, as well as Walter Reuther and A. Philip Randolph, whose political allegiances had been forged in the wake of the Russian Revolution, younger trade unionists were motivated by struggles against fascism and imperialism abroad and economic and racial inequality at home. "Black folks didn't get caught up in the syndrome of looking under the rug in every room for a red," Hayes recalled. "We wanted to get free."[8]

Those generational differences were evident in black trade unionists' responses to the rejection of Randolph's resolution at the founding convention of the AFL-CIO, which began in New York City on December 5, 1955. Having battled the AFL for three decades, Randolph was pleasantly surprised by the few concessions that he won. Delegates adopted a constitution that declared that "all workers without regard to race, creed, color, national origin or ancestry shall share equally in the full benefits of union organization." They also passed resolutions calling on Congress to pass an FEPC law and urging affiliated unions to include fair employment clauses in their collective-bargaining demands. Randolph and Willard Townsend, of the Transport Service Employees union, were elected vice-presidents of the AFL-CIO, along with twenty-five white union leaders, an outcome that gave them a voice but little real power in the federation. On the basis of those results, Randolph told a group of civil rights activists in New York that he "expected the AFL-CIO to step up its fight against racism both in and out of the labor movement." Younger activists were not so optimistic, however, noting that the new federation still refused to expel segregated unions. In contrast, they pointed to the Teamsters, one of the largest and most powerful affiliates of the AFL, which had been denied representation on the executive council and the AFL-CIO on the grounds that it was controlled by the Mafia. Young CIO activists feared that the merger with the larger and more established AFL would overwhelm what progress they had achieved toward making their own unions more egalitarian since the 1930s. "We wish to state here and now, that Negro workers of America are in no mood to continue as foot mats in industry and step-children within the house of labor," declared the Michigan Association of Negro Trade Unionists, which was formed by 500 trade unionists in Detroit shortly before the merger.[9]

Rebuffed at the national level, black trade unionists turned back to their local communities, where they sought to unite local unions and civil rights organizations around the concerns of working-class African Americans. Ernest Calloway, the draft resister who had created the CIO's Committee to Abolish Racial Discrimination in 1942, left Chicago in 1950 to direct the education program for the Teamsters in St. Louis. In 1955 he was elected president of the NAACP chapter and, with his wife, DeVerne, and activists from the Brotherhood of Sleeping Car Porters, created a vibrant labor-based civil rights movement in the city. In 1956 Cleveland Robinson formed a "United Labor Committee" to mobilize union members in local elections in New York City. The efforts of black trade unionists were bolstered by Herbert Hill, a Jewish trade unionist who headed the Labor Department of the

NAACP's national office in New York City. Seeking to increase cooperation between civil rights and labor leaders in local communities, Hill encouraged local branches to form Labor and Industry Committees that could support efforts to unionize black workers and to fight employment discrimination by local unions and employers.[10]

Despite the support they received from Herbert Hill and other leaders of the NAACP, black trade unionists found they often had to form new protest organizations like those created in Montgomery and other southern cities. In 1956 Willoughby Abner won a heated contest for president of the Chicago NAACP, defeating a candidate backed by Chicago's moderate black congressman William Dawson. "When we got active, the NAACP was called a 'tea-sipping' organization, silk-stocking," recalled a Packinghouse union activist who worked on his campaign. In Detroit, a similar effort was launched by United Auto Worker activists Horace Sheffield and Robert Battle, both of whom were veterans of the effort to strengthen the FEPC during the Second World War. Having risen to positions of power within the union's largest local in the Motor City, they created the Trade Union Leadership Council in 1957. Focused initially on challenging discrimination within the union, the TULC expanded its agenda to address a broad range of racial and economic problems facing working-class African Americans in Detroit. "We figured that the problem of job discrimination and discrimination within the unions were problems that should be dealt with within the community as well as within labor," Battle recalled. Setting up a headquarters and clubhouse in an abandoned hardware store, Battle and Sheffield hosted public speakers and discussion groups, conducted voter registration campaigns, published a monthly newsletter, and operated a bar to defray expenses. They worked closely with Reverend C. L. Franklin, a Baptist minister who sought to "give recognition to other leadership," nurture "some new strategies of organization," and, according to one supporter, "quite frankly, to get around the discipline of the NAACP."[11]

In addition to fighting discrimination in their own communities, black trade unionists strengthened their ties to grassroots activists in the South. When Martin Luther King called for the "Prayer Pilgrimage" at the Lincoln Memorial on the third anniversary of the *Brown* decision, Cleveland Robinson's District 65 committed to bringing 1,000 union members to Washington, and the United Auto Workers reserved an entire hotel for union members who travelled to Washington. Charles Hayes arranged for Martin Luther King to address a national conference of the United Packinghouse workers in Chicago on October 2, 1957. "With the coming together of the powerful influence of labor and all people of goodwill in the struggle for freedom and human dignity," the young minister predicted, "I can assure you that we have a powerful instrument." Members of District 65 voted to increase their monthly dues to raise funds for the southern movement, generating $40,000 for civil rights organizations by 1959. In 1958 a group of black autoworkers in Milwaukee invited Birmingham SCLC leader Fred Shuttlesworth to address a mass meeting after police shot a young black man—an incident that some compared to Emmett Till's murder three years earlier. Frustrated by the NAACP's refusal to support mass protests following the killing, the trade unionists formed the Crusaders Civic and Social League to lead a boycott against stores that refused to hire black workers in the city.[12]

Having established bases of support in working-class communities across the urban North, black trade unionists renewed their fight against segregation and discrimination within the AFL-CIO. In July 1959 A. Philip Randolph called a meeting of black trade unionists who had travelled to New York City for the fiftieth annual convention of the NAACP. The meeting was closed to the press and overshadowed by the controversy surrounding Robert F. Williams' call to "meet violence with violence." Nevertheless, over sixty black trade unionists attended, including Horace Sheffield and Robert Battle from Detroit and a leader of the Packinghouse Workers in Chicago. Pointing out that more than a million black workers belonged to unions affiliated with the AFL-CIO—constituting the largest membership of African Americans outside the black church—Randolph urged the assembled to organize themselves for leadership in the "struggle for economic equality and the pressing needs for civil rights." The group resolved to introduce a resolution at the national convention of the AFL-CIO later that year, calling for the expulsion of any union that did not drop racial bars on membership and integrate segregated locals before June 1960. They also decided to form a more formal network to coordinate their activities in various cities. Cleveland Robinson presided over a public labor session at the convention, featuring speeches by Randolph and Walter Reuther, the president of the United Auto Workers and vice-president of the AFL-CIO. Randolph began on a positive note, pointing to the unprecedented number of black workers and the rise of nonwhite trade unionists to positions of leadership in the union movement. He also praised Reuther, President George Meany, and the Executive Committee of the AFL-CIO for their personal commitments to civil rights. But he closed by blasting the federation for its "quite inadequate and much too slow" progress toward realizing those ideals and demanded that it "require labor organizations at all levels to comply with its constitutional provision outlawing race and religious discrimination."[13]

Randolph's speech at the NAACP convention set the stage for a major confrontation at the AFL-CIO convention in San Francisco on September 23, 1959. Randolph introduced two resolutions, one calling for the expulsion of any unions that did not drop bans on nonwhite members within six months and the other ordering the "liquidation and elimination" of any segregated locals in unions affiliated with the AFL-CIO. Drawing a parallel to President Eisenhower's reluctance to enforce the *Brown* decision in the South, a delegate from the Packinghouse Workers said black workers were tired of hearing that unions just needed "a little more time." Tensions rose the following day when a leader of a building trades union stated that black tradesmen had maintained segregated locals for half a century and had "no desire to have Mr. Randolph tell them they had to go out of business." George Meany, who had led the Building Trades Council in New York City before joining the leadership of the AFL in 1939, added that he was familiar with the union in question and knew it had a strong record of racial equality. When Randolph objected that unions should not be able to segregate locals "merely because the members want it," Meany defended "the democratic rights of Negro members to maintain the unions they want." He then demanded to know "Who the hell appointed you as the guardian of all the Negroes in America?" Randolph attempted to respond, but Meany continued, accusing him of arrogance and hypocrisy. "Just a minute, brother president, we don't have to become emotional about it," Randolph said when he regained the floor. "I just don't believe members of a union have the right to maintain a Jim Crow local." Meany was forced to concede that Communist-led unions would be expelled even if their members objected, but delegates still rejected Randolph's resolution. Congressman Adam Clayton Powell sent a telegram to Randolph's Brotherhood of Sleeping Car Porters, stating that "Randolph most assuredly does speak for all Negro trade unionists" and declaring that George Meany "has lost his usefulness and has publicly declared himself a Negro hater." The NAACP's national office informed Meany that it "fully supports" Randolph's demands and condemned the AFL-CIO for failing to "implement its own democratic professions."[14]

Despite the influence that black trade unionists had gained within organized labor, it was clear that they could not win by fighting within the AFL-CIO. Meeting in Cleveland in December 1959, Randolph and others resolved to build a national organization of black trade unionists. Horace Sheffield and Robert Battle volunteered to host a founding convention in Detroit the following May, and black trade unionists began chartering buses and trains to take delegates from their respective cities to the meeting. "Already we have established local councils in twenty-five key cities," Randolph told reporters in early May 1960, speculating that 1,000 trade unionists were prepared to make the trip. Participants in the Cleveland meeting appointed a provisional steering committee consisting of twenty-five trade unionists from across the country, including Sheffield and Battle as well as Cleveland Robinson, Maida Springer, Dorothy Robinson, Willoughby Abner, and Ernest Calloway. Also nominated was Richard Parrish, who had led the youth delegation of the March on Washington in 1941. After graduating from the City College of New York in 1947, Parrish had gone to work in the New York public schools, joined the American Federation of Teachers, and, in 1956, led a successful fight to expel its segregated locals. While the union lost nearly 7,000 members, it made a powerful statement to AFL-CIO leaders who refused to do the same. The same year that he joined the steering committee, Parrish helped merge several unions in New York City to form the 40,000-member United Federation of Teachers. He was elected vice-president of that group and, in an indication that he and Randolph had overcome their differences, took a leadership role in the black trade unionists' group as well. In addition to drafting a constitution and permanent leadership structure to be ratified at the convention, the steering committee arranged speeches by Martin Luther King, Roy Wilkins, and Daisy Bates, the NAACP leader from Little Rock. George Meany declined an invitation to speak, citing a prior engagement, but Walter Reuther agreed to address a mass meeting on the opening night of the convention.[15]

Fifteen hundred men and women attended the founding convention of the Negro American Labor Council on May 28, 1960, attesting to the strength of local networks that black trade unionists had established in the previous decade. Randolph called the convention to order with a militant yet foreboding keynote. "Fellow trade unionists, delegates, and workers, we have come here today from various areas of our country; we have come from the mills and mines, factories and farms, rails and seas," he began. "We are here because we are the victims of the problem of the color line; the color line in labor unions, industry, government, schools, housing, the professions, the arts and sports." Providing a detailed account of the persistence of segregation and discrimination by unions affiliated with the AFL-CIO, he charged that such practices meant that black workers had few opportunities for training and promotion into the skilled trades, were denied seniority protections from layoffs, and earned roughly half the average wages of their white counterparts. Although Randolph had battled those problems since the 1920s, he contended that the cost of discrimination had increased with the rapid automation of manufacturing following the Second World War. Pointing out that manufacturing employment had declined by nearly half a million jobs since the early 1950s, even as production had increased, Randolph warned that black workers were concentrated in unskilled positions that were most vulnerable to elimination. "Unless there is a halt to this trend of excluding Negroes from craft unions and apprenticeship training courses," he declared, "Negroes may wind up, not only as unskilled and unemployed, if not unemployable, but as the forgotten slum proletariat in the black ghettos of the great metropolitan centers of the country, existing within the grey shadows of a hopeless hope."[16]

As he had at the NAACP convention a year earlier, Randolph urged black trade unionists to view their battle against employment discrimination as a critical component of the broader struggle for racial equality. "In the first place, a racially segregated union is basically no different from a racially segregated school, train coach, bus, house, or seat in a theatre," he stated, arguing that organized labor should be held to the same legal standards that the *Brown* decision had established for schools and other public services. While unions were "private, voluntary organizations," Randolph explained that federal labor laws had imbued them with "governmentally derived privileges, position and power" that gave them influence comparable to that of public institutions. As a result of the social and economic policies of the New Deal, he insisted, "powerful economic organizations, such as corporations and labor unions and their philosophy, program and practices, have public effects." Such sentiments were echoed in the opening lines of the constitution that the steering committee proposed to delegates at the founding convention: "The philosophy, ideals, and principles and program of the Negro American Labor Council stem from the concept that labor leadership is a sacred trust, a great moral responsibility." Adopting the Trade Union Leadership Council's model of linking labor struggles to a broader agenda for social reform, founders of the NALC stated that although their "primary objective" was to reach "every Negro who is a member of a bona fide trade union," they would grant membership to any "applicant who is a worker or a potential wage earner."[17]

In addition to linking their cause to the broader struggle for racial equality in the United States, black trade unionists viewed their effort in the context of an international movement against imperialism. "The year 1960 marks that momentous point in history when the rising winds of the civil rights revolution are sweeping the continents of America and Africa with ever increasing force and challenge," read the official call to the founding convention. "Nothing can stop it. No one can escape it." That international perspective appealed to foreign-born trade unionists such as Maida Springer and Cleveland Robinson, who maintained close ties to anticolonial movements in the Caribbean and Africa; but it also reflected a long-standing belief among African Americans that their problems were, as NAACP founder W. E. B. Du Bois described it, "but a local phase of a world problem." Having referenced Du Bois' famous critique of the "color line" in his keynote address to the Detroit convention, Randolph reminded his audience that "the color line is the line which divides the Negro and white populations in the United States, in Africa, in Asia, the Isles of the Sea, and wherever white and colored races live."[18]

In rejecting the color line, black trade unionists did not deny that their primary goal was to organize black workers. The *Chicago*

Defender reported that invitations to the founding convention were sent "only to Negro union leaders" and "consistently sang the refrain that, 'the struggle for freedom cannot be delegated, it is first business for the oppressed.'" While "a sprinkling of white delegates was to be seen at the convention," the newspaper contended that some observers, both black and white, feared the organization would become a "black nationalist group of a go-it-alone black union federation." While this must have reminded Randolph of similar criticism of the March on Washington in the 1940s, or his clash with Marcus Garvey in the 1920s, the comment reflected a growing concern about a resurgence of black nationalism in the 1950s. In July 1959, on the weekend of the NAACP's fiftieth annual convention, a television station in New York aired a documentary about the Nation of Islam, a small but growing religious sect that combined Islamic symbolism and Protestant moralism with the racial self-reliance of Marcus Garvey. Timed perfectly to build on the anxiety produced by Robert Williams' call for violence, and provocatively titled *The Hate That Hate Produced*, the documentary exaggerated the size and influence of the apolitical and peaceful sect and inspired a nationwide surge of reporting on the "black racists." Randolph addressed those fears in his keynote address, stating that the NALC "rejects black nationalism as a doctrine and practice of racial separatism." But he also maintained the position, taken by the March on Washington Movement nearly twenty years earlier, "that history has placed upon the Negro, and the Negro alone, the basic responsibility to complete the incompleted Civil War Revolution through keeping the fires of freedom burning in the Civil Rights Revolution." Defending the group's focus on African Americans, he declared that "while the Negro American Labor Council has not and will not have a color bar, we do not hesitate or apologize for pointing out that the primary and sole purpose of this movement is to organize Negro trade unionists to eradicate the evil of racial discrimination from which they alone suffer."[19]

Randolph enjoyed tremendous prestige at the founding convention, but younger trade unionists did not hesitate to challenge him when disagreements surfaced. The first serious debate emerged around the politics of anti-Communism. Adopting a rhetorical strategy that he had employed since the 1940s, Randolph insisted that the struggle to reform organized labor was critical to victory in the Cold War. "Free labor unions are essential to the strength, health and progress of our democratic society and are one of the prime assets of the United States in its struggle with Communist totalitarian tyranny," he declared in his keynote address to the Detroit convention. While younger trade unionists agreed that the new organization must be "anti-Communist, anti-Fascist, anti-racist and anti-colonialist," several spoke out against a proposal, introduced by officers of Randolph's Brotherhood of Sleeping Car Porters, instructing the NALC to "design programs to fight racism, communism, corruption and racketeering in the trade union movement." They did not object to such programs in principle, but viewed issues other than racism as the responsibility of "white unionists," who had far more resources and influence than the NALC. The standoff was resolved by a more open-ended statement that "the NALC will unequivocally support and defend democracy and freedom at home and abroad." Rather than prohibiting Communists from membership, as the March on Washington Movement had, the NALC Constitution stipulated that no local branches would be "officered, controlled or dominated by communists, fascists or other totalitarians." Willoughby Abner, an ardent anti-Communist, urged delegates to accept the compromise and move on lest the press "misinterpret the political nature of the Convention."[20]

The debate at the convention reflected a rising sentiment among black activists that the Communist Party no longer represented a threat to national security and that the House Un-American Activities Committee and other bodies were now being used purely as excuses to repress legitimate movements for social justice. "By then,

Top, Left: A. Philip Randolph promotes unions for black workers in Chicago, May 9, 1937. (Courtesy of the Newberry Library, Chicago. Call # Pullman 06/01/04, Box 17, Folder 491) *Top, Right*: "The War's Greatest Scandal," pamphlet published by March on Washington Movement, 1943. (Courtesy of the Hoover Institution Archives, Pathfinder Press Collection, Box 26) *Bottom*: Ella Baker (second from left) and Cleveland Robinson (far right) mend ties between the NAACP and District 65 of the Retail, Wholesale and Department Store Workers union, 1953. (Photo by Roland Willoughby, United Automobile Workers of America, District 65 Photographs, Tamiment Library, New York University)

Rosa Parks attends workshop on desegregation at Highlander Folk School on July 24, 1955, four months before she started the Montgomery bus boycott. (Photo by Emil Willimetz, Wisconsin Historical Society, WHS-56309, Courtesy of Joanna Willimetz)

Congressman Adam Clayton Powell addresses Garment Center Labor Rally, New York City, October 11, 1955. Cleveland Robinson, who organized the rally, sits third from left. (Laynes Studio, New York, Library of Congress, Prints and Photographs Division, Visual Materials from the NAACP Records [LC-DIG-ppmsca-08093], Courtesy of Barbara Layne Hicks)

Eleanor Roosevelt, Autherine Lucy, Tallulah Bankhead, and Rosa Parks at "Salute and Support the Heroes of the South" rally in Madison Square Garden, May 31, 1956. (Photo by Dudley Foster, United Automobile Workers of America, District 65 Photographs, Tamiment Library, New York University)

Delegation of garment workers leaves New York for Prayer Pilgrimage at Lincoln Memorial on May 17, 1957, to mark the third anniversary of the *Brown* decision. (Kheel Center, Cornell University)

Chicago Packinghouse union leaders Charles Hayes and Addie Wyatt with NAACP Labor Secretary Herbert Hill (center, left-right) at NAACP convention in 1957. (Wisconsin Historical Society, WHS-3943)

Top: Martin Luther King, Jr., faces tough crowd at AFL-CIO Convention on December 11, 1961. George Meany is taking notes. (Kheel Center, Cornell University) *Bottom*: Malcolm X speaks at Hospital Workers rally in New York, 1962. A. Philip Randolph and Anna Arnold Hedgeman sit on stage. (Photo by 1199SEIU, Kheel Center, Cornell University)

Cleveland Robinson at March on Washington headquarters in Harlem, 1963. (*World Telegram & Sun* photo by O. Fernandez, Library of Congress, Prints and Photographs Division)

Right: A. Philip Randolph, Roy Wilkins, and Anna Arnold Hedgeman plan route for March on Washington, August 3, 1963. (Bettmann/Corbis)

Below: Bayard Rustin addressing members of the Guardian Association, which coordinated security for the March on Washington, August 1963. (Bettmann/Corbis)

Left: Bill Mauldin, "Powder Keg," *Chicago Sun-Times*, August 24, 1963. (Copyright by Bill Mauldin [1963]. Courtesy of the Bill Mauldin Estate LLC) *Below*: Women gather at National Council of Negro Women headquarters before joining the March on Washington, August 28, 1963. (Fred Harris Photographer, National Council of Negro Women Records, National Archives of Black Women's History)

POWDER KEG

Delegation of postal workers leaves New York for March on Washington, August 28, 1963. (New York Metro Postal Union Photographs Collection, Tamiment Library, New York University)

The first "Freedom Train" arrives at Union Station early in the morning on August 28, 1963. (Pictoral Parade, Archive Photos, Getty Images)

Retail, Wholesale and Department Store Workers delegation at the March on Washington, August 28, 1963. (District 65 Photographs Collection, Tamiment Library, New York University)

Leaders scramble to the front after the March on Washington started without them. In black suits, from left to right, are John Lewis, Mathew Ahmann, Floyd McKissick, Martin Luther King, Cleveland Robinson, Joachim Prinz, Joseph Rauh, Whitney Young, Roy Wilkins, A. Philip Randolph, and Walter Reuther. (AFP, Getty Images)

The optimism created by the March on Washington was tempered by the wave of racist violence that followed. Members of the Retail, Wholesale and Department Store Workers union hold a moment of silence to mourn the deaths of Addie Mae Collins, Cynthia Wesley, Carole Robertson, and Denise McNair in a church bombing in Birmingham, Alabama, on September 15, 1963. (District 65 Photographs Collection, Tamiment Library, New York University)

the Committee was like a tiresome uncle who insists on telling his old ghost stories in broad daylight to nephews with other things on their minds," wrote a journalist who covered hearings conducted by the HUAC in the early 1960s. Black activists grew particularly critical as federal authorities pursued any allegation of Communist subversion within the civil rights movement yet seemed unable to stop the escalation of white supremacist violence in the South. Early in 1961, Martin Luther King and sixteen other civil rights leaders drafted a petition protesting the imprisonment of Carl Braden, a white leftist who was investigated by the HUAC after selling a house to a black family in Louisville, Kentucky. "Braden was called before the Committee simply for his integration activities," King charged, warning "that if the Un-American Activities Committee is to have the power to subpoena everyone they will misuse the power to stand in the way of integration." Over 3,000 Americans signed King's petition, including the staunchly anti-Communist A. Philip Randolph.[21]

Having softened his stance on anti-Communism, Randolph faced a more difficult challenge over the representation of women in the leadership of the NALC. Maida Springer and Dorothy L. Robinson were the only women on the twenty-four-member steering committee, and Randolph provoked an angry rebuke when he proposed to replace that provisional body with a board of vice-presidents composed entirely of men. "I am sick and tired of you men discriminating against me as a woman," yelled L. Joy Jennings, a United Auto Worker activist from Chicago. She was seconded by Jeanette Strong, of the United Steel Workers of America, who grabbed a microphone on the convention floor and refused to stop talking when Randolph struck his gavel and informed her that she had exceeded the five-minute period allotted to comments on the issue. "A stocky woman in a brown sweater, she became the center of a milling throng of angry male and female delegates," reported the *New York Times*. "Arms swung, bodies crashed into one another, the gavel kept thundering and, through it all, Mrs.

Strong kept talking." She was supported at the microphone by Jennings and three other women from Chicago.[22]

Initially Randolph attempted to stonewall the opposition, but he backed down in the face of an expanding revolt. "The 71-year old chairman, his patriarchal calm unruffled by the clamor," demanded a voice vote on his original proposal and then announced a slim victory in his favor. Women booed and jeered from the floor when he tried to move on, however; and, according to the *Chicago Defender*, "For once Randolph was at a loss." NAACP leader Daisy Bates, who had received enthusiastic applause for her address the night before, negotiated a compromise that allowed seventy-five female delegates to elect two additional vice-presidents. After caucusing for ten minutes in a separate room, the women returned and nominated Lola Belle Holmes, a Garment Workers union activist from Chicago, and Agnes Willis, who belonged to the CIO Electrical Workers union in Brooklyn. "We were somewhat amused and pleasantly pleased at the way the women demanded (and received) a voice in the destiny of the new Negro American Labor Council which took its first tottling steps this week under the firm hand of A. Philip Randolph," the *Amsterdam News* editorialized with the mix of praise and condescension that was typical of both black and white newspapers' reporting on the incident. The editors attributed the settlement primarily to Randolph's "gallant bow to the ladies," but conceded that "when all is said and done, it is altogether fitting and proper that they have a voice in this new civil rights labor organization for which all of us hold such high hopes."[23]

The founding convention did not resolve disagreements over anti-Communism and women's leadership, but black trade unionists established a sufficient level of unity that they could return to their communities and to building the new organization. Lacking a paid staff, the NALC relied on its eighteen vice-presidents to maintain communication between local branches and the national office, which operated out of the headquarters of the Brotherhood of Sleeping Car Porters in

Harlem. A. Philip Randolph maintained the office with assistance from NALC secretary Theodore Brown, who had been Randolph's administrative assistant for ten years before joining the staff of the AFL-CIO's Civil Rights Department; and Richard Parrish, who was elected treasurer. The three of them published a national newsletter with reports on local activities in several cities, and planned a series of regional meetings to coordinate local activities into a national program.[24]

As established branches had before the convention, new ones focused initially on reaching out to black members of local unions, studying conditions for black workers in the area, and mobilizing to improve them. The Indianapolis council recruited representatives from every union local in the city, conducted a survey of "discriminatory practices in certain locals," and cooperated with the local NAACP to convince the Central Labor Union Council to elect a Civil Rights Committee with an NALC member as chairman. In Cleveland local activists focused on employment discrimination in restaurants and on pressuring local building trades unions to open apprenticeships to black workers. Working closely with the NAACP and a group of local ministers, the Los Angeles chapter persuaded the International Longshore and Warehouse Union to reserve two-thirds of the spaces in an apprenticeship program for black workers in an effort to compensate for years of discrimination. "The historical process of bringing black workers together in an organization of their own represents the initial step in the creation of working class solidarity between black and white workers," Randolph observed in his first annual report to the NALC. "Through the unspectacular drive to build local chapters, the future of black workers takes on tremendous meaning."[25]

The NALC took shape during the presidential campaign of 1960. John F. Kennedy made few overtures to African Americans, but it was not hard for him to distinguish himself from Eisenhower. Running on the promise of a "New Frontier" of liberal and assertive leadership, he suggested that this would apply at least partly to civil rights. Some black voters were distraught that he chose Lyndon Johnson, a white Texan, as his running mate, but Johnson had supported the 1957 Civil Rights Act and made his own sincere appeals to black voters. In the end Kennedy won 70 percent of the black vote, which provided him with a critical edge in an extremely tight election. The new president acknowledged that support in his inaugural address on January 20, 1961, in which he affirmed the nation's commitment to "human rights . . . at home and around the world." His speech focused primarily on foreign affairs, but even there he dwelled on supporting the independence movements in Africa and Asia that many African Americans viewed as part of the same global struggle as theirs. A. Philip Randolph and other civil rights leaders also noted Kennedy's promise to restore economic growth, and saw an opportunity to inject a discussion of how black workers would fit in. "And without progress on civil rights, we shall be unable to achieve the full utilization of our manpower resources so indispensable to accelerated economic growth," Roy Wilkins wrote in a memorandum to Kennedy on February 6. Those hopes were bolstered by Adam Clayton Powell's appointment to chair of the House Committee on Education and Labor, the highest position ever held by an African American in Congress.[26]

Wasting no time in taking advantage of those openings, the NALC planned a two-day Workshop and Institute on Race Bias in Trade Unions, Industry and Government starting on February 17 in Washington, D.C. Working with local trade unionists and NAACP activists, the NALC invited workers to present testimony at a hearing on discrimination by employers and unions in the nation's capital. Modeled on FEPC hearings during the Second World War, the workshop was chaired by Cleveland Robinson and presided over by law professors from Howard and Yale. Martin Luther King, Roy Wilkins, and Congressman Adam Clayton Powell addressed the meeting, as did President Kennedy's new secretary of labor, Arthur Goldberg. Kennedy sent a telegraph stating: "I fully share your deep concern over the grave issue of unemployment and over the added burdens carried by those who suffer from the racial bias that still unhappily remains in our midst." On March 6 the president issued an executive order requiring government agencies and federal contractors to take "affirmative action" to ensure that workers were treated "without regard to their race, creed, color or national origin," which Randolph considered the NALC's first victory in Washington. The Committee on Equal Employment Opportunity, which was charged with enforcing the order and chaired by Vice-President Lyndon Johnson, considered adding sex and age to that list but concluded it would "throw the committee into complete chaos." The following week Labor Secretary Goldberg authorized Assistant Secretary of Labor Esther Peterson to initiate a separate Commission on the Status of Women, which Kennedy empowered with a second executive order on December 14, 1961.[27]

In addition to raising expectations about progress in the new decade, the Washington meeting energized local efforts to build the NALC. "Here were hundreds of Negro trade unionists, men and women from all over the country—and they were together!" recalled a delegate from Connecticut, stating that the experience in Washington inspired his chapter to organize a mass rally against discrimination and unemployment. The Bay Area council organized conferences in San Francisco and Oakland, addressing problems created by automation of longshore jobs, the shortage of apprenticeship positions for "Negro youth," and the failure to include black workers in efforts to unionize agricultural workers in the region. Black trade unionists conducted an investigation into employment discrimination in Philadelphia, and worked with the Pennsylvania Fair Employment Practice Commission and the city's Commission on Human Relations to develop a plan for ending discrimination by unions and employers. "It is our opinion, based on hard-won experience, that only to the extent that we win the Negro men and women trade unionists in the shops can we successfully build a real movement," wrote the leadership of the New York

NALC, boasting that "rank-and-file trade unionists" from eight local unions attended a day-long Unemployment Action Conference in June 1961. Randolph reported that "several hundred Negro longshoremen" joined the New York council during a campaign to expose discrimination against black workers at the port of New York City.[28]

Having won a small place in the national leadership of the NALC, black women mobilized to assert their influence at the local level. Lola Belle Holmes, L. Joy Jennings, and other women who had led the revolt at the founding conference established a Women's Department in the Chicago branch. Welcoming participation from all NALC members as well as wives of members, they organized a speaker's series featuring black women in the civil rights and labor movements. Holmes's fellow vice-president, Agnes Willis, chaired a similar group of NALC women in New York. While they supported efforts to eliminate barriers to training and employment, they prioritized fights against discrimination in unions that already had large numbers of black women in their membership. Women were elected officers of local councils in Jersey City, Philadelphia, and Oakland. When A. Philip Randolph issued a call for a second national convention of the NALC in Chicago, Holmes and Jennings cautioned that "a serious oversight has been made by not providing a Convention committee to look into the acute and peculiar forms of discrimination practiced against and suffered by Negro women trade unionists." Seeking to avoid a repeat of the Detroit conflict, Randolph agreed to create such a committee. "May I say that I am in accord with your ideas," he wrote Holmes, adding, "we do not want our Negro sisters to feel that we are separating them from the brothers of the Negro American Labor Council."[29]

Like the Southern Christian Leadership Conference, the NALC was a network of leaders rather than a mass organization like the NAACP or a union. Membership ranged from 5,000 to 10,000 in the early 1960s, but it was composed of staff and elected officials from local unions and civil rights groups who wielded tremendous influence in their communities. While they focused initially on organizing black workers, NALC chapters reached out to a broad range of potential allies in the battle for fair employment. San Francisco trade unionist James Herndon reported that NALC conferences served to unite "a coalition of peace, labor, liberals and minorities" around efforts to create full employment in the Bay Area. In Milwaukee, the Crusaders Civic and Social League became the local chapter of the NALC and teamed with the Congress of Racial Equality to launch a boycott against local businesses that discriminated against black workers. The Trade Union Leadership Council, which kept that name after becoming the local chapter of the NALC, worked with the NAACP and other black organizations to protest police brutality in Detroit. When the mayor resisted their demands, black trade unionists launched a campaign to defeat him in the 1961 election. Despite endorsements from major newspapers, business groups, and the United Auto Workers, the incumbent lost to Jerome Cavanagh, a relative newcomer whose "most important institutional ally" was the Trade Union Leadership Council. Pointing out that the NALC had no paid organizers, Randolph reported that the establishment of local chapters was "left to those dedicated bands of Negro trade unionists who had the conviction, strength and courage to forge an organization out of the conditions and circumstances provided by history."[30]

The NALC was strongest in New York, where it enjoyed support from the national office as well as the leaders of several civil rights and labor groups. The local council kicked off its Unemployment Action Conference in June 1961 with a mass rally cosponsored by the New York office of the SCLC. Representatives from the NAACP, the U.S. Department of Labor, and the New York Department of Welfare shared the podium with Randolph and other national leaders of the NALC. In September the NALC initiated the Emergency Committee for Unity on Social and Economic Problems to protest discrimination in employment and housing and the failure of local police to counteract the proliferation of drug dealing in black communities. Randolph agreed to chair the committee but delegated responsibility for organizing to his old friend Anna Arnold Hedgeman, who was employed as an aide to New York mayor Robert Wagner. Drawing on deep roots in New York's civil rights and labor movements, and her experience heading the National Council for a Permanent FEPC, Hedgeman expanded the group to represent an impressive array of labor, civil rights, and religious groups in the city. In addition to longtime allies Cleveland Robinson and NAACP branch president Percy Sutton, she recruited Malcolm X, a young minister with the Nation of Islam. Reporting on the success of the Emergency Committee in August 1961, the *NALC Newsletter* claimed that it "indicates how the building of unity required an understanding of the historic role to be played by the black working class, and demonstrates the pressing and urgent need and desire of the people for solidarity."[31]

As the *NALC Newsletter* suggested, Malcolm X's participation in the Emergency Committee demonstrated that despite significant divisions over goals and tactics, black trade unionists could unite a broad spectrum of activists around a response to the economic crisis facing black working-class communities. The thirty-five-year-old minister had emerged as the most effective spokesman for the Nation of Islam in the wake of the controversy created by *The Hate That Hate Produced* in 1959. His ascendancy was due in part to his ability to exploit the paranoia generated by the film, but also to the fact that he was far more interested in political engagement than the sixty-three-year-old leader of the sect, Elijah Muhammad. The son of Garveyites, Malcolm X had lived in Harlem, Boston, and Detroit before going to prison for petty theft in 1946. Two of his brothers belonged to the Nation of Islam, which reminded them of Garvey's Universal Negro Improvement Association, and by the time he was released in 1952, Elijah Muhammad had become his spiritual and intellectual mentor. By 1961 that relationship had begun to fray. It was becoming increasingly apparent to

Malcolm that Muhammad did not hold himself to the standards of morality that he expected of his followers, and Malcolm X found it hard to stay focused on spiritual and personal development at a time when mass protests seemed to be erupting all around him. That tension was evident in the speech that he gave at a "Mass Rally for Unity" that Anna Hedgeman organized in Harlem on September 6, 1961. While he criticized the police and city officials for allowing crime and violence to spread in Harlem, he opposed a mass march on the police station on the grounds that black people should take responsibility for their own problems.[32]

Despite its influence in black working-class communities, the NALC made little headway with the AFL-CIO. At the meeting in Washington following Kennedy's inauguration, trade unionists called on the AFL-CIO to set firm timelines for affiliates to drop racially exclusive language from their bylaws, expand opportunities for black workers in union leadership and apprenticeship programs, and integrate "qualified Negro office and staff workers into all departments of the general headquarters of the AFL-CIO." George Meany did not respond to these requests, but noticed that the NALC letterhead listed Theodore Brown, who was the assistant director of the AFL-CIO's Civil Rights Department, as secretary of the NALC. On April 30, 1961, Meany fired Brown on the grounds that he had charged the federation for unauthorized travel to civil rights meetings. Brown responded that the meetings were consistent with his duties, and accused Meany of punishing him for fulfilling those duties.[33]

Black trade unionists responded to Brown's dismissal by calling for a march on the AFL-CIO's national headquarters in Washington. L. Joseph Overton, an NALC vice president who also headed the Manhattan branch of the NAACP, announced that other NALC leaders would meet in New York on May 7 to plan a "national work stoppage" or a "mass mobilization" at the AFL-CIO headquarters. Cleveland Robinson opened the meeting "with a great burst of anger," calling

George Meany "a racist" and stating that other white labor leaders were "just like Hitler." Some proposed suing the AFL-CIO under the Labor-Management and Disclosure Act, or Landrum-Griffin Act, which Congress had passed in 1959 to fight corruption and organized crime in the labor movement. The law was seen by most union activists as an attempt to discredit unions by associating them with the Mafia, and A. Philip Randolph objected that using it would only bolster conservative attacks on the labor movement. Several reiterated Overton's proposal for a mass march and pushed to build support by circulating a petition in black working-class communities across the country. Predicting that Brown's firing would "prove to be the straw that broke the camel's back," Overton declared: "Let's march on Washington." At Horace Sheffield's suggestion, they resolved to delay plans for a march until Randolph could discuss the issue with Meany and other AFL-CIO leaders at a meeting of the AFL-CIO Executive Council in June.[34]

Tensions only grew when Randolph showed up at the Executive Council meeting with a detailed memorandum calling for stronger civil rights policies in the AFL-CIO, describing the growing problem of unemployment in black communities, and lamenting the "widening gulf between negro and labor communities." He also presented reports on discrimination by unions at the port of New York City and the practice of segregating housing and social events at state AFL-CIO conventions in the South. Reporting that the Virginia AFL-CIO had agreed to desegregate its convention that year after NALC activists threatened a boycott, Randolph announced a nationwide campaign to ensure that "all AFL-CIO State Federation Conventions are completely desegregated." In August George Meany expressed support for a bill sponsored by Adam Clayton Powell to restrict federal funding from vocational schools that were not open to all workers. Although a spokesman from the U.S. Labor Department complained it would be too costly to enforce, Meany endorsed the bill "as a start toward the larger goal of legislation on fair practices" in employment. When the Executive Committee met again on October 12, however, Meany blamed Randolph, rather than discriminatory unions, for "the gap that has developed between organized labor and the Negro community." At his suggestion, the white members of the Executive Committee voted to censure Randolph for making "incredible assertions, false and gratuitous statements, and unfair and untrue allegations" against organized labor. They also prepared a motion to expel the black union leader from the Executive Council at the AFL-CIO convention in December. Both motions were drafted by the president of the Brotherhood of Railway Clarks, which maintained segregated locals and seniority systems for black workers. Detroit NALC leader Horace Sheffield called it "the largest jim-crow union in America."[35]

On October 13, 1961, the day after the AFL-CIO censured Randolph, the U.S. Commission on Civil Rights issued a 246-page report on employment that "in effect upheld most of Mr. Randolph's charges." While it praised the Packinghouse, Auto, and Garment unions for taking "forceful steps" against discriminatory locals, the commission found that "most international unions have failed to exhibit any profound concern over civil rights problems." Investigators were particularly critical of craft unions in the building trades, where black workers were routinely denied access to apprenticeship programs and employment in skilled jobs. "Within the labor movement itself civil rights goals are celebrated at the higher levels," the commission observed, "but fundamental internal barriers tend to preserve discrimination at the workingman's level." Concluding that current "federal law has little impact on the discriminatory practices of labor organizations," the commission recommended that Congress and the president take stronger measures to prohibit discrimination by any agency, contractor, or union involved in a federally financed project, require state employment offices to ensure equal access to jobs and training programs, and deny collective bargaining protections to unions that denied membership to "any person because of race, color, creed or national origin." In an editorial printed on October 15, the *New York Times* pointed out that the AFL-CIO's statements about civil rights were contradicted by the fact that "Negroes were barred, by a Washington electricians' local, from work on the construction of the AFL-CIO national headquarters" in 1959.[36]

Adam Clayton Powell responded to the report by holding congressional hearings on employment discrimination in cities across the country. Speaking before a hearing in Chicago on October 23, Horace Sheffield cited the AFL-CIO's attack on Randolph and the Civil Rights Commission report as evidence of "the imperative need for the enactment of strong federal equal employment practices legislation and for the necessity of trade unionists like myself to speak candidly about the issues involved around this proposed legislation and why it should be passed." Citing evidence from Detroit to support the commission's findings, he claimed that the number of black apprentices enrolled in a vocational school controlled by the building trades unions had dropped from 59 to 37 from 1957 to 1960. Furthermore, nearly all of them were in masonry programs, which promised lower pay than plumbing, electrical, sheet metal, or ironworking, where no black apprentices were enrolled. He pointed to similar patterns in the auto industry, where apprenticeship programs were controlled by management. While there was one black apprentice enrolled in a program operated by General Motors Corporation in Detroit, there were none at Chrysler or at GM in Flint, Michigan. Pointing out that this practice concentrated black workers in "unskilled and semi-skilled" jobs that were being eliminated by mechanization of the auto industry, Sheffield cited figures showing that 30 percent of black workers in Detroit were unemployed. He argued that this problem would be addressed by Adam Clayton Powell's bill on apprenticeship programs but insisted that stronger measures were needed. He suggested amending the Landrum-Griffin Act to prohibit unions from refusing membership to or segregating workers on the basis of race, color, religion, or national origin.[37]

Ironically, the report from the Civil Rights Commission seems to have given Meany reason to seek common ground with Randolph. On November 10, 300 angry black trade unionists gathered in Chicago for the NALC's second annual convention. "This was a show of power to demonstrate to Negro union members that they represent nothing when it comes to setting policies in the labor movement even though they pay dues," Richard Parrish said of Randolph's censure, asking why liberal labor leaders such as United Auto Workers president Walter Reuther or David Dubinsky, of the Garment Workers, had not stopped it. Rejecting Overton's plan for a March on Washington, delegates resolved to work through their local unions and labor councils to elect delegates who would oppose Randolph's expulsion at the AFL-CIO convention a month later. By the time they got to the convention, however, they discovered that Meany had invited Martin Luther King to address the three-day meeting at Bal Harbour, the Miami resort where AFL leaders had gathered every winter since 1951.[38]

Martin Luther King did not know what to expect as he flew to Miami from Los Angeles, where he had spoken at a major rally sponsored by a black businessmen's club and a Baptist church. "Segregation is on its deathbed," he had told nearly 2,000 supporters in the Santa Monica civic auditorium on December 8. "But history has proven that the status quo is always on hand with an oxygen tank to keep the old boy alive." King got a "tumultuous standing ovation" by ending the speech with a line that he planned to use in Miami. Quoting a traditional spiritual, he looked forward to the day when he could truthfully sing: "Free at last, free at last. Thank God Almighty, I'm free at last." King had grown close to Randolph, Cleveland Robinson, and other black trade unionists since 1956, and had spoken to interracial meetings of District 65 and the Packinghouse and Auto Workers unions. But this was his first encounter with the 3,000 white men, a few women, and "a handful of Negro delegates" who headed the House of Labor. George Meany received a standing ovation when he opened the meeting on Saturday, December 9. President Kennedy gave a blistering talk about the threat of Communism and enlisted unions in the fight for freedom. Delegates rejected the proposal to expel Randolph and adopted what Randolph called "the best resolution on civil rights the AFL-CIO has yet adopted." They also applauded when George Meany pinned a union button on King's lapel and introduced him for the closing address on Monday, December 11. Then they were silent.[39]

"Less than a century ago the laborer had no rights, little or no respect, and led a life which was socially submerged and barren," King began, reaching out to his audience by asserting that the "inspiring answer to this intolerable and dehumanizing existence was economic organization through trade unions." Pointing out that many had opposed unions at the time, the young minister noted: "Now everyone knows that the labor movement did not diminish the strength of the nation but enlarged it." Exhausted from the long flight, King relied heavily on the text that he had prepared in consultation with Stanley Levison, his advisor from In Friendship. He continued by recounting how workers had been "emancipated" by the Wagner Act and other New Deal laws only to discover that they "tended merely to declare rights but did not deliver them." Now that African Americans found themselves in a similar situation, he declared, it was "not an historical coincidence" that they looked to labor for support. "Negroes are almost entirely a working people," King declared, and thus had the same interest as other workers in decent wages and working conditions; quality housing; health, education, and welfare policies; and pensions. That also led black organizations to support labor's legislative agenda and to "fight laws which curb labor." King won applause by pointing out that the same politicians who attacked unions were usually the ones who also rejected civil rights, and by calling on employers to ensure that automation does not "grind jobs into dust as it grinds out unbelievable volumes of production."[40]

King moved cautiously toward a more direct criticism, urging a "thoughtful examination of Mr. Randolph's criticism of labor's efforts to end discrimination within its own ranks." Asking the AFL-CIO to "accept the logic of its special position with respect to Negroes and the struggle for equality," King urged Meany and the others to follow through with their 1956 pledge to donate $2 million to the civil rights movement. He also noted that when "a Negro leader who has a reputation of purity and honesty which has benefited the whole labor movement criticizes it, his motives should not be reviled nor his earnestness rebuked." Then he closed with an uplifting refrain that he would use frequently in the next few years, asking labor leaders to join him in the struggle to "bring into full realization the dream of American democracy—a dream unfulfilled." Emphasizing economic concerns that could unite the two movements, King described a "dream of equality of opportunity, of privilege and property widely distributed; a dream of a land where men will not take necessities from the many to give luxuries to the few . . . the dream of a country where every man will respect the dignity and worth of human personality—that is the dream."[41]

The motive behind Meany's invitation to King became evident a month later, on January 24, 1962, when the AFL-CIO president testified before Adam Clayton Powell's Labor and Education Committee. "In our view, Mr. Chairman, the time is overdue to establish a policy—by the enactment of an enforceable statute—dealing with discrimination in employment for the United States as a whole," Meany began. As he continued it was clear that this was not a sudden conversion to Randolph's side, but a realization that federal legislation would free him from the burden of confronting the Jim Crow unions himself. Brushing aside Horace Sheffield's complaints about discrimination in apprentice programs run by the building trades unions in Detroit, the former president of the New York Building Trades Council insisted that the "overwhelming instances of employment discrimination in this country are caused by the hiring and other personnel policies of employers." He conceded that "discrimination does exist in the trade union movement," but declared that the AFL-CIO was "a generation or more ahead of the employers" in the fight against discrimination. Besides, Meany added, when "the rank-and-file membership of a local union obstinately exercises its right to be wrong, there is very little we in the leadership can do about it, unaided."[42]

Recognizing the calculation behind Meany's overtures to the civil rights movement, NALC leaders continued to strengthen their base in Harlem and other working-class communities across the urban North. In January 1962 the New York chapter of the NALC sponsored a "Gala Benefit Show" at the Apollo Theatre in Harlem. Featuring appearances by musicians Art Blakey and Nina Simone, actors Ossie Davis and Ruby Dee, and boxing champion Archie Moore, the event raised $5,000 to support efforts to combat unemployment in Harlem. In July 1962 A. Philip Randolph and Anna Hedgeman joined Malcolm X on the stage of a mass rally organized by the Hospital Workers Union Local 1199, which had launched a strike to win collective-bargaining rights for 20,000 mostly black and Latino workers at non-profit hospitals in New York. A few weeks later Malcolm X invited Randolph, Hedgeman, Cleveland Robinson, and Bayard Rustin to sit on the platform at a Nation of Islam rally. "Conditions in Harlem have deteriorated to the point where the religious, political, business and civic leaders must now take an intelligent and unselfish stand," he told 2,500 followers at Harlem Square, taking a more political stance than he had the previous year. "The fuse has already been lit," the minister warned, "the crisis has been reached and if something is not done immediately there will be an explosive situation in the Negro community more dangerous and destructive than a hundred megaton bomb."[43]

Harlem remained the center of such activities, but by 1962 NALC chapters were operating in twenty-three cities. Most were northern industrial centers such as Philadelphia, Gary, and Los Angeles, but chapters also operated in Atlanta, Tampa, and Randolph's hometown, Jacksonville, Florida. In February 1962 Horace Sheffield wrote to the

SCLC office in Atlanta that Randolph had authorized NALC branches to raise funds for a Voter Education Project that Martin Luther King's group, the NAACP, CORE, and the National Urban League had launched to increase registration rates of black voters in the South. Expressing confidence that this "most significant development" would "give real impetus to the civil rights struggle," he stated that the NALC "wholeheartedly endorses and supports" the registration drive. In May 1962 Randolph accepted an invitation to address a mass rally in Oakland, California, where the NALC was backing a "minority slate" for leadership of a building trades union that had no black officers despite the fact that 75 percent of its 3,500 members were black. The slate was defeated, but Randolph called it "the most exciting union election in local Labor history." In June the NALC chapter in Newark, New Jersey, played a central role in defeating the "machine candidate" to elect a reformist mayor. "We cannot sit back and expect the fruits of our political activity to be handed to us on a silver platter," branch officers wrote soon after the election, inviting leaders of other local groups to join them at a planning meeting on July 7. Among the issues they intended to address were "de-facto school segregation," "police brutality," dilapidated public housing and medical clinics, and discrimination in apprenticeship programs and city government. "Newark can be a model community in this respect," the trade unionists insisted. In Milwaukee the NALC supported a group of twelve high school students who picketed three A&P groceries to protest the "small percentage" of black employees in stores that served neighborhoods that were nearly entirely African American. "It's an obvious case of discrimination," the chapter president told the Wisconsin State Conference of NAACP Branches. "If they hired more Negroes, this would keep Negro dollars in a Negro area, thereby making a more prosperous community." The following year the Wisconsin NAACP established a Direct Action Committee to coordinate picket lines and a Legal Redress Committee to prepare a lawsuit, and asked the Labor and Industry Committee to investigate hiring employment practices at A&P stores and Retail Union locals across the state.[44]

While black trade unionists built a broad base of support in those communities, they maintained the strict exclusion of Communists from official positions in the NALC. In September 1961 the president of the NALC branch in Buffalo informed the national office that he had resigned after members of the group invited the president of the local Communist Party to speak at an NALC picnic. Charging that the decision was made during an unannounced meeting by a trade unionist whose mother was a prominent local Communist, he informed Randolph that membership in the branch had fallen dramatically since then. Alarmed that local leaders had turned control of the branch over to suspected Communists, Randolph urged them to reconsider. "I need not tell you that any propaganda that causes the public to feel that the Buffalo NALC is under communist domination is tantamount to the 'kiss of death' to the movement in that area," he wrote, adding that "it will render it impossible for the local chapter to get cooperation from the AFL-CIO and other responsible agencies in that section." Caught up in the debate with George Meany, the NALC Executive Committee did not act until January 1962, when L. Joseph Overton and another vice president were sent to investigate the situations in Buffalo and Cleveland, where a similar conflict had erupted. In addition to the threat that Randolph saw in Buffalo, he may have been motivated by increased scrutiny of Martin Luther King's ties to Stanley Levison, who FBI director J. Edgar Hoover claimed was still a Communist. The charges surfaced soon after King's address to the AFL-CIO, which Hoover claimed to have been authored solely by Levison. King rebuffed the Kennedy administration's request that he cut all ties to Levison, but Hoover was authorized to wiretap Levison and monitor his interactions with King. With George Meany voicing support for an FEPC law, Randolph was certainly not going to let a few Communists in Buffalo and Cleveland spoil his détente with the AFL-CIO.[45]

L. Joseph Overton succeeded in reorganizing the Buffalo branch under new leadership, but faced resistance in Cleveland. In June 1962 the president of the Cleveland NALC informed Randolph that he had ended the investigation into Communist infiltration and stopped asking branch members to sign affidavits testifying to their political affiliations. "Our program has suffered as members prepare either to join the attack or defend against it," he explained, and "fear, confusion and suspicion have made it difficult for member to work with member for the common goals." Citing Randolph's endorsement of Martin Luther King's petition against the House Un-American Activities Committee in 1961 and charging that HUAC "enjoyed the support of every reactionary, anti-labor, anti-Negro group in the land," the Cleveland trade unionist argued that the investigation was only aiding "our enemies." Randolph disagreed, stating that he would not permit "Communist infiltration" of the NALC on the "unsound assumption that a Communist is less a Communist because he or she happens to be pointed out by the anti-Communist and anti-liberal Un-American Activities Committee." On July 6 he authorized an NALC vice president in Cleveland to suspend the branch and reorganize it under new leadership.[46]

The same week that Randolph suspended the Cleveland branch, he faced a renewed debate over a legal remedy to employment discrimination. A year earlier, NAACP labor director Herbert Hill had filed a complaint with the New York State Commission for Human Rights, which was charged with enforcing the FEPC law that the National Council for a Permanent FEPC had helped to pass in 1945. The case involved a black worker at a garment factory in Queens who claimed that the Garment Workers, one of the most diverse and egalitarian unions in the country, had deprived him of wages and benefits by not allowing him to join the local union. After a fifteen-month investigation ending the first week of July 1961, the commission confirmed that in addition to denying membership to the worker, leaders of the local had ordered his dismissal from the plant after he filed the complaint. Finding no evidence that managers had any part in the discrimination, they ordered the union to secure the worker's reinstatement and warned that they would continue to monitor the situation. While Herbert Hill was pleased with the outcome in that particular case, he charged that it represented a broader pattern of discrimination in even the most egalitarian unions. Testifying before Adam Clayton Powell's Labor and Education Committee that August, he reiterated Horace Sheffield's insistence that the Landrum-Griffin Act be amended to deprive collective-bargaining protections to any union found to have discriminated against workers on the basis of race, religion, or national origin.[47]

Black trade unionists were unanimous in their condemnation of the Queens local, but many were troubled by the broader implications of Hill's testimony. Authored by vehemently anti-union senators from Michigan and Georgia in 1959, the Landrum-Griffin Act was widely seen as the centerpiece of a conservative backlash against New Deal labor law in the postwar era. Justified on the premise that unions were inherently corrupt, the law imposed strict regulations on the internal finance of unions, the actions that union leaders could take against members or locals that violated union policies, and the ability of unions to picket or boycott employers. Employing the language of the civil rights movement, supporters of the law called it a "bill of rights" for workers who were abused by "union bosses," but they also argued that it would help preserve "the Southern way of life" by preventing unions from organizing black workers. Knowing that history, black trade unionists were reluctant to legitimate the law by using it as a weapon against the AFL-CIO. "We of the Negro American Labor Council know that this investigation is long overdue," read a pamphlet distributed by NALC members in New York City, who urged black workers to document similar cases of discrimination and bring them before Powell's committee. The flyer did not mention the Landrum-Griffin Act, but Hill's position gained support from Horace Sheffield, L. Joseph Overton, and other activists in the CIO Auto, Retail, and Clothing Workers unions who felt it was worth the risk of destroying a few unions in order to save the rest. Maida Springer, who had dedicated thirty years to building the Garment Workers Union, did not agree. "This is an industry I know," she wrote to Hill and a CIO activist who criticized her for defending her union during a hearing by Powell's committee on August 24. While she "would never deny its sins," she knew "enough of its virtues to be able to stand up and be counted as a member and former officer of this union." Randolph took a similar position at the same hearing, stating that the NALC was "uncompromisingly opposed to race bias in all labor unions and industry but also opposed to any witch hunt against a bona fide union." Finding common ground with George Meany, he argued that "the basic remedy" was not the destruction of unions but "the enactment of federal fair employment practice legislation."[48]

Randolph responded to the growing divide within the NALC by asking Meany, who faced a similar crisis in the AFL-CIO, to address a banquet at the NALC's third national convention in New York City on November 15, 1962. The *Amsterdam News* acknowledged that the invitation "may have surprised those outside the labor movement who have at times pictured the NALC as being at odds with the AFL-CIO," but pointed out that the two men had worked together since the 1930s and that "the areas of their agreement are much greater than the areas of their differences." Furthermore, the newspaper reported that Meany's previous statements led many to expect that he would use the event to lay out a civil rights program for the AFL-CIO—perhaps even calling for a fair employment law—and that broad interest in Meany's position "virtually assured a sellout audience" for the banquet. "The main issue before our convention is to expand and strengthen the lines of cooperation between the AFL-CIO and the NALC," Randolph told reporters, stating that he had offered to arbitrate the dispute between the NAACP and the Garment Workers. "Randolph made it clear, on more than one occasion during the convention, that he was in full sympathy with the NAACP," and "commended Herbert Hill" for his work on behalf of black workers. But he rejected Hill's plan for Landrum-Griffin. Accusing the press of exaggerating the differences between black and white trade unionists, Randolph maintained that "basically, the way bias is going to be eliminated in the labor movement is through unions and the leadership of unions."[49]

George Meany had none of the eloquence and grace that Martin Luther King had displayed in Bal Harbour a year earlier, but he served Randolph's purpose. "When anyone tries to say that the trade unions are the chief barrier to the economic opportunities of Negroes in this country, I resent it and I reject it, for it is simply not true," he bellowed. Vowing to stop all contributions to the NAACP in retaliation for Herbert Hill's "political attack," he called the Garment Workers "a union whose record shines like a beacon in the history of human progress." After hearing Meany's outburst, Roy Wilkins remarked that the AFL-CIO had never contributed to the NAACP. Despite "much talk and few deeds on civil rights," the NAACP leader charged, "even today, a Negro worker needs the patience of Job, the hide of an elephant, plus a crowbar to get into Mr. Meany's own union—the plumbers." When the NALC delegates debated a resolution endorsing Hill's Landrum-Griffin plan, however, Cleveland Robinson introduced an amendment that defended the NAACP without taking a specific position on Hill's proposal. "The enemies of labor would have been happy to see us make such a move because they would use it as a means of dividing and perhaps destroying the labor movement," he stated after his amendment was adopted by a narrow margin. "We were on the brink of disaster."[50]

While he resolved the debate over Landrum-Griffin, Randolph faced a renewed conflict over anti-Communism. In contrast to the relatively small branches in Buffalo and Cleveland, this time it occurred in one of the largest and most respected branches in the country. Shortly before the NALC convention in November, Randolph received a terse letter from Chicago branch president Timuel Black, a public schoolteacher and activist in the Chicago Federation of Teachers. Born in Alabama, Black had moved to Chicago as a baby in 1919. After completing high school in 1935 he worked at various jobs before serving in Europe during the Second World War. He started in teaching in 1954, after working in a packinghouse while completing college. During that period he joined the United Packinghouse Workers and the Congress of Racial Equality and, like many in those groups, worked closely with Communists. Black did not belong to the Communist Party in 1962, but he objected to Randolph's willingness to take action against NALC members on the basis of testimony from people "who, for selfish or other motives, are dedicated to the suppression of the democratic principles of Freedom, Equality and Justice." During the convention, Black and other leaders of the branch explained to Randolph that NALC vice president Lola Belle Holmes had revealed that she was a paid informant for the FBI and was preparing to testify at a federal hearing on "Communist infiltration" of the NALC, the NAACP, and other organizations in Chicago. Holmes argued that her actions were consistent with the anti-Communist policies of the NALC, but L. Joy Jennings, who had helped her lead the revolt of women at the founding convention, called her actions "disgraceful, shameful and extremely damaging to the Negro people's movement as a whole and to the NALC in particular."[51]

Combined with his opposition to Herbert Hill's proposal, Randolph's handling of the dispute in Chicago sparked a small revolt from the NALC. On January 24, 1963, Lola Belle Holmes testified as promised and explained that the FBI had paid her to join the Communist Party in 1956 and to report on the activities of Communists in the NALC and other groups in Chicago. When confronted by angry activists as she left the hearing, Holmes stated: "I expect to get more of this treatment, but it's worth it. It is the price of freedom." Randolph removed Holmes from leadership of the NALC, but still sent Joseph

Overton to investigate her charges about Communist infiltration. Out-raged that the national leadership was taking seriously allegations from an "admitted communist and government spy," Timuel Black declared: "we certainly do not intend to stand idly by and watch honest per-sons vilified and slanderized." Randolph was able to mend his ties to Black and other leaders of the Chicago NALC, but James Haughton, a thirty-three-year-old activist who had worked as Randolph's assis-tant since the founding of the NALC, quit the organization in disgust. Claiming that membership had declined because of "the present lack of militant leadership," he accused Randolph, Overton, Robinson, and "other lackeys" of "serving as agents for a white, reactionary, labor leadership that is playing a vicious and unprincipled role in the struggle of all workers, black and white." After leaving the NALC, Haughton was elected president of the Labor and Industry Committee of the New York NAACP and utilized that position to fight employment discrimi-nation. He continued to cooperate with Randolph and other leaders of the NALC, but charged that anti-Communist stances and deference to white labor leaders had destroyed the group's ability to advance the interests of black workers.[52]

Randolph was certainly more vehemently anti-Communist and more loyal to George Meany than most members of the NALC, but Haughton's criticism misrepresented the nature of that divide. Few black trade unionists disagreed with his concern that a direct attack on the AFL-CIO might undermine an institution that was critical to the economic security of thousands of black workers. That his hesitation was shared by Cleveland Robinson, who had roots in the left wing of the old CIO and who had pushed for a mass march against Meany just a year earlier, demonstrated that the convention debate was driven more by strategy than by ideology. As he had repeatedly throughout his life, Randolph responded to the mounting frustration within the NALC by calling for a march on Washington. In January 1963 he asked his old friend Bayard Rustin, who was working for the left-wing War

Resisters League, to prepare a proposal that could win support from civil rights and labor leaders for a "mass descent" on the nation's capital. Excited by the opportunity to revive mass-based protest, Rustin spent the next month planning Randolph's demonstration. He worked closely with Norman Hill, an NALC member who was employed by CORE, and Tom Kahn, a young white Socialist who was on vacation from Howard University. At the end of January they delivered a three-page memorandum outlining an ambitious campaign to draw attention to "the economic subordination of the Negro," create "more jobs for all Americans," and advance a "broad and fundamental program for economic justice." Their plan centered on a massive lobbying campaign, in which 100,000 people would shut down Congress for one day while presenting legislators and the president with their legislative demands, followed the next day by a "mass protest rally." Randolph liked the idea, and the NALC vice presidents approved it on March 23. By then the plan had expanded to include a mass march from the Capitol to the Lincoln Memorial, where they hoped that President Kennedy would address the crowd.[53]

CHAPTER FIVE

FOR JOBS AND FREEDOM

I N THE LAST week of March 1963, A. Philip Randolph, Cleveland Robinson, L. Joseph Overton, and Richard Parrish invited Anna Arnold Hedgeman and Reverend Thomas Kilgore, who had coordinated the Prayer Pilgrimage in 1957, to help them organize a "March on Washington for Jobs." Having led the Emergency Committee for Unity on Social and Economic Problems two years earlier, and having talked to teachers and students in public schools, Hedgeman "knew intimately the apathy and sense of despair" that marked the lives of young African Americans in Harlem and other cities across the United States. Even when black students earned admission to prestigious universities like Columbia, a mile away, they retained a "sense of isolation" from other students and displayed little knowledge of African Americans' "history of involvement in whatever is good in the U.S." Reminded, perhaps, of her own work for the YWCA or the National Council for a Permanent FEPC, she thought "a March on Washington might well be a way of giving young people a new picture of their leadership and a new sense of their dignity." She recalled Randolph stating, in "his usual calm, quiet fashion," that it was "time for the masses of people to move again," reminding her and the others that although "a war had been fought for democratic aims," it had "poisoned our society" with the same "racial attitudes" that had motivated the fascists. He pointed to Congress' failure to pass "a postwar FEPC" and noted that a century after the Emancipation Proclamation black workers were still concentrated in low-wage jobs, sharecropping, and impoverished ghettos. Hedgeman was intrigued.[1]

But she had "mixed emotions." Having "witnessed the death of the March on Washington Movement in 1946," the sixty-four-year-old activist wondered if they could raise the funds or sustain the "local organization" required to change federal policy. Randolph was seventy-four, and with membership in his union plummeting as a result of the decline of passenger rail, he "would have a larger load to carry than we ought to expect of him." Most importantly, she wondered, how "would a March for Jobs held in Washington affect the southern movement?" Would southern leaders and their followers have the time or money to attend? "Would they consider the march useful?" Those concerns were shared by Reverend Kilgore, who had taken a six-week leave of absence to organize the Prayer Pilgrimage in 1957—a much smaller undertaking than Randolph was now proposing. Both Hedgeman and Kilgore recalled the personal and institutional rivalries that had marked the movement in the 1950s, and were particularly concerned that Roy Wilkins and other leaders of the NAACP would not "be willing to participate in a mass movement." They knew that Martin Luther King's SCLC was planning to launch a major campaign the following week in Birmingham, Alabama, with the hope of reviving the southern movement that had limped along, with bursts of energy here and there but few victories, since 1958. SNCC was weathering a storm of violence in Greenwood, Mississippi, where its headquarters had been burned to the ground and eight leading activists thrown in jail. The student organization planned to mark its third anniversary in two weeks by reassessing its commitment to nonviolence and electing new leadership at a conference in Atlanta, where John Lewis was the leading candidate for chairman. Hedgeman and Kilgore knew that leaders of all three groups shared Randolph's concern about the economic crisis facing black America, but they doubted whether any of them would support his objectives over their own battles in the South.[2]

The trade unionists did not wait to find out. In March Randolph removed himself from organizing because of the illness of his wife, Lucille, who died on April 12. In the meantime Cleveland Robinson asked Hedgeman and Kilgore to join an Administrative Committee for the Emancipation March on Washington for Jobs, along with Overton, Bayard Rustin, and Reverend George Lawrence, who represented Martin Luther King's SCLC in New York City. Robinson and Overton secured funding from their union, District 65, and set up an office in the union's headquarters in midtown Manhattan. They also drew up a detailed plan of action, which included the establishment of local organizing committees in cities across the country, outreach to churches, civic groups, and newspapers that might support the mobilization, and production of signs and placards to publicize their demands. As Hedgeman had expected, Roy Wilkins urged Randolph to focus on formal lobbying rather than waste their time with a protest. The Urban League's new director, Whitney Young, expressed "great sympathy and emotional support for the effort," but he feared that his allies in Washington "would look with some suspicion, if not confusion, on our participation in the March." Young had his own plan for addressing the economic crisis facing black America. By April 1963 he had already begun seeking support from business, organized labor, and government for a massive "Marshall Plan for the Negro"—modeled on the $17 billion effort to rebuild Europe following the Second World War—to improve housing, education, health care, and employment opportunities in cities across the United States.[3]

After failing to gain support from the nation's oldest civil rights groups, Anna Hedgeman made two suggestions for expanding the base of support for the demonstration. The first was to invite her old friend Dorothy Height, who was by then the president of the National Council of Negro Women, to join the official leadership of the March on Washington. Height was in the news that spring for her leadership of an investigation into "the special needs of Negro women," sponsored by President Kennedy's Commission on the Status of Women. Authored by prominent women in the civil rights and labor movements, including Dorothy L. Robinson of the NALC, the study detailed the low wages, poor working conditions, and discrimination that black women faced in the labor market. In her statements to the press, however, Height insisted that those problems could be addressed by ending employment discrimination against black men. "If the Negro woman has a major underlying concern, it is the status of the Negro man and his position in the community," Height stated at a press conference on April 30, 1963, "and his need for feeling himself an important person, free and able to make his contribution in the whole society in order that he may strengthen his home." Despite this affirmation of Randolph's belief in the centrality of winning jobs for black men, he and other male leaders refused to add Height to the official leadership of the march. "As usual, the men must have discussed the matter in my absence," Hedgeman recalled, "and when the first leaflet was printed, I was embarrassed to find that I was still the only woman listed."[4]

Hedgeman's second proposal was more successful. Although southern activists had been focused on campaigns in Alabama and Mississippi, their attention shifted to Washington after the Kennedy administration refused to intervene against flagrant violations of federal authority in the South. In late May, a group headed by author James Baldwin lashed out at Attorney General Robert Kennedy, the president's brother, for failing to protect southern activists from violence. A few days later, Martin Luther King scolded the administration for allowing Alabama governor George Wallace to defy a federal court order requiring him to admit three black students to the state university. "In his broadest attack to date on President Kennedy's civil rights record," the New York Times reported, King warned that the SCLC and other groups were prepared to organize "a march on Washington, even sit-ins in Congress" to force the federal government into action. Recognizing an opportunity to coordinate with the southern movement, Hedgeman brought a newspaper story about King's statement to Randolph and set up a meeting where the two men resolved to march under the slogan "For Jobs and Freedom." They soon won support from John Lewis, who had been elected chairman of SNCC, as well as James Farmer of CORE.[5]

The debate over the leadership and strategy of the March was complicated by President Kennedy's endorsement, on June 11, of a moderate civil rights bill focused narrowly on ending segregation and discrimination in public accommodations in the South. While Kennedy's statement affirmed Wilkins' and Young's position that federal officials could be moved through lobbying, it also underlined the gap between the president's proposal and the broader agenda of the civil rights movement—a disparity that was illustrated tragically by the assassination of Medgar Evers, who headed the NAACP in Mississippi, in his driveway early in the morning following Kennedy's announcement. Leaders of the NALC and SCLC pushed forward with their plans for the March on Washington, although they shifted their target from the White House to Congress and expanded their agenda to demand federal protection of civil rights activists in the South. They also agreed to discuss their differences with Young, Wilkins, and Dorothy Height at a June 20 meeting arranged by the Taconic Foundation, a group of wealthy white donors who had supported all the major civil rights groups since its founding in the late 1950s. Fearing that strategic and interpersonal rivalries threatened to destroy the civil rights movement at a moment when it seemed to be gaining traction, leaders of the foundation convinced black leaders to mediate their differences through regular meetings of a new Council for United Civil Rights Leadership.[6]

The Taconic meeting did not resolve differences among civil rights leaders, but it created a framework in which they could move forward.

On June 21, Cleveland Robinson and Reverend George Lawrence issued the first official announcement of the March on Washington, stating that the NALC and SCLC were organizing 100,000 people to descend on the nation's capital in early August to pressure Congress into action on civil rights. Almost immediately, President Kennedy asked Randolph and King to meet him in the White House, along with Wilkins and James Farmer. In a move that must have reminded all those assembled of Randolph's meeting with Franklin D. Roosevelt two decades earlier, Kennedy attempted to persuade civil rights leaders that a mass demonstration would harm their cause by raising the potential for violence and giving opponents of his bill "a chance to say that they have to prove their courage by voting against us." Randolph, King, and Farmer defended their plans, stating that protests were already breaking out across the country, and asked whether it wasn't preferable to have them "led by organizations dedicated to civil rights and disciplined by struggle rather than to leave them to other leaders who care neither about civil rights nor about nonviolence." Wilkins maintained that the NAACP would not join the March unless conservatives filibustered Kennedy's bill, but agreed to discuss the issue further at a luncheon hosted by United Auto Workers president Walter Reuther.[7]

Wilkins and Reuther still hoped to talk Randolph and the others out of marching, but within a week both of them would commit their organizations to the mobilization. An important cause of their reversal was the success of a mass march in Detroit on June 23. Organized by the Trade Union Leadership Council and Reverend C. L. Franklin, the "Walk to Freedom" faced intense resistance from NAACP and Urban League leaders, who feared a militant protest would disrupt their ties to white leaders in the city. Brokering peace between Franklin and established civil rights groups, as well as between black militants and white labor leaders, Horace Sheffield, Robert Battle, and other black trade unionists ensured that the march integrated efforts to support civil rights activists in the South with demands for fair employment, better wages, working conditions, housing, and education in the urban North. Over 125,000 people packed Detroit's broad Woodward Avenue and marched through downtown to a massive rally at Cobo Hall, making it the largest civil rights demonstration yet. After speeches by Mayor Jerome Cavanaugh, Walter Reuther, and other local leaders, Martin Luther King delivered a rousing ode to the "magnificent new militancy within the Negro community all across the nation." Stating that the best way for northerners to support the southern movement was "to work with determination to get rid of segregation and discrimination" in their own communities, he insisted: "We've got to come to see that the problem of racial injustice is a national problem." Elaborating a theme that he had introduced in his speech to the AFL-CIO's national convention in 1961, King concluded by describing a vision of social justice that gave him optimism in the face of unceasing opposition. Giving a local flavor to that vision, he added, "I have a dream this afternoon that one day, right here in Detroit, Negroes will be able to buy a house or rent a house anywhere that their money will carry them and that they will be able to get a job."[8]

Recognizing that the March on Washington would take place even without their participation, and assured that the demonstration would be as peaceful and orderly as the Walk to Freedom, Wilkins and Young finally came on board. With leaders of the NALC, SCLC, CORE, and SNCC, they met in New York on July 2 and pledged to mobilize local chapters of their respective organizations to bring their membership to Washington on August 28, the eighth anniversary of Emmett Till's murder. Bayard Rustin presented a detailed set of demands for the demonstration, including a federal jobs creation program, raising the minimum wage, a Fair Employment Practice law, and support for Kennedy's civil rights bill. He anticipated that they could get 100,000 people to participate and estimated that the event would cost $65,000. Wilkins agreed to the general outline, but insisted that Rustin not remain the primary spokesman for the effort. "He's got too many scars," the NAACP leader told Randolph, citing Rustin's ties to the Communist Party in the 1930s, his draft resistance during the Second World War, and his arrest for homosexuality in the 1950s. Randolph insisted that Rustin was the best man for the job but avoided a conflict by agreeing to be listed as the official director of the march and appointing Rustin as his deputy. Cleveland Robinson was elected to chair the Administrative Committee, which expanded to include representatives from all sponsoring groups. Joseph Overton and Norman Hill were charged with coordinating local organizing committees in northern cities, and the NAACP, SNCC, CORE, and SCLC appointed southern administrators in Mississippi, Alabama, North Carolina, and Georgia, respectively. Reverend Thomas Kilgore donated the Utopia Neighborhood Club House, a recreation center connected to his Friendship Baptist Church in Harlem, to serve as the national headquarters of the mobilization.[9]

Historians have marveled at Rustin's ability to build the march "out of nothing" in less than two months, but that assessment overlooks the rich organizational networks that he built upon. Robinson and Overton asked trade unionists to establish local organizing committees in cities where they had influence, and Norman Hill spent the months of July and August travelling across the country to coordinate their efforts. Roy Wilkins wrote to every NAACP branch, youth council, and state conference asking them to organize "no less than 100,000" people to participate in the March, and he dispatched NAACP labor secretary Herbert Hill to help them do that. Anna Hedgeman was charged with reaching out to religious groups. She took particular pride in recruiting white Christians from the South who "feel concern but have all too little opportunity to express it in their home place," stating that the March would give them a chance to meet "white allies" from other regions while also demonstrating that African Americans were not completely alone in the South. She also convinced the National Council of Churches to hold its annual convention in Washington the week of August 28 and encourage its 80,000 members to attend the March. When asked whether Protestant churches objected to the inclusion of fair employment and public works alongside the "civil rights" demands of the March, she pointed out that they had a long history of working toward economic justice and would not "have been willing to cooperate" had they not agreed with the agenda. The American Jewish Congress and the National Catholic Conference for Interracial Justice endorsed the March on Washington, along with seventeen international unions, several state and municipal labor councils, and the Industrial Union Department of the AFL-CIO. By the end of July, Rustin reported that local organizing committees had chartered 2,000 buses, twenty-one trains, and ten airplanes—enough to carry 115,000 marchers to Washington.[10]

The one major liberal body that rebuffed Randolph's request for support was George Meany's AFL-CIO, but by that point the March was clearly prepared to move forward without it. Randolph and Walter Reuther pushed for the endorsement at a meeting of the executive council just two weeks before the March, but met resistance from union leaders who feared "that there would be disorder, that people would get hurt, and that it would build up resentment in Congress." Some pushed for outright rejection of the March, but Meany negotiated a compromise that expressed support for its goals and allowed affiliated unions to participate but withheld an official endorsement from the federation itself. "We are convinced that the AFL-CIO can make its major contribution to victory by continuing its all-out legislative activity on Capitol Hill and its efforts in cooperation with other like-minded groups to bring an end to segregation and inequality of opportunity in the local communities of America," read the resolution, exaggerating significantly the resources that labor leaders were currently devoting to lobbying for a civil rights law. Calling the statement a "masterpiece of noncommittal noncommitment," Randolph made it clear that it had no bearing on the March. "The leaders of the federation do not understand that the Negroes, who are the victims of racial bias, have the responsibility to lead the attack on racial bias," he declared, pointing out that "many Negroes feel that the legislation is inadequate anyway, which lessens the importance to them of its enactment."[11]

Some complained at the time that reliance on moderate organizations forced leaders of the march to temper their demands and reduce the militancy of the demonstration. Rachel Horowitz, a young radical who volunteered in the national office, recalled that staffers were dismayed when Rustin agreed to changes demanded by leaders of the NAACP and the National Urban League. Further concessions came when representatives of the United Auto Workers, the American Jewish Congress, the National Catholic Conference for Interracial Justice, and the National Council of Churches joined the official leadership of the protest. In early August, Rustin announced that the demonstration would include no civil disobedience and that lobbying would be restricted to formal meetings between leaders of the sponsoring organizations and Kennedy and Congress while other marchers were encouraged to leave Washington immediately following the March.[12]

The most vocal criticism of those changes came from Malcolm X, the Nation of Islam minister who had worked closely with Randolph, Hedgeman, and other leaders of the March on Washington just a year before. He was particularly concerned that the Taconic Foundation, which had close ties to the Kennedy administration, had helped raise nearly $800,000 to support the organizations sponsoring the March. Initially, Malcolm X announced that Nation of Islam leader Elijah Muhammad would attend the March on Washington to ensure that "there will be no skull-duggery, no flim-flam, no sell-out," charging that changes in the program demonstrated that the mobilization had been hijacked by "the white man." He revised that position a few weeks later, stating that the demonstration already had been "taken over by the government and is controlled by the government and is being used for political expediency." Muslims were authorized to sell papers to marchers as they boarded buses in New York and other cities, but Malcolm X announced that "Muslims who follow the Honorable Elijah Muhammad won't have anything to do whatsoever with the March."[13]

While the specifics of the demonstration were certainly adjusted in consultation with newcomers, both black and white, the charge of co-optation underestimated the degree to which control over the March remained in the hands of Randolph, King, and other initiators of the protest. Despite Roy Wilkins' objections, Bayard Rustin retained primary control over planning and preparing for the demonstration. Urban League leader Whitney Young "was continually concerned" that the "Randolph clique" had the ability to make key decisions between meetings of the official leadership. Journalist Reese Cleghorn looked into Malcolm X's charge that the Taconic Foundation was "infiltrating the revolution with money," and found that wealthy donors placed no restrictions on the funding other than to use it for thoughtfully planned protests and well-audited organizations. "The capitalists are not trying to inject Adam Smith into the revolt, just Price Waterhouse," Cleghorn wrote in the left-wing *New Republic*. Furthermore, civil rights leaders agreed to earmark nearly half of the Taconic funds for the NAACP, which bore the brunt of legal costs generated by civil disobedience in the South, while giving only a small portion to the SCLC and none to the NALC or directly to the March on Washington. "So far no one has complained about receiving the new money," Cleghorn concluded."[14]

Journalist Harvey Swados, a former union organizer who visited the national headquarters frequently in the weeks leading up to August 28, argued that far from being restrained by collaboration, the goals of the March on Washington "simultaneously broadened and become more specific" as the mobilization unfolded. "The March itself, after all, came into being in a merging of two streams of thought and action," Swados wrote in *The Nation*, crediting Randolph and King with linking black trade unionists' twenty-year struggle for fair employment with the southern struggle against Jim Crow. Chiding other journalists for focusing on petty differences among the leadership or charges that "Communists and Black Muslims are trying to take over the March," Swados complained that such stories prevented readers from "getting an understanding, in depth, of the new American revolution." He attempted to counteract that shortcoming through detailed portraits of Rustin, Cleveland Robinson, Anna Hedgeman, and other organizers at the national headquarters. "Mrs. Hedgeman was not alone in feeling that in a revolution, new leadership emerges on all sides and from all strata, and cannot be contained," he reported, suggesting that organizers of the March were not concerned about co-optation by moderate organizations or liberal donors.[15]

As Swados observed, the demands of the March expanded as new groups joined. They included a "comprehensive and effective" civil rights law, which would guarantee that all Americans had access to public accommodations, "decent housing, adequate and integrated education, and the right to vote." The federal government was also to withhold funding from any discriminatory program, desegregate all school districts by the end of the year, enforce the Fourteenth Amendment by reducing congressional representation from states in which citizens were disfranchised, bar discrimination in housing projects supported by federal funding, and grant the attorney general authority to issue injunctions when "any constitutional right is violated." Finally, the demands included a "massive federal program to train and place all unemployed workers—Negro and white—on meaningful and dignified jobs at decent wages," raising the minimum wage to "give all Americans a decent standard of living," extending the Fair Labor Standards Act to domestic service and other employment sectors that had been excluded from the law, and "a federal Fair Employment Practices Act barring discrimination by federal, state, and municipal governments, and by employers, contractors, employment agencies, and trade unions." The official statement included a qualification that support for the March did "not necessarily indicate endorsement of every demand," since the list had grown too quickly for every group to "take an official position" on every issue.[16]

Ironically, the one demand that Randolph and Rustin would not agree to was Hedgeman's request to include representatives from women's organizations in the leadership of the demonstration. Learning just a week before the March that no women were even included in the official program, Hedgeman met with NALC activists Corrine Smith and Geri Stark to draft an angry letter to Randolph. "In light of the role of Negro women in the struggle for freedom and especially in light of the extra burden they have carried because of the castration of our Negro men in this culture, it is incredible that no woman should appear as a speaker at the historic March on Washington Meeting at the Lincoln Memorial," they wrote, suggesting that at the very least a woman be allowed to make a short statement and introduce a few "Heroines" of the movement. Randolph ignored the letter but, after Hedgeman read it aloud at the next meeting of the Administrative Committee, he agreed to allow wives of civil rights leaders to sit on stage at the Lincoln Memorial, to invite Little Rock NAACP leader Daisy Bates to speak briefly, and to recognize Rosa Parks and other women for their contributions to the struggle. "We grinned, some of us," Hedgeman recalled, "as we recognized anew that Negro women are second-class citizens in the same way that white women are in our culture."[17]

Other women were not so resigned to that conclusion, and continued to push for representation during the days leading up to the March. Pauli Murray, who had helped organize the March on Washington Movement in the 1940s, planned to picket A. Philip Randolph when he spoke before the all-male National Press Club in Washington on August 26. NALC leader Maida Springer allowed Murray to use her Washington apartment as "a combination of secretariat and public relations office," but refused to join the protest on the grounds that it would detract attention from the broader goals of the movement. Randolph avoided further conflict by insisting that the club relax its prohibition on allowing women to sit on the main floor during his speech. Height convinced Murray not to picket Randolph, but invited her and other women to discuss the issue at the National Council's headquarters in Washington the evening of August 28. Pointing out that this proposal violated Randolph's request that marchers leave Washington immediately after the demonstration, Height recalled that the conflict made women "much more aware and much more aggressive in facing up to sexism in our dealings with the male leadership in the movement."[18]

While organizers of the March grappled with conflicts over funding and women's leadership, the press was preoccupied with the possibility that the March would result in violence. Randolph addressed those fears in his speech to the National Press Club, stating that organizers had taken every step possible to avoid conflict and that participants "certainly are not going to provide anything that would discredit the movement." His assurances were counteracted by statements from the American Nazi Party, which encouraged hundreds of its members to travel to Washington on August 28 despite the fact that local authorities had denied their request for a permit to hold a counterdemonstration. Local authorities banned the sale of alcohol at bars, restaurants, and package stores for the forty-eight hours surrounding the demonstration, and cleared prisoners from local jails "to make room for possible troublemakers." Six thousand police, firefighters, and soldiers were assigned to "crowd and trouble control duties," and the Pentagon stationed 4,000 soldiers at nearby bases, "ready to cross the Potomac in helicopters if they were needed for riot duty." The *Chicago Tribune* reported that "public officials were reluctant to speak publicly about it, but fear of violence was always in the background," noting that "Smoothly and almost silently, they prepared for the worst." The front page of the *Los Angeles Times* read: "Washington Gets Jittery over March."[19]

Preparations for violence reflected a broader sentiment among even relatively supportive observers that the March on Washington was a "futile, risky" endeavor. The *Wall Street Journal* interviewed hundreds of whites in dozens of northern and western cities, "where civil rights demonstrations could be expected to provoke the most sympathetic reaction," and found that nearly two-thirds of them opposed the demonstration. "A lot of the sympathy I had before is being whittled away," stated a white schoolteacher from Pennsylvania. "I've always pushed for equal rights myself, but I don't approve of this mass and mob thing." While a "vocal minority of whites" supported the demonstration, most "talk in a general way of the need to go slow, of the importance of Negroes' preparing themselves better for jobs and of the desirability of calm negotiations." The *Los Angeles Times* concurred that the "vast majority" of Americans supported "demands for equality by Negroes and other minorities" but were concerned "that the march could somehow miscarry, that the very numbers participating will make it vulnerable to disorder." An Illinois congressman said that the March "held little hope for accomplishing any substantial legislative ends," adding that "it could have quite the opposite effect" if marchers did not behave themselves. The *Chicago Sun-Times* ran a cartoon depicting rows of well-dressed marchers converging like a fuse on a "Powder Keg" labeled Washington, D.C.[20]

Alongside such measured criticism, journalists discovered more overt hostility toward the March on Washington. "Negroes are looking for the easiest way to make a living, and they think by demonstrating they may get something for nothing," said a Bostonian. Charging that the marchers "just want to take everything over," a Detroit pipefitter maintained that African Americans "should be segregated." Criticism of the goals of the March often accompanied the claim that the mobilization was a pretext for insurrection. "Beware marching techniques," warned nationally syndicated columnist William S. White, who charged Bayard Rustin and other "Negro 'militants' " with manipulating the civil rights movement "to promote their own economic and political lines." White stopped short of calling the March a "Communist plot," but warned that Rustin's approach to mass mobilization was "strictly within the operating tradition of the Communist and Fascist marching movements." The president of the American Council of Christian Churches, a fundamentalist group that claimed over a million members, called the March "the largest company of Communists and communist-sympathizers ever to meet in one place in America." A congressman from South Carolina compared the protest to the Fascist "March on Rome," which led to Benito Mussolini's seizing control of Italy in 1922.[21]

Such hyperbole contributed to the eerie silence that greeted journalist Russell Baker when he arrived in downtown Washington on Wednesday morning, August 28, 1963. "At 8 a.m., when rush-hour traffic is normally creeping bumper-to-bumper across the Virginia bridges and down the main boulevards from Maryland, the streets had the abandoned look of Sunday morning," Baker reported in his weekly column for the *New York Times*. Local authorities estimated that a majority of the 160,000 federal and city employees who worked nearby stayed home that day, while nearly half of local businesses were closed. Tourists also avoided the city, leaving twice the typical number of vacant rooms in local hotels. Businesses that did open suffered "hundreds of thousands of dollars" in losses, and normally bustling department stores "resembled a railroad station at 3 a.m." Even many taxicab drivers took the day off. "For the natives," Baker wrote, "this was obviously a day of siege and the streets were being left to the marchers."[22]

As Randolph had explained to President Kennedy a month earlier, the March on Washington was peaceful not because its participants were co-opted or naïve but rather because they were well-organized and "disciplined by struggle." From the start of the mobilization, Rustin, Robinson, and others in the national office took every precaution to ensure that marchers understood and complied with the principles of nonviolent protest. They sent detailed newsletters and organizing manuals to local organizing committees, explaining the goals and plans for the March and instructing them on the process for bringing supporters to Washington. Marchers were discouraged from travelling in private cars, and every chartered vehicle was required to have a captain who could keep track of passengers, explain the procedures of the demonstration, and take responsibility "for the welfare and discipline of their groups—on the road and in Washington." Local organizers were also required to report the name, address, and phone number of every marcher, along with the total number of vehicles departing from their city. The local organizing committee in Chicago, which was headed by NALC leader Timuel Black, asked train captains to comfort "demonstrators who appear lonely" and recruited banjo players, guitarists, and even a three-piece jazz combo to "combat boredom" during the eighteen-hour ride to Washington.[23]

Such procedures were particularly effective because they built on organizational networks that already linked most participants in the March. Cleveland Robinson arranged transportation for thousands of marchers through his union, which chartered three trains and eighteen buses and then assigned blocks of tickets to union members to sell in their workplaces and neighborhoods. The union provided each rider with a boxed lunch and supper, and hats and pins marked with the official logo of the March. Maida Springer's Garment Workers union chartered a sixteen-car train and eight buses to carry its members from New York, Newark, Philadelphia, Baltimore, and other cities. The union hired doctors and nurses to care for passengers and gave marchers a send-off in the Manhattan Center before a 6:30 A.M. departure from nearby Penn Station. Three hundred members of the United Church of Christ gathered for a midnight prayer service in midtown Manhattan before departing on eleven chartered buses for the nation's capital. Corrine Smith, the NALC activist who had coauthored Hedgeman's letter protesting women's exclusion from the speakers' list, organized a "Midnight Benefit Show" at the Apollo Theatre in Harlem. Lining up performances by Tony Bennett, Quincy Jones, "Little" Stevie Wonder, and other stars, she helped raise over $30,000 to send unemployed workers to the March. One journalist noted that buses converging on the capital were "full of heads covered with caps printed with their organizations' names." Other buses were decorated with red-white-and-blue signs reading "Erie, Pa., Branch, NAACP," "Inter-Church Delegation, Sponsored by the National Council of Churches of Christ in the U.S.A Commission on Religion and Race," and "District 26, United Steelworkers of America, Greater Youngstown AFL-CIO Council, Youngstown, Ohio."[24]

Even movie stars arrived in a well-organized contingent. Marlon Brando had formed a Hollywood committee to protest housing discrimination in Los Angeles. With support from the local CORE and NAACP branches, he invited Charlton Heston, Debbie Reynolds, and other actors to discuss further actions in his bungalow at Revue Studios. Heston hosted a second meeting, where they resolved to use their contacts to recruit other celebrities and pressure television studios to cover the March on Washington. Concerned that their fame would detract from serious engagement with the goals of the demonstration, they emphasized that they would march "as citizens" who "wish to be part" of what they viewed as a historic event. They also stressed that the demonstration was aimed at discrimination in the West and North, and not just in the South. Not all their co-workers agreed, and some released an unsigned letter urging stars not to join the March. "The event is unpredictable," stated the dissenters, warning that "the momentum generated by this colossal demonstration could open the floodgates to unprecedented violence and race riots later on." Over sixty performers joined Brando's Hollywood Committee, however, including Dean Martin, Judy Garland, Lorraine Hansberry, and Kirk Douglas. While most flew directly from Los Angeles, Sidney Poitier, Joanne Woodward, and Paul Newman headed east a few days early to appear at Corrine Smith's benefit at the Apollo.[25]

In addition to preparing marchers for the trip to Washington, sponsoring organizations provided infrastructure that was critical to keeping the demonstration orderly and effective. Anticipating that many marchers would overlook the organizing manual's instruction to pack two meals for the journey, Anna Hedgeman asked the National Council of Churches to organize three shifts of volunteers to prepare 80,000 box lunches and pack them into refrigerated trucks for sale at reduced price in Washington. She also persuaded New York mayor Robert Wagner, whom she had worked for in the 1950s, to declare an official city holiday on August 28 so that city employees could use their holiday time to attend the demonstration. Bayard Rustin convinced the Garment and Auto Workers unions to donate $20,000 for a state-of-the-art sound system so that marchers could hear the speeches from the Washington Monument, which was nearly a mile from the Lincoln Memorial. "We cannot maintain order where people cannot hear," he stated, explaining that "a classic resolution" to the problem of controlling a crowd was to "transform it into an audience." Rustin also recruited the Guardian Association, a fraternal organization of black police officers in New York City, to serve as "the Internal Security Force of the March on Washington for Jobs and Freedom." Reaching out to similar associations in New York, Connecticut, New Jersey, and Pennsylvania, Guardian president William H. Johnson recruited nearly 2,000 police, firefighters, and prison guards to meet buses, trains, and planes arriving in the capital, guide marchers to and from the demonstration, and "help maintain peaceful, nonviolent behavior by setting an example for others."[26]

The threat that some observers saw in the March on Washington stood in marked contrast to the jovial spirit that marchers brought with them to the nation's capital. "I feel good because the Negroes are on the march and nothing is going to stop us," yelled organizer George Johnson as he signaled the departure of twenty-four buses that CORE had arranged to carry nearly 1,000 passengers from New York City. Journalist Marlene Nadle recorded the scene in Harlem as marchers boarded the buses at two in the morning, noting that riders responded with "tongue-in-cheek parody" to Johnson's exasperated commands not to change buses or save seats and to write down emergency phone numbers in case they got lost in Washington. She climbed aboard with ten other CORE members, including James Peck, a white activist who had been beaten brutally in Birmingham, Alabama, and unemployed workers whose transport had been sponsored by CORE to demonstrate the need for jobs. There were also six Peace Corps volunteers who had joined the demonstration before leaving for an assignment in Nigeria. Once the bus departed, passengers got into heated debates ranging from the potential for passing Kennedy's civil rights bill and the impact of the Cold War on race relations to the sincerity of white participants in the movement. As tensions rose, one rider "cheerfully yelled, 'Everybody sing.'" Another responded: "You're nuts! At seven o'clock sane people don't even talk."[27]

As the CORE delegation approached Washington it joined an "unending caravan of buses" from New York and other cities. Police estimated that 1,500 chartered buses carried marchers to the capital that day, in addition to regularly scheduled routes. Organizers in New York City and Philadelphia reported that 400 buses came from each of those cities, carrying a combined total of nearly 60,000 marchers. Eleven came from North Carolina, ten from Boston, six from Alabama, four each from St. Louis and Atlanta, three each from Kansas City, Cleveland, Houston, and Jackson, Mississippi, and two each from New Orleans and Tulsa, Oklahoma. One bus drove all the way from San Francisco. Just after 8 A.M. the first of thirty-two chartered "Freedom Trains" arrived at Union Station, each of them carrying 1,000 people. Fourteen trains arrived from New York City. Another moved up the southern seaboard, starting in Tallahassee, Florida, and making stops at Brunswick and Savannah, Georgia, and Charleston, South Carolina. Two trains came from New Orleans, one from Detroit, and two from Chicago. *Time* magazine reported that the new arrivals looked "weary, bewildered and subdued" until their spirits were lifted by the Florida contingent, which "piled off the train singing the battle hymn of the

Negroes' 1963 revolution, *We Shall Overcome*." With trains arriving every eleven minutes, station employees encouraged marchers to move quickly to waiting shuttles or to begin the two-mile walk to the Washington Monument.[28]

The vast majority of marchers came by bus or train, but others arrived any way they could. Delegations walked from New York, Philadelphia, Baltimore, and as far away as Gadsden, Alabama. One man came on roller skates from Chicago, and another rode a bicycle from Los Angeles. As the CORE bus approached Washington, Marlene Nadle spied "a beat-up old cab with six people in it and March on Washington posters plastered on all its doors." Hundreds of marchers traveled by airplane. SNCC activist Eleanor Holmes took the first flight out of La Guardia Airport, after spending the night answering phones at the March headquarters in Harlem. Harry Belafonte and Marlon Brando arrived at National Airport with an interracial delegation of thirty "show business people" from Los Angeles, while Charlton Heston and Sidney Poitier flew with a group of luminaries from New York. Singer Josephine Baker, writer James Baldwin, and actor Burt Lancaster flew in from Paris with a petition signed by fifteen other Americans who supported the goals of the March. March organizers arranged for shuttles to meet them at the airport and deliver them to the National Mall.[29]

Some marchers headed for the Capitol to seek a meeting with their representatives, and a small group went to picket Attorney General Robert Kennedy at the Justice Department; but for the most part they were content to leave the formal lobbying to Randolph, King, and other representatives of the Big Ten organizations. Even the official leaders received a cold reception. Senator Everett Dirksen, an Illinois Republican whose support would be critical to overcoming resistance from southern Democrats, insisted that legislators had "a responsibility to render an independent judgment on these matters" and thus could not allow themselves to be swayed by demonstration. Minnesota

Democrat Hubert Humphrey, "one of the most enthusiastic" supporters of the March, agreed that it "probably hasn't changed any votes
on the civil rights bill," although he insisted that it was "a good thing
for Washington and the nation and the world." South Carolina senator
Strom Thurmond, who had vowed to lead a filibuster against Kennedy's bill, dismissed the demonstration as "totally unnecessary and
uncalled for," claiming that civil rights leaders had exaggerated the
extent of racial discrimination in the United States and "distorted in
the eyes of the whole world the view of freedom as it actually exists in
America." Most legislators simply ignored the delegation, saying they
were focused on passing a bill aimed at averting a strike by the five railway brotherhoods that, ironically, Randolph had spent the past forty
years battling over racial discrimination. March leaders attempted to
appear optimistic, telling the New York Times that they were "particularly encouraged" by the willingness of Congress to consider adding
a fair employment clause to Kennedy's civil rights bill, but only a few
lawmakers accepted their invitation to be introduced during the program at the Lincoln Memorial.[30]

By 9:30 A.M., 40,000 people had gathered at the base of the Washington Monument. Scattered groups sat on the grass or posed for pic-
tures "like tourists on a rare visit to the capital," while individuals
broke off to ride the elevators to the top of the monument and women
"concentrated on feeding babies." Russell Baker recognized black trade
unionist Peter Ottley, who led a union of hospital and nursing home
workers in New York City, holding a press conference with 100 union
members wearing yellow hats reading BSEIU. The union leader was
flanked by six young boys holding an American flag, a union flag, and
a long banner marked "Local 144." Smaller groups sang protest songs
or displayed signs, but Baker saw "no cohesion in the crowd." In the
distance, a loudspeaker summoned one marcher to claim his lost child
and asked for assistance locating singer Lena Horne, who was scheduled to perform at the Lincoln Memorial later in the day.[31]

Although a "fair grounds atmosphere prevailed," Baker noted that several southern delegations displayed "an uncharacteristic note of bitterness." Seventy-five SNCC activists huddled together wearing black armbands and singing "of the freedom fight in a sad melody." A fifteen-year-old boy explained that they were "mourning injustice in Danville," Virginia, where a few weeks earlier police had attacked nonviolent demonstrators with clubs and fire hoses before arresting their leaders on charges of "inciting the colored population to acts of violence and war against the white population." Protesters from Albany, Georgia, where a series of violent clashes between police and protesters had tested many SNCC activists' commitments to nonviolence, held placards listing casualties of the conflict: "Milton Wilkerson—20 stitches. Emanuel McClendon—3 stitches (Age 67). James Williams—broken leg." Another held a sign asking: "What is a state without justice but a robber band enlarged?" A group from Cambridge, Maryland, kneeled in prayer before rising to belt out a gospel hymn. "We know truly that we will—we shall—overcome—someday," declared a minister from the small town, just ninety miles from Washington, where the national guard had been called in repeatedly in the previous year to break up battles between police and protesters.[32]

The open resentment displayed by young southerners reflected a broader undercurrent of frustration among the marchers, from every region of the country, with the refusal of so many white Americans to support even the most modest steps toward racial equality. "I have no faith in the white man," stated the previously optimistic George Johnson soon after the CORE caravan left New York City, expressing skepticism that the March would result in passage of Kennedy's civil rights bill. Johnson supported CORE's use of nonviolent civil disobedience, but admitted, "as far as I'm concerned, anything done to get our rights is O.K." A teenager sitting near Johnson was not so averse to violence. "If this thing comes to violence, yours will be the first throat we slit," he shouted to a white Peace Corps volunteer on the bus, adding, "We don't need your kind." Conrad Lynn, who had grown increasingly critical of the civil rights movement since defending Robert Williams in 1959, handed out pamphlets calling for the creation of an all-black Freedom Now Party. "If our revolt means anything," a party activist declared, "it is our rejection and repudiation of the white liberals whom we have permitted for too long to dictate what we ask for, when, where, and how." The most cynical assessment came from Malcolm X, who told a reporter that he travelled to Washington but ended up watching the protest on television in a hotel room nearby.[33]

Writing in *Ebony* magazine a few months later, author Lerone Bennett chided journalists who "went away and wrote long articles on 'the remarkable sweetness' of the crowd, proving once again that they still do not understand Negroes or themselves." He may have read the story in *Newsweek*, which reported: "From the first, it was plain that the marchers were neither the rabble army that detractors had predicted nor the volatile mix that had even some friendly onlookers crossing their fingers," adding that the "careful months of planning by the 'Big Ten' command coalition of civil rights, church, and union leaders plainly had paid off in the cathedral solemnity on the mall." Perhaps Bennett was referring to *Time* magazine's claim that Nazi Party leader George Lincoln Rockwell stood across 15th Street from the Washington Monument with fifty followers muttering, "I can't stand niggers" and "I can't stand to hear *We Shall Overcome*" but, getting no response from marchers, "led his ridiculous group away from the vicinity in an agony of frustration." What such reports overlooked, according to Bennett, was the "wonderful two-tongued ambivalence" that characterized the crowd. "Many moods competed, but two dominated: a mood of quiet anger and buoyant exuberance. There was also a feeling of power and a certain surprise as though the people had discovered suddenly what they were and what they had."[34]

Journalists were so surprised by the orderly nature of the crowd that some delighted in pointing out that the "only breach in the marching orders" occurred when the March actually began. As protesters approached the Washington Monument they were greeted by women wearing white dresses and blue sashes, who asked them to sign pledge cards committing themselves "unequivocally and without regard to personal sacrifice, to the achievement of social peace through social justice." The ushers then directed marchers across Constitution Avenue to the Ellipse where, at 10 A.M., actor Ossie Davis began a preliminary program on a small stage in front of the White House. Announcing that police estimates now placed the crowd at over 90,000, Davis introduced folk singers Joan Baez, Odetta, Bob Dylan, Josh White, Peter, Paul and Mary, and the SNCC Freedom Singers. Between songs, Davis acknowledged celebrities and movement heroes including actress Lena Horne, Rosa Parks, Socialist Party leader Norman Thomas, and Bayard Rustin, who received the most enthusiastic applause of the day so far. Because the stage was close to the ground, Rustin had recruited a contingent of NALC activists to form a barrier to protect performers from the crowd. He later asked the trade unionists to go reserve seats for congressmen and other "honored guests" at the Lincoln Memorial, but as they departed he noticed that others were following them with the hope of getting a good seat for themselves. "My God, they're going," Rustin cried, as he rounded up Randolph, King, and other official leaders who had just returned from their meeting in Congress. "We're supposed to be leading them." A contingent of Guardians succeeded in slowing the March and creating space for the Big Ten to walk arm in arm behind a truck carrying television cameras, but the leadership was still surrounded by "oceans of bobbing placards." One of King's staffers remarked, "A revolution is *supposed* to be unpredictable."[35]

With its chaotic start, the March displayed the full spectrum of emotions that protesters brought with them to the nation's capital. "Some marchers wept as they walked," *Time* magazine reported, adding that "the faces of many more gleamed with happiness." A group of young people from Louisiana danced the entire way. Organizers had attempted to control the message by asking protesters to carry signs that either identified a sponsoring group or stated an official slogan, but they were only partially successful. "What's after college for me?" asked a sign carried by a ten-year-old boy, whose cousin wore a sandwich board reading: "Must we wait 100 or 200 more years for equality?" Several groups guided coffins symbolizing the death of Jim Crow. Even the official signs displayed a wide array of concerns: "An End to Bias," "Jobs for All," "Integrated Schools," "Decent Housing," "Voting Rights," "Higher Minimum Wage Coverage for All Workers," "An FEPC Law"—all punctuated with a bright red "NOW!" Organizational signs displayed the remarkable breadth of support for the mobilization: "I.U.E. AFL-CIO for Full Employment," "Southern Christian Leadership Conference of Danville, Va.," "Emma Lazarus Federation of Jewish Women's Clubs," and "Detroit Catholics for Equality and Freedom." In what may have been an impromptu protest against their exclusion from the Big Ten, Daisy Bates, Rosa Parks, and three other women led a group of marchers across the Mall and down Independence Avenue while the male leaders walked directly down Constitution Avenue toward the Lincoln Memorial. Anna Arnold Hedgeman walked with two members of her staff from the National Council for a Permanent FEPC. E. Pauline Myers, who had headed the March on Washington Movement two decades earlier, marched until she collapsed from exhaustion and was forced to watch the rest on television from a friend's house nearby.[36]

Having swelled to more than 200,000, the two streams of the March converged into a broad semicircle around the base of the Lincoln Memorial and pushed back on both sides of the Reflecting Pool and all the way back to the Washington Monument. Waiting nearly an hour and a half for the marchers to travel less than a mile, journalists and radio and television crews interviewed public officials and celebrities who gathered on the steps leading up to the temple containing the massive statue of Abraham Lincoln. New York mayor Robert Wagner walked down the steps while Jackie Robinson, who had integrated major league baseball two decades earlier, found a seat with his teenage son, David. Inside the memorial, journalists lined up for interviews with Harry Belafonte, Charlton Heston, and Burt Lancaster. Ossie Davis reclaimed the microphone and began introducing the celebrities to the crowd. Alabama civil rights leaders Fred Shuttlesworth and Ralph Abernathy brought greetings from "down in Egypt Land." "We are determined in the South and in America today to say to the pharaohs to let God's people go free," Abernathy said to loud applause. Singer Josephine Baker, who had vowed never to return to the United States after being denied service in a New York nightclub, said, "I'm glad that in my homeland where I was born in love and respect, I'm glad to see this day come to pass." Sociologist Ralph Bunche, who had helped A. Philip Randolph form the National Negro Congress in the 1930s and currently worked as a diplomat for the United Nations, called the March "one of the truest and finest expressions of American democracy at work." Harry Belafonte and Burt Lancaster read statements from their respective groups, in Hollywood and Paris, and comedian Dick Gregory joked that the last time he had seen so many black people was in a Birmingham jail. Their remarks were interspersed with performances by Joan Baez, Bob Dylan, and the other folk singers.[37]

It was nearly 2:00 P.M., and marchers were fading in the summer heat. Some sought shelter under the trees or wandered off to "walk dreamily in the sun," but they were drawn back to attention by the arrival of Randolph, King, and the other leaders of the Big Ten organizations. Ossie Davis asked people at the back of the crowd to stop pushing forward, as those in front were getting crushed. Red Cross volunteers distributed ice cubes and started carrying away people who had been overwhelmed by the heat. Nevertheless, marchers leapt to their feet and cheered as Randolph came to the podium and introduced opera singer Camilla Williams to sing the "Star-Spangled Banner." After an invocation by Reverend Patrick O'Boyle, the archbishop of Washington, D.C., Randolph came back to the microphone and, looking out over the sprawling crowd with obvious pride, declared: "We are gathered here today for the largest demonstration in the history of this nation. Let the nation and the world know the meaning of our numbers." Addressing those who dismissed the marchers as "a pressure group" or "a mob," he declared: "We are the advance guard of a massive moral revolution for jobs and freedom." Trained in the speaking style of a pretelevision era, Randolph appeared as if he were conserving his energy for a two-hour speech before a union convention. Marchers responded with polite applause, showing their fatigue and, perhaps, taken aback by Randolph's moderate tone and what one journalist called his "perfect Oxford diction."[38]

Despite his awkward start, Randolph won over the crowd with the boldness of his message. Emphasizing that the "civil rights revolution" was "not confined to the Negro," or even "to civil rights," the labor leader insisted that "we know that we have no future in a society in which six million black and white people are unemployed and millions more live in poverty." He clarified that while the March demanded federal laws guaranteeing access to public accommodations, an end to employment discrimination, and "integrated public schools," those victories would be insufficient without measures to ensure that people could afford those accommodations, that jobs were not destroyed by "profit-geared automation," and that schools were properly funded. Randolph spoke quickly, giving the crowd little time to digest ideas that he had contemplated over a lifetime; but he got their attention when he cited a concrete example of the philosophical and institutional changes that he had in mind. "For one thing we must destroy the notion that Mrs. Murphy's property rights include the right to humiliate me because of the color of my skin," he stated in reference to the hypothetical homeowner who, conservatives claimed, would be forced by Kennedy's civil rights bill to rent a room to any stranger who wanted to live in her house. For the first time in his speech Randolph had to pause while the applause subsided. Then he declared: "The sanctity of private property takes second place to the sanctity of the human personality."[39]

Drawing on decades of experience as a Socialist and union president, Randolph placed that specific example in the context of a broad vision of American history. Tracing the origins of the contemporary struggle to the cultural legacy of slavery, he argued that African Americans had a particular interest in reasserting "this priority of values because our ancestors were transformed from human personalities into private property." As "the worst victims of unemployment," the labor leader contended, "it falls to us to demand new forms of social planning, to create full employment, and to put automation at the service of human needs." History had placed African Americans "in the forefront of today's movement for social and racial justice, because we know we cannot expect the realization of our aspirations through the same old anti-democratic social institutions and philosophies that have all along frustrated our aspirations." But as he had since his days stumping for Eugene V. Debs nearly half a century earlier in Harlem, Randolph insisted that African Americans were not the only ones with a stake in that revolution. "The March on Washington is not the climax of our struggle," he declared, "but a new beginning not only for the Negro but for all Americans who thirst for freedom and a better life."[40]

By that point Randolph was losing his energy, faltering at times and repeating his words, but the audience roared with approval when he defended the tactic of mass mobilization. "The plain and simple fact is that until we went into the streets the federal government was indifferent to our demands," he observed, crediting demonstrations and civil disobedience in the South as well as picketing of discriminatory employers in the North with forcing Congress to finally consider civil rights legislation. "Those who deplore our militance, who exhort patience in the name of a false peace, are in fact supporting segregation and exploitation," he charged. "They would have social peace at the expense of social and racial justice. They are more concerned with easing racial tension than enforcing racial democracy." Pointing out that Kennedy's civil rights bill was opposed by the same "coalition of Dixiecrats and reactionary Republicans" that had opposed Medicare, Social Security, minimum wage laws, and federal funding for education, he insisted that mass protests would continue in Washington and across the country "until total freedom is ours." Lacking the energy to emphasize his final sentences, Randolph received only scattered applause from an audience that seemed unsure whether his speech had come to an end.[41]

His uneven delivery notwithstanding, Randolph set a militant tone that would resonate throughout the afternoon. After a brief pause, he announced the arrival of 150 "outstanding members of the House and Senate" who walked down the steps of the Lincoln Memorial. While some protesters clapped and cheered, a rhythmic chant of "pass the bill, pass the bill, pass the bill" started in the front of the crowd and "rolled back, rank by rank, through the massed thousands." A similarly bois-terous applause greeted Bayard Rustin, whom Randolph introduced as the "executive director of the Committee of the March on Wash-ington, the man who organized this whole thing," and Rosa Parks, who was introduced "almost casually," according to Anna Hedge-man. Bob Dylan received a tepid response when he performed a new ballad about Byron De La Beckwith, the white supremacist who had been arrested for shooting Medgar Evers two months earlier. Scattered applause suggested that few marchers appreciated the raw cynicism of "Only a Pawn in Their Game," which asserted that De La Beckwith "can't be blamed" for the murder because he was "a poor white man" who was manipulated by race-baiting politicians and an unjust social system. The crowd burst into applause, however, when Daisy Bates pledged the support of "the women of this country" and gave awards to SNCC activists Diane Nash Bevel and Gloria Richardson, Ms. Her-bert Lee, whose husband had been murdered for attempting to vote in Mississippi, Mrs. Medgar Evers, and Rosa Parks.[42]

Randolph seemed genuinely appreciative of the women, but also anxious to move on to the other speeches. Eugene Blake, of the National Council of Churches, spoke first, followed by opera singer Marian Anderson, who had been scheduled to sing the national anthem but got caught in traffic and arrived too late. Few knew it at the time, but the next speech had been the subject of intense debate among March leaders over the previous twenty-four hours. The previous evening, SNCC activists had circulated a draft of the address that their chairman, John Lewis, planned to deliver at the March on Washington. Drafted in collaboration with several leaders of the group and Rustin's aide Tom Kahn, the text captured the spirit of young radicals who had been risking their lives on the front lines of struggle in Mississippi, Alabama, and other southern states. Denouncing Kennedy's civil rights bill as "too little, and too late," Lewis planned to point out that it did nothing to "protect our people from police brutality," to protect the right to vote, or to "insure the equality of a maid who earns $5 a week in the home of a family whose income is $100,000 a year." Lewis' speech echoed Randolph's reference to a "civil rights revolution," which the elderly trade unionist had used repeatedly in his speeches to the NALC and other groups. "The revolution is at hand," Lewis planned to say, "and we must free ourselves of the chains of political and economic slavery." But it also employed a violent imagery that Randolph had always insisted was counterproductive to social transformation. "We will march through the South, through the heart of Dixie, the way Sherman did," the SNCC document read, referring to the Union general who had burned cities and destroyed crops in Georgia at the end of the Civil War. "We shall pursue our own 'scorched earth' policy and burn Jim Crow to the ground," the text read, adding that all this would be done "non-violently."[43]

Randolph had spent much of the previous twenty-four hours mediating between Lewis and other leaders of the March about the SNCC speech. He dismissed Cardinal Patrick O'Boyle's complaints about "communist" language such as "revolution" and masses," stating, "I've used them many times myself." Randolph took more seriously the objections of Walter Reuther and others who argued that such harsh criticism would make it impossible to strengthen and pass Kennedy's civil rights bill, which, even with its flaws, remained one of the mobilization's central objectives. Randolph also agreed with Rustin and King that SNCC's references to violence, even as metaphor, violated the spirit of Gandhian nonviolence that had defined the March on Washington Movement since the 1940s. Rustin and Lewis worked through much of the night discussing alternatives, and Randolph convinced the SNCC leader to accept them. "I've waited all my *life* for this opportunity," Lewis recalled the aged radical pleading, nearly in tears; "please don't ruin it." The incident was seen by some as further evidence that white liberals had co-opted the March, but, after dropping explicit references to violence and agreeing to support Kennedy's bill with "great reservations," Lewis and other SNCC activists felt "our message was not compromised." He still reminded marchers that they were "involved in a serious social revolution," and denounced a political system based on "immoral compromise" and dominated by "political, economic and social exploitation." Newspapers and magazines carried detailed accounts of the debate, even comparing passages from both versions of the speech, so the controversy drew far more attention than Lewis might otherwise have received. "He finally gave in," *Time* magazine reported, "but not much."[44]

What was most remarkable about Lewis' message was how consistent it was with the other speeches that day—not just Randolph's but also those of the more moderate leaders who followed Lewis to the microphone. "I am here today with you because with you I share the view that the struggle for civil rights and the struggle for equal opportunity is not the struggle of Negro Americans but the struggle for every American to join in," white union leader Walter Reuther declared, echoing Randolph's appeal for an interracial struggle for both racial and economic justice. While he called Kennedy's civil rights bill "the first meaningful step," Reuther reiterated Lewis' complaint that it did not go far enough. "The job question is crucial," he insisted, "because we will not solve education or housing or public accommodations as long as millions of American Negroes are treated as second-class economic citizens and denied jobs." Like the others, Reuther viewed the March on Washington as the beginning of a nationwide mobilization for "freedom and justice and equality and first-class citizenship for every American, not just for certain Americans, not only in certain parts of America, but in every part of America, from Boston to Birmingham, from New York to New Orleans, and from Michigan to Mississippi."[45]

Representatives of CORE, the Urban League, and NAACP leveled similar critiques at the civil rights bill, drew the same linkages between racial equality and economic justice, and echoed Randolph, Lewis, and Reuther's vision of an interracial and nationwide movement. CORE chairman Floyd McKissick read a letter from his colleague James Farmer, who had been scheduled to speak at the March but refused to post bail after he and 200 other activists were jailed for protesting segregation in Louisiana. "We will not come off of the streets until we can work at a job befitting of our skills in any place in the land," McKissick read. "We will not stop our marching feet until our kids have enough to eat and their minds can study a wide range without being cramped in Jim Crow schools." Urban League director Whitney Young urged marchers to help transform "the rat-infested, overcrowded ghettos" into "decent, wholesome, unrestricted residential areas," to address racial disparities in infant mortality and life expectancy, and to integrate and provide funding to "congested, ill-equipped schools which breed dropouts and which smother motivation." Roy Wilkins leveled a scathing attack at the White House, asking how it was possible that the United States government could not protect civil rights activists from being "beaten and kicked and maltreated and shot and killed by local and state law enforcement officers" and calling Kennedy's civil rights proposals "so moderate an approach that if it is weakened or eliminated, the remainder will be little more than sugar water." Demanding that Congress take up an FEPC bill as well, the NAACP leader declared: "We want employment and with it we want the pride and responsibility and self-respect that goes along with jobs."[46]

By the time Martin Luther King came to the stage, he may have felt that the other speakers had focused too much on specifics, whether social or political. It was nearly 4:00 P.M., and some marchers had already been forced to head back to Union Station so they would not miss their train home. Gospel singer Mahalia Jackson warmed up the crowd by singing the defiant spiritual "I've been 'buked and I've been scorned," which King had requested, and when Randolph introduced the young minister he got only as far as "the leader of the moral revolution" before the crowd erupted into applause for the man who was already recognized as the movement's most powerful speaker. King began with a scripted speech that emphasized the links between economic justice and racial equality, albeit more poetically than others, that had dominated the afternoon. "In a sense we've come to our nation's capital to cash a check," he stated, pointing out that 100 years after Lincoln had freed the slaves their descendants were "still sadly crippled by the manacles of segregation and the chains of discrimination," and restricted to "a lonely island of poverty in the midst of a vast ocean of material prosperity."[47]

King continued along the same themes as the other speakers—denouncing those who called for patience, emphasizing the national scope of the problem, and urging marchers to return home "knowing that somehow this situation can and will be changed." Halfway into the prepared text, however, he pushed his notes aside and delivered an improvised version of the "I Have a Dream" refrain that he had pioneered at the AFL-CIO convention in 1961 and elaborated in several settings before delivering it at the Detroit "Walk to Freedom" a month earlier. Mahalia Jackson was heard shouting from behind him, "Tell them about the dream, Martin," although it is not clear whether he heard her. Whatever his inspiration for the shift, it provided King with an ideal ending for the most important speech of his career. "So even though we face the difficulties of today and tomorrow," he stated sternly, "I still have a dream. It is a dream deeply rooted in the American dream. I have a dream that one day this nation will rise up and live out the meaning of its creed: We hold these truths to be self-evident, that all men are created equal." The audience roared.[48]

King's "I Have a Dream" speech is justifiably remembered as the most powerful and effective address given at the March on Washington; but, taken out of context and often viewed as the only speech, it was the least representative or attentive to the specific goals and demands of the mobilization. Writing in the *New York Times*, journalist E. W. Kenworthy noted that while the other speakers "concentrated on the struggle ahead and spoke in tough, even harsh language . . . paradoxically it was Dr. King—who had suffered perhaps most of all—who ignited the crowd" with a utopian vision of the future. Looking to a day when "the sons of former slaves and the sons of former slave-owners will be able to sit down together at the table of brotherhood" and expressing a messianic confidence that "the rough places will be made plain, and the crooked places will be made straight and the glory of the Lord shall be revealed," the preacher delivered a much-needed respite to marchers who had endured a long day of intense political engagement. Ending with a picture of "that day when all of God's children—black men and white men, Jews and Gentiles, Protestants and Catholics—will be able to join hands and sing in the words of the old Negro spiritual, 'Free at last, free at last, thank God Almighty, we are free at last,' " King emanated an infectious optimism that brought even the most hardened and cynical SNCC activists to their feet, "laughing, shouting, slapping palms, hugging," and wiping tears from their eyes.[49]

After several minutes of roaring applause, Bayard Rustin returned to the podium and refocused the crowd on the specific tasks ahead. "The moment in that afternoon which most strained belief," according to journalist Murray Kempton, was the sight of the "radical pacifist" reciting the official demands of the March while "every television camera at the disposal of the networks was upon him." A. Philip Randolph followed Rustin to the stage and led the crowd in a mass pledge to "join and support all actions undertaken in good faith in accord with the time-honored democratic tradition of non-violent protest, of peaceful assembly and petition, and of redress through the courts and the legislative process." Each marcher vowed to "carry the message of the march to my friends and neighbors back home and to arouse them to an equal commitment and an equal effort," to march, write letters, demonstrate and vote, and "work to make sure that my voice and those of my brothers ring clear and determined from every corner of our land." Restating the pledge that ushers had asked them to sign as they arrived at the Washington Monument, protesters dedicated their hearts, minds, and bodies, "unequivocally and without regard to personal sacrifice, to the achievement of social peace through social justice." Close to 5:00 P.M., the March ended with a benediction led by Benjamin Mays, Martin Luther King's mentor from Morehouse College.[50]

Exhausted, marchers boarded shuttles or began walking back to buses, trains, planes, and cars. Bayard Rustin's sound system blasted "We Shall Overcome" from an organ at the Lincoln Memorial, but most marchers were too tired to sing along. Cleve Howell, a forty-year-old butcher from the Bronx, settled on the lawn outside Union Station to wait for his train. Gesturing toward the Capitol across the street, he remarked: "I hope those guys over there got the message." A white union leader from Pennsylvania insisted that the impact of the March had already been felt by those who joined it. "We came here with about fifty members," he told a reporter, "and I'm not sure most of them were awakened to the real issue until we started to march and sing." Marlene Nadle boarded the CORE bus with other passengers from Harlem, and, as they drove slowly toward the highway, black Washingtonians stood on their doorsteps raising their "fingers in a victory sign," clasping their hands "over their heads in the prizefighter's traditional gesture," or simply clapping, cheering, and smiling. "We'll be back," the bus captain remarked. "If this doesn't work, we'll bring 500,000, and if that doesn't work, we'll bring all 20 million." By sundown the National Mall was deserted, save for the team of 400 city employees charged with picking up garbage, dismantling stages, and hauling away the portable toilets. Rustin had offered to recruit volunteers to do this, but city officials seemed eager to get the crowds out of town. Organizers of the March were happy to oblige. "We've got to get back home and finish the job of the revolution," CORE chairman Floyd McKissick declared as he left the Lincoln Memorial.[51]

McKissick in fact had one final duty to perform before leaving Washington, and, with Randolph, Rustin, King, and other March leaders he climbed into a shuttle for the short ride up Constitution Avenue to the White House. President Kennedy congratulated them for keeping order and sending a clear message to Congress but, in his excitement, seems to have forgotten that his guests had been working since early that morning. "Mr. President, I wonder if I could have just a glass of milk," Randolph asked politely, and Kennedy sent for sandwiches and refreshments before they settled into a sixty-minute conference with Vice-President Lyndon Johnson, the secretary of labor, and the head of the Civil Rights Division of the Department of Justice. Afterward Kennedy joined the March leaders for a press conference on the White House lawn, where he vowed to continue his work toward "translating civil rights from principles into practices," and promised to expand that struggle to ensure "increased employment and to eliminate discrimination in employment practices, two of the prime goals of the march." Echoing Randolph's insistence that such policies would benefit

Americans of all races, Kennedy declared that the March on Washington had advanced the cause of 20 million African Americans, "but even more significant is the contribution to all mankind." Randolph concurred, expressing confidence that Congress would not only pass Kennedy's pending civil rights bill but a Fair Employment Practices Act as well. Celebrating "one of the biggest, most creative and constructive demonstrations ever held in the history of our nation," he called it an achievement of which "every American could be proud."[52]

CHAPTER SIX

BATTLE LINES DRAWN

I N PROJECTING A sympathetic image of the civil rights movement, the March on Washington was an unmitigated success. In stark contrast to the predictions of violence before the March, positive reports of the protest filled airwaves and print media in the hours and days following August 28, 1963. Even southern newspapers gave gave "extensive coverage and prominent display" to the demonstration and, although five of the region's eighteen largest newspapers "expressed disapproval of the march or its goals or both," the remainder either "praised the marchers for their orderliness" or "carried no comment." The nation's three major television networks broadcast the entire event live, aired recorded footage in the late afternoon, and carried extensive commentary during the evening news. The A. C. Nielsen Company reported a nearly 50 percent jump in television viewership over the same time period a week before. Telstar communications satellites, which had been launched into orbit just a year before, transmitted footage of the protest to Europe. Russian television stations cancelled the broadcast at the last minute, leading American journalists to speculate that Soviet authorities had hoped to show scenes of violence and police repression; but detailed reports of the demonstration were still broadcast throughout the Soviet bloc. "If any viewers turned to the march with the thought that there might be violence or disorder, they were disappointed," the *New York Times* reported. "No television show has ever been less violent."[1]

Celebrating the peaceful, interracial, and patriotic nature of the protest, journalists and others were optimistic that their reporting would ensure the realization of the March on Washington's demands. "More significant than the immediate effect the Washington civil rights march would have on the Congress of the U.S., more remarkable than the spectacle itself, was the Negroes' orderly demonstration of their potential as a moral force," read an issue of *Life* magazine that was devoted almost entirely to photographs of marchers. Michigan senator Philip A. Hart, who previously had expressed doubts that the demonstration would aid passage of Kennedy's civil rights bill, conceded that "if the spirit captured by news stories and television is correct, it could produce increased public awareness and public support" and "in turn could produce support in Congress." Like many observers, *Atlanta Constitution* editor Eugene Patterson identified Martin Luther King's "I Have a Dream" speech as the clearest and most effective expression of this "new vision of the Negro's destiny in America." Impressed by the "tremendously positive and upbeat" tone of King's address, Patterson suggested that many white Americans shared the view of a white airline stewardess whom he met on the flight home to Georgia. "I haven't been for this civil rights stuff and I've never liked King," she told him, "but I watched him on TV, and after it was over I was proud of the Negro and proud of America. I'd thought they were just going to criticize us white people. He made my country seem so beautiful I felt like I wanted to shake his hand."[2]

King and other participants in the March were not so confident that their message had been heard. "This demonstration, I am certain, has already done a great deal to create a coalition of concern about the status of civil rights in this country," the minister told an interviewer at the Lincoln Memorial. When pressed as to whether the mobilization had "changed the mind of one bigot," however, he admitted that this was not clear. King's skepticism was confirmed by isolated acts of violence against marchers as they made their way home from the nation's capital. Six buses were pelted with stones while they passed through Baltimore the evening following the protest, and the window of a bus from Philadelphia was shattered by a bullet. Later that night, "nightriders" surrounded the home of a minister who had led a large delegation of marchers from Lynchburg, Virginia, and smashed his windows with stones. The worst attack occurred early the next morning, when two marchers got off a bus in Meridian, Mississippi. After ordering breakfast at a lunch counter in the bus station, the black men were surrounded by a mob of white men who dragged them outside and beat them mercilessly while police officers stood by and watched. "Our people were returning from a tremendous affirmation of faith in democracy and received wonderful treatment in the nation's capital," the Mississippi NAACP wrote in a protest to the Interstate Commerce Commission, "only to return to harassment, intimidation and unjust treatment contrary to ICC regulations in their home state."[3]

Direct attacks on marchers were sporadic and restricted primarily to the South, but they reflected a broader undercurrent of opposition toward the March on Washington and its objectives. *Newsweek* magazine closed its otherwise positive coverage of the demonstration with the story of Horace and Sara Baker, a young black couple who were prevented from moving into a six-room row house in suburban Philadelphia the day after the protest. Greeted by "a howling, bottle-tossing, egg-slinging mob," the Bakers relented and returned to their apartment in "the Negro ghetto in the City of Brotherly Love." The following day the couple returned under the protection of sixty police officers and local civil rights leaders but found that vandals had smashed the windows, torn out the plumbing and furnace, and painted "Nigger's house" across the front of their new home. Five hundred people circled the house shouting and throwing eggs, rocks, and at least one homemade bomb as police guided the couple into the basement, where they spent the night. An "uneasy calm" prevailed the following day, while 100 state police patrolled the neighborhood. "Under the law, no one can refuse to deal with anyone else because of race or religion in this state," a defiant Mr. Baker told a reporter. "We have no malice toward those who damaged the house. All we desire is to show goodwill toward others and for that goodwill to be returned toward us." A few months later, Horace Baker was hospitalized for a nervous breakdown, and after three years of "constant harassment" the couple moved back to the city. In startling counterpoint to images of the interracial crowd gathering peacefully in the nation's capital, *Newsweek* printed a photograph of neighborhood boys, "barely in their teens," chanting "Two-four-six-eight, we don't want to integrate" as they circled the Bakers' car with belts wrapped around their fists.[4]

Aware that sympathetic images alone would not by themselves change the minds of people like the Bakers' new neighbors, A. Philip Randolph and other leaders of the March insisted that success for the movement depended on their ability to strengthen and expand the coalition that had helped them build the demonstration in the first place. "We need allies," Randolph stated the day after the protest, explaining that while "people who are victims must take the leadership" in struggles for equality, "the Negro cannot win the fight alone, no more than the Jew or labor leader could" defeat anti-Semitism and exploitation without support from others. Writing in the *New York Times*, journalist James Reston observed: "The first significant test of the Negro march on Washington will come in the churches and synagogues of the country this weekend," when white ministers and rabbis would have an opportunity to impress on their flocks the moral urgency of the fight for racial equality. "If the preachers said what they really thought about this racial crisis and even half of those who heard and believed them wrote their honest convictions for or against racial equality to Capitol Hill, the political balance on racial equality might easily be transformed," Reston claimed. "If, however, the churches do not react and the march on Washington is regarded by the religious community as just another TV show, the political battle for civil rights could easily be worse off than before."[5]

As with the March on Washington Movement, the first concrete actions to strengthen the March on Washington coalition were initiated by women who had been excluded from the official leadership of the protest. Defying Bayard Rustin's request that sponsoring groups refrain from holding meetings in Washington before or after the March, the National Council of Negro Women invited representatives of the National Council of Jewish Women, the National Council of Catholic Women, and the National Association of Colored Women's Clubs to address the question "After the March, What?" at a two-day conference starting the morning of August 29. In addition to a "Write for Rights" campaign aimed at increasing support for Kennedy's civil rights bill and a boycott of products made by discriminatory employers, the interracial gathering created a Community Caravan to "help local communities assess their specific needs and utilize existing resources to meet them more effectively" and a Youth Emergency Fund to "aid youthful leaders in non-violent demonstrations for civil rights." They also planned to reconvene at a Leadership Conference in November, where attorney and former March on Washington Movement organizer Pauli Murray was invited to address the legal basis of demands for equality between women and men. "Over and above the planned agenda, women talked freely of their concern about women's participation," NCNW president Dorothy Height recalled, noting that "women became much more aggressive in facing up to sexism in our dealings with the male leadership in the movement."[6]

Male leaders also reached out to allies on the day after the March, although they displayed less urgency than the women. Randolph and King addressed a Socialist Party conference in Washington, along with CORE chairman Floyd McKissick and John Lewis of SNCC, announcing that leaders of the March would meet within two weeks to plan a nationwide campaign aimed at strengthening and passing Kennedy's civil rights bill. "We will need to continue demonstrations," Randolph told the mostly white audience, explaining: "You can't move Senators and Congressmen just because a measure is right. There has to be pressure." King and the others expressed support for Randolph's plan, but stated that each of their individual groups would also launch separate campaigns. King's SCLC was considering a direct action campaign in Alabama or Virginia, while SNCC hoped to mobilize "hundreds of students" to protest the slow pace of desegregation in "such relatively progressive Southern cities as Atlanta, Nashville and Durham," North Carolina. CORE had no specific plans of its own, but McKissick urged the Socialists to volunteer "to work in the South, where you are needed." Meanwhile leaders of the NAACP and Urban League distanced themselves from both Randolph and King, insisting on the need to focus on registering voters and lobbying Congress to pass the civil rights bill. King explained: "There is a need for all these organizations, a need for a diversified approach."[7]

Both the strengths and limitations of the March on Washington coalition were demonstrated by a Labor Day parade organized by the Central Labor Council of New York the Monday after the protest. Nearly 20 percent of the participants in the March on Washington had come from New York City, a significant portion of them in delegations representing unions affiliated with the Labor Council, and union leaders emphasized their agreement with the goals of the March on Washington by organizing their Labor Day celebration around the theme of "full employment and equal opportunity." More than 100,000 union members walked in the parade, while 700,000 supporters came out to cheer them on from the sidewalks. Not all union leaders were pleased with the show of support for the civil rights movement, however; and leaders of the powerful Building Trades and Construction Council announced that they were boycotting the parade out of frustration with the Central Labor Council's failure to support them in disputes with civil rights groups. The leader of one building trades union explained that he did not expect the council to defend him from charges of discriminating against black workers, but felt that labor leaders had gone "overboard the other way." Despite the impressive showing from garment, retail, and health care unions that had supported the March on Washington, organizers admitted that the size of the parade was only half of what it had been in previous years.[8]

Conflict among union leaders in New York City had direct implications for efforts to realize the March on Washington's agenda. Impressed by the size and discipline of the civil rights demonstration, which may have been the largest gathering of union members in U.S. history, AFL-CIO president George Meany placed the full weight of his office behind efforts to add a fair employment clause to Kennedy's civil rights bill. "While all parts of [the law] are extremely important in the crusade for equality, none is more important than FEPC," Meany wrote to all members of the House Judiciary Committee, explaining that "without equal opportunity for employment, minority groups will find themselves unable to enjoy many of the other opportunities we seek to guarantee them." The union leader toned down that rhetoric, however, as he prepared to greet the parade in New York City, where he had begun his career as a plumber and leader of the Building Trades Council. "Joblessness aggravates race discrimination and race discrimination weakens the economy," he explained, suggesting that federal authorities should prioritize tax cuts aimed at expanding the economy over civil rights laws that would ensure African Americans equal access to jobs and services. Meany reiterated that point in his official Labor Day speech, stating his support for Kennedy's civil rights bill but making it clear that "until the nation can solve unemployment, it cannot deal effectively with the struggle for civil rights and equal job opportunity."[9]

For A. Philip Randolph and other black trade unionists, the ambivalence of white union leaders reinforced the need to sustain a broad

coalition that could link struggles for racial equality and economic justice. "Only the unity of the civil rights organizations and their white
allies could have produced that spectacular success," Bayard Rustin
wrote to leaders of the Big Ten in a detailed evaluation of the March
on Washington. Frustrated that news reports of the demonstration had
often overlooked the specific demands of the protest, particularly those
related to economic reform, Randolph and Rustin proposed to remind
the public of their agenda by organizing a series of smaller demonstrations in cities across the country. Anticipating that conservatives would
filibuster Kennedy's civil rights bill once it was introduced to Congress,
they also called for a "People's Congress" that would bring marchers
back to Washington for public hearings on the need for civil rights
legislation. "The civil rights movement has now to face the fact that
it has to go deeper into the economic and social questions," Bayard
Rustin wrote soon after the Labor Day parade. "What is required now
is an alliance between the trade union movement and the civil rights
movement and the unemployed to face this problem of jobs directly."[10]

The coalition strategy was strained by increasing evidence that large
numbers of whites, even in relatively liberal northern cities, rejected
the most basic demands for racial equality. Two weeks after the March
on Washington, the City Council of Chicago passed an ordinance barring racial discrimination in the sales, rental, or financing of housing.
While most city officials celebrated the law, over 4,000 white home-
owners marched on City Hall waving signs asking: "Is My House My
Castle?" and chanting: "I'll pick my own neighbors; I'll sell to whom
I choose." Mostly housewives, "pushing infants in strollers or leading
older children by hand," the protesters circulated petitions demanding
that the law be subjected to a statewide referendum, a move that the
leader of the Chicago Urban League predicted would result in its rejection. Mathew Ahmann, who had spoken on behalf of Catholics at the
March on Washington, warned that similar campaigns were mounting
against open housing laws in Michigan and California. A survey of

white northerners conducted by the *Saturday Evening Post* revealed that most believed a homeowner should have the right to discriminate against potential buyers or tenants on the basis of their race. The same study found that a majority of white northerners believed that African Americans were already treated "around right" and that "a surprising 16 per cent of the people interviewed were convinced that whites are innately superior to Negroes." On the basis of those results, the pollsters concluded: "The white North is no more ready to accept genuine integration and real racial equality than the deep South."[11]

Equally disturbing were signs that Kennedy's support for a moderate civil rights law was damaging his prospects for reelection in 1964. The president's approval ratings had dipped following the announcement of his civil rights bill in June, and they dropped sharply after he endorsed the March on Washington in August, reaching their lowest point since his election in 1960. Attorney General Robert Kennedy conceded that support for civil rights legislation was "having an adverse political effect on his brother's chances of re-election in the North as well as the South," although he insisted that his brother's proposal was "a necessary step" for moving the country beyond racial conflict. The biggest beneficiary of that backlash was Arizona senator Barry Goldwater, who made opposition to the civil rights bill a central feature of his bid for the Republican nomination for president. While Kennedy retained a comfortable lead in the general election, polls showed Goldwater well ahead of his more moderate opponent in the Republican primary and beating the president by ten percentage points in the South. "The civil rights issue has already materially affected the political situation in the South and may have an important effect on the views of Northern white voters in the month ahead," the *Los Angeles Times* reported two weeks after the March on Washington, noting that three-quarters of white southerners and half of white northerners said that the Kennedy administration was "pushing integration too fast."[12]

As was often the case, events in Alabama revealed the full intensity of the racist backlash that rumbled across the United States in the wake of the March on Washington. In the first week of September, NAACP attorneys secured a federal court order requiring public schools in the state to admit students regardless of their race. Governor George Wallace ordered state troopers to keep black students out of white schools, as he had with the University of Alabama earlier that year, but backed down after President Kennedy federalized the Alabama national guard and ordered it to escort black students into the schools of their choice. Schools in Mobile, Huntsville, and Tuskegee integrated without incident, but when two black girls entered Birmingham's West End High, nearly 300 white students marched out chanting: "We hate Kennedy! We hate niggers! We want Wallace!" Teachers stood at the windows smiling at the demonstrators, and a group of white mothers stood outside cheering and encouraging other students to join them. Police dispersed the crowd, but students continued to roam the neighborhood waving Confederate flags and placards with segregationist slogans. The incident touched off a wave of racist violence in Birmingham, including the bombing of two homes and several rallies sponsored by the Ku Klux Klan. Five days later, on September 15, a bomb ripped through the 16th Street Baptist church, which had been a center of civil rights activity, killing four young girls and wounding dozens of worshippers who were preparing for Sunday service.[13]

Infuriated by the failure of local officials to protect black citizens and their property, while openly supporting white resistance to federal authority, black Birmingham exploded in outrage after the church bombing. Some local residents helped police carry the wounded from the building, but others started throwing stones at officers and any whites who happened to drive by. Rioting spread across the city after white teenagers, who were returning from a white supremacist rally nearby, cruised around in cars decorated with Confederate flags and slogans such as "Negroes Go Back to Africa." Even after a thirteen-year-old black boy was shot and killed by two older whites, local authorities continued to ignore white aggressors while arresting, and in at least one case shooting, black rioters. Martin Luther King rushed to Birmingham from Atlanta and, with SCLC leader Fred Shuttlesworth, begged President Kennedy to intervene. "There is a breakdown of law and order in Birmingham and we need Federal troops," Shuttlesworth wrote to the White House. Kennedy agreed to meet with civil rights leaders in the White House, but refused to send federal troops to the southern city. "I am convinced that if something isn't done to give the Negro a new sense of hope and a sense of protection," King insisted, "there is the danger that we will face in that community the worst race riot that we've ever seen in this country."[14]

The threat that King saw in Birmingham spread quickly as news of the killings there reached black activists across the country. SNCC activist Diane Nash Bevel urged southern activists to drop other projects and mount a massive civil disobedience campaign at the Alabama state capitol in Montgomery. By surrounding government buildings, refusing to pay state and local taxes, lying down on runways and railroad tracks, and organizing a "general work strike," she proposed, a "nonviolent army" could paralyze George Wallace's' government and force Kennedy to intervene. In New York City, writer James Baldwin formed a Committee of Artists and Writers who sponsored a memorial service for victims of the bombing and street violence in Birmingham, organized a demonstration seeking intervention from the United Nations, and called for a nationwide boycott of Christmas shopping to get the attention of business leaders and save money that could be sent to aid activists in the South. The intensity of outrage was palpable as several hundred activists gathered in Richmond, Virginia, on September 24 for the seventh annual convention of the SCLC. "We have been duped—or have duped ourselves—into believing the chains have been broken, when in truth we have only been chained more securely," declared SCLC leader Wyatt Tee Walker, arguing that a nationwide strike and boycott of discriminatory companies was necessary to push federal authorities into action. Martin Luther King tried to calm the crowd, insisting that those "who call for retaliatory measures do not represent the Negro masses and their leaders," while Roy Wilkins assured them that despite the setbacks Congress would soon pass a strong civil rights bill. Congressman Adam Clayton Powell disagreed, charging that Kennedy's bill had no chance of passing that year and that white authorities had already given all they ever would to the civil rights movement. The *New York Times* reported that delegates left the meeting with a rough outline of future actions to be clarified at a meeting of SCLC leaders a few weeks later but noted that many "voiced disappointment that the high hopes inspired by the Aug. 28 March on Washington were not materializing."[15]

By October even moderate civil rights leaders began to abandon the hope—expressed by so many just over a month before—that the March on Washington could usher in a new era of interracial cooperation. Early that month Whitney Young revived the Urban League's campaign for a Marshall Plan for the Negro, which had been put on hold during preparations for the March. But rather than emphasizing the degree to which federal investments in housing, education, health care, and job creation would benefit both black and white Americans, as he had before, Young now described the program as compensation for slavery, Jim Crow, and other racially specific forms of oppression. "For more than 300 years the white American has received special consideration, or 'preferential treatment,' if you will, over the Negro," he wrote in the *New York Times*. "What we ask now is that for a brief period there be a deliberate and massive effort to include the Negro citizen in the mainstream of American life." Framing a debate over "affirmative action" that continues fifty years later, Young's proposal met strong criticism from those who supported the idea of a massive antipoverty effort but worried that policies aimed exclusively at African Americans would undermine the racially inclusive appeal that many viewed as critical to the March on Washington's success.

"Negroes would of course be the chief beneficiaries of an educational and economic crash program, because of the predominant number of deprived Negroes," wrote the editor of *Christian Century*, a white Protestant magazine that strongly endorsed the civil rights movement. "But a domestic [Marshall Plan] aimed at the needs of *all* the nation's backward peoples would close rather than widen the nation's racial cleavage." Young's proposal was also at odds with a rising sentiment among Kennedy's economic advisors that "disadvantaged groups other than Negroes now deserve our attention."[16]

The problem for civil rights leaders was that race-neutral anti-poverty programs, which Whitney Young's Urban League had been pushing for longer than any other civil rights group, would have little impact on African Americans unless coupled with decisive measures to prevent racial discrimination. In mid-October the Kennedy administration pressured liberals on the Judiciary Committee of the U.S. House of Representatives to vote against a draft of the civil rights bill that included a fair employment clause and increased federal authorities' ability to prosecute cases of discrimination in public accommodations, voting rights, and employment. The president voiced support for the employment measure, but urged Congress to debate it as a separate bill so that opposition would not derail his original civil rights plan, while Attorney General Robert Kennedy warned that the new enforcement powers could lead to abuse by federal authorities. Civil rights leaders were outraged by this retreat from measures that most viewed basic to any viable civil rights policy. "The tragic and frightening history of the past seven years . . . should be warning enough that by delaying overall action we are playing with human lives as well as with the nation's welfare and strength," NAACP director Roy Wilkins told a gathering of white liberals in the Kennedys' home state of Massachusetts. He credited the administration with risking more than its predecessors, conceding that they "probably have lost some southern states because of their civil rights stand," but blasted the president for backing down on enforcement and fair employment. "Negro unemployment rates are now approaching three times that of the white worker," Wilkins declared, arguing that fair employment policies were needed more than ever before. "Yet the Kennedys hesitate. Why?"[17]

In addition to increasing tensions between civil rights activists and their white allies, the impasse over the civil rights bill deepened rifts within the movement itself. After failing to win support for their March on Montgomery in September, SNCC activists threw their energies behind a voting rights campaign that had been jointly sponsored by the NAACP, CORE, SNCC, and SCLC in Mississippi. Bob Moses, a twenty-eight-year-old former schoolteacher from New York, proposed to hold a mock election, in which disfranchised voters could cast ballots for an interracial slate of candidates, a few days before the official statewide election in November. Other civil rights organizations responded enthusiastically to the effort, preparing over 80,000 supporters to participate in the "freedom vote," but controversy erupted over a decision to recruit nearly 100 white volunteers from Yale, Stanford, and other elite universities to assist with canvassing and conducting the election. Moses and other SNCC leaders argued that the support allowed them to reach more voters and draw much-needed attention from the national press, but some activists complained that white volunteers had "taken over" local campaign offices and undermined efforts—central to SNCC's mission since its founding—to develop indigenous black leadership in the South. Despite the success of the campaign, it set off a debate over the possibilities of interracial cooperation that would grow more intense within SNCC and other civil rights organizations over the next few years.[18]

Divisions over interracial collaboration also erupted in Detroit. Reverend C. L. Franklin, who had invited Martin Luther King to give an early version of his "I Have a Dream" speech at the massive Walk for Freedom five months earlier, sought to recapture the optimism of that event by inviting activists from across the country to chart a path forward on the first weekend in November. King sent representatives prepared to discuss the formation of a northern civil rights group modeled on the SCLC, and Adam Clayton Powell and Mahalia Jackson agreed to headline a mass rally at the city's famous Cobo Hall. Two weeks before the event, however, several key supporters quit the organizing committee after Franklin accused them of turning the program over to "black nationalists and other radical groups." While Franklin insisted that the "mathematics of such a proposition" made it impractical for a "black minority" to declare "political warfare against a white majority," his opponents charged that he was naïve to believe that the crisis facing African Americans could ever be addressed through interracial cooperation. Organizing a competing conference on the same weekend as Franklin's, they drew nearly 2,000 people to a Sunday evening rally headlined by the charismatic and controversial Malcolm X.[19]

It is doubtful that many in the audience shared Malcolm X's religious views, but his defiant tone and biting cynicism appealed to activists who had lost hope for achieving even the most modest demands on the March on Washington's agenda. Repeating his charge that black leaders had allowed white liberals to infiltrate the mobilization and tone down its militancy, the Nation of Islam minister insisted that the only solution was for black people to set aside their political differences and wage a bloody war for independence from white America. "There's no such thing as a nonviolent revolution," he declared, scoffing at the notion of a "revolution in which the goal is a desegregated lunch counter, a desegregated theater, a desegregated park, and a desegregated public toilet; you can sit down next to white folks on the toilet." Malcolm X ignored Randolph's repeated insistence that integration represented only a small part of a broader economic and political transformation. He provided no specifics on what a true revolution would look like, other than to make the puzzling claim that its primary objective would be to control land. He also predicted that its victims would include not only whites but also Randolph, King, Roy Wilkins, and other "Uncle Toms" who, he claimed, had been fooled into feeling loyalty for the United States. Distributed on an LP record and in numerous newsletters, his "Message to the Grassroots" served as a manifesto for the rising tide of black nationalism that would sweep through the civil rights movement in the following decade.[20]

While male leaders clashed over the role of white liberals in the civil rights movement, an equally pressing question was raised a few days later at the twenty-eighth annual convention of the National Council of Negro Women in Washington, D.C. As planned at the meeting that NCNW president Dorothy Height had called in response to women's exclusion from the leadership of the March on Washington, the convention featured a discussion of black women's role in the civil rights movement led by attorney and veteran activist Pauli Murray. "Recent disquieting events have made imperative an assessment of the role of the Negro woman in the quest for equality," Murray declared, asserting that the same feelings of frustration that led many activists to question the influence of white liberals in the civil rights movement had also produced "a new male aggressiveness against the Negro woman." In addition to shutting women out of "the partnership role in the civil rights movement which they have earned by their courage, intelligence and dedication," she observed, "the undertone of news stories of recent efforts to create career opportunities for Negroes in government and industry seems to be that what is being talked about is jobs for Negro men only." While black women had often prioritized men's access to jobs in the past, she insisted, they could "no longer postpone or subordinate the fight against discrimination because of sex to the civil rights struggle but must carry on both fights simultaneously." Dorothy Height recalled later that Murray's speech "really captured the feelings of the moment and it galvanized the women." Like Malcolm X's "Message to the Grass Roots," it was "widely reported in the black press," reprinted in newsletters and journals, and cited frequently in discussions of sexism in the civil rights movement. "It was invaluable that Pauli Murray had lifted the situation to the context of equality," Height wrote four decades later. "It forced us to take a hard look at the actual treatment we received at the March on Washington and the public recognition" that black women received for their contributions to the civil rights movement.[21]

The disillusionment that drove debates over race and gender relations in the movement turned to despair on November 22, when John F. Kennedy was gunned down in Dallas, Texas, during a trip aimed at shoring up his flagging approval ratings in the South. Having held out hope that the president was preparing to take a stronger stand on the civil rights bill, Martin Luther King was literally sickened by the news. News of Kennedy's death was made worse by the knowledge that he would be succeeded by Vice-President Lyndon Johnson, a southern Democrat who had devoted much of his two decades in Congress to blocking any effort to undermine the Jim Crow system. When Johnson had broken ranks with his fellow southerners in 1957 and supported President Eisenhower's nearly meaningless Civil Rights Act, many assumed that he did so only to placate northern Democrats who might block his bid for the presidential nomination in 1960. King responded optimistically when reporters asked for his assessment of the new president at Kennedy's funeral. "I am sure he plans to take the same position as President Kennedy," he stated, insisting that the assassination "does not at all mean a setback." He equivocated, however, when one reporter asked if civil rights leaders were concerned about Johnson's southern roots. "Naturally this question will be raised," he conceded. Roy Wilkins was more openly distraught. "Everything's in a state of suspension for the moment," he told the *New York Times*. "The bullet that killed Kennedy paralyzed the civil rights drive."[22]

Few civil rights leaders predicted that Johnson would become a more passionate supporter of their cause than Kennedy had ever been. The day after the assassination, Roy Wilkins received a call from the White House asking him to meet with the president and discuss a strategy for passing the civil rights bill. Similar calls were made to Whitney Young, Martin Luther King, A. Philip Randolph, and James Farmer. On November 27 Johnson made civil rights a focus of his first major address as president. Against the advice of aides, who warned him not to waste time and political capital on a bill that had little hope of becoming law, he told a joint session of Congress that "no memorial oration or eulogy could more eloquently honor President Kennedy's memory than the earliest possible passage of the civil rights bill for which he fought so long." Most importantly for civil rights leaders, Johnson made it clear that he intended to sign the version that the House Judiciary Committee had drafted in October, including a fair employment clause and stronger enforcement measures, rather than the much weaker bill that Kennedy had originally proposed in June. Johnson's actions were calculated to win votes from northern liberals and African Americans who saw him simply as a southern Democrat; but he also acted out of a sincere hatred for injustice and exploitation. In stark contrast to John F. Kennedy, who came from one of the richest families in New England, the new president had grown up in relative poverty on a small farm in southwest Texas; and in addition to making Johnson a staunch supporter of Franklin D. Roosevelt's New Deal in the 1930s, that background also gave him an acute appreciation of the linkages between economic and racial inequality in the 1960s.[23]

Roy Wilkins met with Johnson on Friday, November 29, and left the White House more optimistic about passing the civil rights bill than he had been in months. Calling leaders of the Big Six organizations (NAACP, NALC, SCLC, CORE, SNCC, and National Urban League), as well as Dorothy Height of the National Council of Negro Women, Wilkins asked them to meet in New York the following Tuesday to coordinate their lobbying efforts. While each of those groups had suspended demonstrations temporarily in the wake of Kennedy's assassination, he asked them to consider declaring a moratorium on protests while the bill worked its way through Congress. To the dismay of Bayard Rustin, who stood to lose his only official position within the civil rights movement, the others also agreed to close the March on Washington's headquarters in Harlem and shift to a more traditional lobbying effort under the direction of the Leadership Conference on Civil Rights.[24]

Not all civil rights leaders were so impressed with Johnson. The only Big Six organization not invited to send a representative to the White House was SNCC, despite the fact that its leadership was already in Washington for the organization's fourth national convention. "Some believe that Johnson may even be more effective than President Kennedy in obtaining enactment of the civil rights bill because of his great experience in Congress," SNCC secretary James Foreman stated as nearly 400 delegates and supporters gathered for the three-day meeting at Howard University. He praised the president for stating that "civil rights legislation should be a memorial to Kennedy," but insisted that "Mr. Johnson, being a Texan, will have to prove himself to Negroes and liberals by his actions." Mississippi activist Bob Moses echoed that skepticism in his opening address to the conference, in which he asked delegates to support a more ambitious version of the Freedom Vote campaign that he and others had organized a few weeks earlier. Explaining that thousands of black and white students would spend the summer of 1964 in Mississippi registering black voters and demanding their right to participate in the Democratic Party primary for the fall election, he stated that the goal of the Freedom Summer was not simply to back Johnson and other supporters of civil rights legislation but to force them into a confrontation with the white supremacists who had controlled the Democratic Party in the South for nearly a century. "It is true the Negroes are blackmailing the Federal Government to force other elements in the power structure to accept a compromise," he declared; "our job is to change the power structure."[25]

SNCC activists did not question Johnson's sincerity; they simply did not believe that he would be any more successful than Kennedy in winning white voters over to the cause of racial equality. In the absence of that political support, they believed, only dramatic confrontations could force federal officials to protect the constitutional rights of black citizens in the South. Bayard Rustin criticized that strategy in his closing address to the SNCC conference, stating that "gimmicks" like blocking streets would not help the movement win support from white voters. "Heroism and [the] ability to go to jail should not be substituted for an over-all social reform program," he told a reporter soon after his speech, insisting that the movement needed to advance an agenda that "will not only help the Negroes but one that will help all Americans." Addressing the concerns about the participation of white students in the Freedom Summer, he suggested that they "could perform a more useful function if they returned home to agitate among the white people." Rustin's critique inspired some white activists to initiate organizing projects in white working-class communities, but most SNCC activists doubted that significant numbers of white workers would ever unite with black workers around shared economic concerns. Without such a hope, James Foreman "took the position that SNCC had to work on discrimination and not worry about the broader economic issues."[26]

The four civil rights leaders who met with Johnson the week after the SNCC convention were more optimistic about the new president, although they agreed with the young militants that further pressure was needed to realize the broader goals of the March on Washington. Johnson asked Whitney Young to prepare a memorandum on the Urban League's Marshall Plan for the Negro, and James Farmer reported that the president expressed "great interest" in his proposal to spend $15 billion on education for "educationally deprived children—mostly Negroes." Martin Luther King's conversation focused on "unemployment and the economic plight of Negroes," and the civil rights leader was "very impressed" with the chief executive's "awareness of the needs of civil rights and the depth of his concern." In a stark reversal of his initial assessment of the Texan, he said: "As a Southerner, I am happy to know that a fellow Southerner is in the White House who is concerned about civil rights." A. Philip Randolph endorsed Young's Marshall Plan, although he insisted that it should "assist all underprivileged—not just Negroes." He also reminded Johnson that "full employment without fair employment" would leave many black workers shut out from economic gains, pointing out that recent improvements in the economy had produced "no discernible decrease" in unemployment among black workers. Despite these productive conversations, civil rights leaders made it clear to the president that demonstrations would resume the following week and continue, as King put it, "until the injustices that have caused them are eliminated." Randolph announced that religious groups were preparing to stage sit-ins at the Capitol in the event of a filibuster against the civil rights bill and urged civil rights organizations to step up demonstrations during the debate. "Even good men need to be pressured," he told a gathering of CORE activists in New York City; "because you only get what you can take."[27]

By the end of 1963, the prospects for linking struggles for racial equality and for economic justice looked better than they had since the March on Washington. Before meeting with Martin Luther King on December 3, Johnson convinced leaders of the House to file a discharge petition that would force conservatives to bring the civil rights bill to a vote before Christmas. He then sent his chief political aide to gather signatures for the petition on Capitol Hill, the first time a sitting president had intervened so closely in the workings of Congress since Franklin D. Roosevelt secured passage of the Fair Labor Standards Act in 1938. The following day Johnson met with AFL-CIO president George Meany, who had never been a reliable ally to the president or the civil rights movement, and asked him to endorse the petition strategy. Meany demonstrated his support by attending a strategy session organized by the Leadership Conference on Civil Rights, stating that labor backed the bill "as a matter of simple justice" and "a memorial to President Kennedy." Randolph called Meany's support for the bill "complete, comprehensive, positive and without reservations," and the

New York Times reported that veteran observers "sense a possible dramatic breakthrough" on the civil rights bill. "It is too turbulent to predict anything certainly now," one congressman stated, "but I've never seen one before where we've had the President going, and the civil rights groups, and labor, and the church people."[28]

The House did not vote on the bill before Christmas, but a major victory came two weeks later, when, in his first State of the Union address, Johnson vowed not only to pass a strong civil rights law but also to couple it with an "unconditional war on poverty in America." The idea of an "attack on poverty" had been floated during the Kennedy administration, but Johnson's program was far more ambitious. Concerned primarily with civil rights and tax assistance for "the middle-income man in the suburbs," Kennedy had insisted that antipoverty programs remain modest and focused narrowly on remedial health and education for poor children and young adults. In contrast, Johnson called for a billion-dollar investment in "better schools, and better health, and better homes, and better training, and better job opportunities to help more Americans, especially young Americans, escape from squalor and misery and unemployment rolls." An economist who advised both administrations on antipoverty policies recalled that Johnson viewed the announcement as a way to counter perceptions that he was more conservative than Kennedy. "If you looked at my record, you would know that I am a Roosevelt New Dealer," Johnson told him the day after the assassination. "As a matter of fact, to tell the truth, John F. Kennedy was a little too conservative to suit my taste." The large scale of the program, however, and the inclusion of policies that had been demanded by the March on Washington—such as a public works program and extending minimum wage laws to all workers—indicated that the War on Poverty was also influenced by the civil rights movement.[29]

The clearest evidence of civil rights leaders' influence on Johnson was his insistence that the War on Poverty would complement rather than compete with policies banning discrimination. "Let me make one principle of this administration abundantly clear," Johnson stated in his State of the Union address. "All these increased opportunities—in employment, in education, in housing, and in every field—must be open to Americans of every color . . . For this is not merely an economic issue, or a social, political, or international issue. It is a moral issue, and it must be met by the passage this session of the bill now pending in the House." Johnson affirmed that synergy between civil rights and economic policies when he invited civil rights leaders to the White House a week after his speech to hear specifics about the War on Poverty and to suggest additional measures "to eliminate economic hardship among Americans." According to James Farmer, Johnson "made it very clear that he feels the fight on poverty and illiteracy is a vital part of the fight on discrimination." Whitney Young agreed that job creation and improved public services were critical to black communities, where nearly a quarter of all workers were unemployed; and although Johnson assured them that the House would vote on the civil rights bill before the end of January, Roy Wilkins stated that discussion of antidiscrimination policies "was only incidental to the main thrust on poverty and the fact that the anti-poverty bill will affect Negroes."[30]

President Johnson's openness to input from civil rights leaders helped to alleviate strategic differences between Wilkins and Young, who favored traditional lobbying, and direct-action advocates such as Randolph, King, and Farmer; but it deepened rifts between those five activists and SNCC leaders, who feared that the emphasis on economic reforms would draw attention from the segregation, disfranchisement, and racist violence that they confronted on a daily basis in Mississippi, Alabama, and other states in the deep South. Johnson exacerbated those differences by excluding SNCC leaders from the White House meetings that were critical to forging a common view of both civil rights and anti-poverty policies during his first few months in office. "Looking around at the setting, the way people were dressed and talked, I knew I would have to stay on my toes not to be swallowed up by this slick band of competitors and circle of distrust," James Foreman wrote of a meeting to discuss fundraising with other leaders of the major civil rights organizations. In early February, SNCC resolved to shift the focus of the Freedom Summer from registering black voters for the Democratic Party primary to creating a new statewide party, called the Mississippi Freedom Democratic Party, which would challenge the segregationist Democratic Party of Mississippi for recognition at the Democratic national convention that fall. Organizers also developed plans to establish "freedom schools" in black communities across the state, which would teach traditional academic skills such as reading, writing, and arithmetic as well as contemporary politics, leadership development, and black history and culture. Although its reliance on white volunteers reflected a lingering attachment to the ideal of interracial cooperation, SNCC was moving increasingly in the direction of developing separate, black-controlled institutions. Writing a week before northern students would start arriving in Mississippi, Foreman explained that the main tasks were to call national attention to "what really goes on in Mississippi" and "to develop and strengthen a home-grown freedom movement that will survive after the 1000 visitors leave."[31]

The appeal of racial separatism also gained a boost from the news that Malcolm X had left the Nation of Islam and was creating a secular organization in cooperation with black nationalists in Detroit, New York, and other cities. "There are many elements in the Negro community—among the working class and among the intellectuals—who, out of the frustration of the current situation, have been deeply attracted to Malcolm's analysis but who reject his synthesis," Bayard Rustin told the *New York Times*, explaining that the new organization would be attractive to those who were "not interested in the separate state idea, or in the back-to-Africa thing, or in the religion" but agreed with his "analysis of the evils that are being practiced on the Negro people." Urban League leader Whitney Young discounted Malcolm X's following, attributing the attention he had received to "an unconscious sympathy on the part of many reporters and others with the notion of separation"; but other civil rights leaders were not so confident. "That cat does have a lot of followers outside the temple," warned CORE leader James Farmer. Rustin observed that Malcolm X's appeal would be diminished only by "the degree to which the established civil rights organizations are more vigorous and develop a program which quite obviously affects the man in the street."[32]

In addition to sparking debates over the possibilities for interracial cooperation, the alliance with Johnson also exacerbated tensions between male civil rights leaders and black women, who were still smarting from their exclusion from the leadership of the March on Washington. Taking office just a few weeks after Pauli Murray's militant speech to the National Council of Negro Women, Lyndon Johnson came under fire for not consulting black women's organizations on his strategy for passing the civil rights bill. In early December the new president invited Dorothy Height to advise him on potential candidates for positions in his administration, but he waited several months before naming one of her suggestions to a "per diem job which pays off more in prestige than in money." NALC activist Dorothy Lowther Robinson resigned from a position in the Department of Labor after complaining about her low pay and lack of influence and, by April 1964, some were suggesting that the president had imposed a bar on black women in positions paying more than $10,000 a year. "The President has announced his intentions of naming more than 50 women to key posts in an effort to utilize untapped female brainpower," reported the *Pittsburgh Courier*. "Therefore, Negro women, especially those who have long been staunch Democratic supporters on the grassroots level, are urging that the time for them to demand top jobs at top pay is NOW, and not later, when the whole 'cake' will have been passed around."[33]

It was not just prominent black women like Height and Robinson who felt pushed aside during the debate over the civil rights bill.

In January 1964 a group of trade unionists formed a Committee for the Defense of Working Women within the New York branch of the NAACP. "All over the city, Negro and Puerto Rican women are working in particularly bad positions, with difficult hours, inadequate pay, and unpleasant working conditions, and often at menial tasks," they wrote, noting that nonwhite women were concentrated almost entirely in domestic service, industrial laundries, garment factories, and public hospitals, "where they are treated with no respect, and where they have little or no job protection." Charging that unions offered little help to such women, and at times colluded with employers to "keep them in their place," the committee demanded that the NAACP pay attention to their concerns. "Already doubly and triply burdened by low wages and care of the home and children, women take on added responsibilities as the job crisis deepens," read a flyer that committee members distributed at an NALC conference on unemployment in June 1964. Rejecting the assumption that black women's concerns could be addressed simply by creating more jobs for black men, they insisted that issues such as access to child care and "discrimination in the hiring of women, especially Negro and Puerto Rican women, must be made a part of all civil rights programs."[34]

Having called for just such discussions in her address to the National Council of Negro Women, Pauli Murray placed them at the center of the debate over how to pass the civil rights bill. In February, after failing to prevent the bill from moving to the floor of the House, an influential conservative introduced an amendment that would have banned employment discrimination based on sex as well as race, ethnicity, religion, and national origin. While he claimed it was a "serious" attempt to aid the "minority sex," most civil rights activists viewed it as a thinly veiled move to discredit the effort. The bill's sponsors attempted to withdraw the legislation and, when that failed, pushed hard to defeat the amendment. Pauli Murray drafted a memorandum, however, arguing that the original law would do nothing to prevent employers from claiming that they hadn't hired a black woman because of her sex rather than her race. Pointing out that women were the primary wage earners in over 20 percent of all nonwhite households, she insisted that "Negro women *especially* need protection against discrimination." Working through her contacts in the President's Commission on the Status of Women, Murray distributed the memo to key figures in the Senate and the White House. A few weeks later she learned that it was critical to convincing Lyndon Johnson and other supporters of the bill to retain the prohibition on sex discrimination.[35]

Lyndon Johnson's machinations helped guide the civil rights bill through the House of Representatives, but, as expected, it required more pressure to win a hearing in the Senate. When the bill came before the full Senate for debate on March 30, Georgia senator Richard Russell led eighteen Democrats and one Republican in a filibuster to prevent it from coming to a vote. It was a desperate measure, but conservatives hoped that by slowing down the process they could force amendments that would make the bill "less offensive," as Johnson himself had done with the civil rights laws of 1957 and 1960. But this time around the president was adamantly opposed to any compromise, as were key allies in the Republican Party, so the prospects of a prolonged stand-off were more likely. Conservatives got a strong signal that this delaying tactic would work in their favor when Alabama governor George Wallace, who had challenged Johnson in the Democratic Party primary for that fall's presidential election, won nearly a third of the votes in Wisconsin; Wallace had little chance of winning the Democratic nomination, but his strong showing bolstered Senator Barry Goldwater's chances of winning the Republican nomination later that summer and indicated that opposition to the civil rights bill reached far beyond the South. The Democratic leader of the Senate predicted that the filibuster would continue past his party's national convention in August, tying up the federal budget and any other business.[36]

Predictably, the filibuster strained the détente that Johnson's support for the civil rights bill and the War on Poverty had facilitated between advocates of mass protests and more traditional lobbying efforts. "The Senators may become so stubborn in their fight against the bill, that civil disobedience will be necessary to dramatize the blatant misuse of legislative processes and to arouse the conscience of the nation," Martin Luther King told reporters during a visit to the Capitol, warning that the SCLC was prepared to launch demonstrations across the country if the bill did not come to a vote before the first of May. Noticing that Malcolm X happened to be standing nearby, King made a dramatic statement by walking over and shaking the black nationalist's hand in full view of the reporters. A. Philip Randolph insisted that protests would have to target Johnson and other supporters of the civil rights bill as well as those who opposed it. "We must recognize that no matter how good any man is, we must still keep the pressure on him," he told a meeting of 200 NALC activists in Chicago. "If the civil rights bill is lost because of the filibuster, there will be trouble in this land," he warned. "We can't wait another 100 years." Roy Wilkins took a more cautious tone, insisting that "civil disobedience has no place in our planning at this time" and explaining that the NAACP would employ the same lobbying tactics that business, farm, and labor groups did to shape legislation. Vowing to employ "every legitimate pressure," he announced that the Leadership Conference on Civil Rights was organizing Catholic, Protestant, and Jewish clergy to lead prayer services each day at a church near the Capitol and then march their flocks over to meet with senators and pack the galleries of the legislature.[37]

Strategic differences sharpened as the stalemate dragged on. In early April, leaders of NAACP and CORE branches in New York City announced that they were asking supporters from across the country to join a massive protest at the World's Fair, which was slated to open a few weeks later in Queens. Most organizers refused to discuss the specifics of the protest, but the Brooklyn branch of CORE distributed flyers asking supporters to drive onto highways with near-empty gas tanks in order to create a blockade when their cars ran out of fuel. City officials were furious, charging that the "stall-in" would "paralyze the whole city" for a week. CORE leader James Farmer also expressed alarm, stating that such tactics would "merely create confusion and thus damage the fight for freedom." He later suspended the branch for holding a news conference after being ordered to halt publicity until they met with him and other national leaders of the organization. The demonstration proceeded without the "stall-in," but conflicts resurfaced after authorities imposed a ban on peaceful picketing at the fair. Farmer vowed to challenge the ban in court after he and nearly 300 other CORE activists were arrested for violating it, but their actions were overshadowed by those of other CORE members who chanted and heckled President Johnson when he spoke at the opening ceremony. "We will not stop now," Farmer stated, warning that demonstrations would continue throughout the two-year run of the fair if needed. But he distanced himself from the hecklers, stating that the president, "like anyone else, has a right to make a speech and have a courteous audience."[38]

Meanwhile "battle lines" were drawn in Mississippi, where activists from SNCC and other organizations were preparing for the arrival of over 1,000 students, the vast majority of them white northerners, who had volunteered to help with education and registration of black voters during the Freedom Summer. Tensions had mounted in recent weeks: many whites viewed the strong turnout for George Wallace in Wisconsin as "proof of growing and national opposition to the civil rights movement and thus reason to draw the lines tighter at home," while civil rights leaders cautioned that it "increase[d] among their people the sense of futility that feeds the urge to seek redress by extra-legal means." Comparing the scene to officers "marshaling their resources like armies in preparation for battle," journalist John Herbers, who had reported from Mississippi for ten years before going to cover civil rights for the *New York Times*, presented Jackson as the epicenter of a broader civil war that threatened to engulf the entire region that sum-mer. "The temper of the Southern Negro was one of increasing dissatis-faction and hostility toward segregation, discrimination in employment and refusal of whites in some areas to allow him full participation in state and local government."[39]

As they had during the impasse with the AFL-CIO in 1962, black trade unionists responded to the filibuster with a mass mobiliza-tion; and this time their proposal was even more ambitious than the March on Washington. On May 2, 1964, NALC vice-president L. Joseph Overton asked the national board of the NAACP to support a "Nation-Wide One-Day Work Stoppage and Prayer Vigil." The NALC executive committee had already approved the proposal, and Ran-dolph sent it to local chapters for their approval at his group's fourth national convention on May 29. Randolph also asked NALC chapters to prepare for the strike by organizing local marches for "Freedom from Poverty through Fair and Full Employment," and by renewing contacts with other civil rights and labor groups in their communities. The primary objective of the action was to push the Senate into action on the civil rights bill, but black trade unionists also hoped to call attention to "the tragic economic plight and widespread and deepen-ing depths of grinding poverty into which Negroes have fallen." Noting that the gross national product hit an all-time high in 1963 and was predicted to increase in 1964, Overton pointed out that 60 percent of all black families still lived below the poverty line, less than 2 percent of the apprenticeships in skilled crafts went to black youth, and mil-lions of black workers were employed in agriculture, domestic service, hospitals, and hotels where they enjoyed no protection from minimum wage laws, social security, or unemployment insurance. The NALC had not set a specific date for the strike, but some suggested August 28, the first anniversary of the March on Washington. NAACP leaders approved Overton's resolution and authorized Roy Wilkins to support the strike if it occurred.[40]

Even as Randolph called for a general strike to break the filibuster, he warned that the civil rights bill would not address all the concerns identified at the March on Washington. Meeting the most pressing demands of the March, the bill would ban discrimination in stores, restaurants, hotels, and other public accommodations, prohibit state and local governments from discriminating in access to public services or the right to vote, and empower the federal government to speed the desegregation of schools. Most importantly for Randolph, the law would create an Equal Employment Opportunity Commission to prevent businesses, unions, and government from discriminating against potential employees on the basis of race, color, religion, national origin, or sex, thus making permanent and expanding the power of the FEPC that President Roosevelt had created to stop the first March on Washington in 1941. While Randolph emphasized the importance of passing the bill, however, he also noted that it was insufficient to overcome the "economic, social, cultural and political deprivation" caused by three centuries of slavery and "semi-feudal serfdom under segregation." The union leader was particularly alarmed by the quickening pace of industrial automation, which was eliminating the entry-level jobs that had been the first step for generations of working-class men into well-paid and unionized jobs in manufacturing. "This is a problem to which Negro leaders must address themselves while there is day, for the night cometh when no man can work," the seventy-five-year-old trade unionist asserted.[41]

While Randolph emphasized the threat posed by automation, it was hardly the only problem left unaddressed by the civil rights bill. In addition to endorsing the strike, delegates to the NALC convention adopted resolutions calling for raising the federal minimum wage and extending it to all workers, organizing domestic workers into unions, the abolition of the House Un-American Activities Committee, and an end to the use of the death penalty against anti-apartheid activists in South Africa. Black trade unionists also resolved to unite civil rights, labor, religious, and student groups behind an American Labor Party, on the grounds that "no basic difference in philosophy" separated the Democrats and Republicans. Agnes Willis, whom Randolph had appointed to the national leadership of the NALC under pressure from women at the founding convention, led a delegation of twenty trade unionists who demanded representation from "at least one woman" on all committees of the organization and at all levels of planning for future campaigns. Acknowledging that theirs and other groups were divided by "internal conflicts and cross currents," black trade unionists proposed to invite a broad spectrum of black organizations, including the Nation of Islam and black nationalists, to a State of the Race Summit in Washington soon after the Senate voted on the civil rights bill. "Some discussion of the tactics and goals by leaders of the major Negro fraternal, civic, women's, student and church movements is essential at this time."[42]

It is not clear what impact the threat of a general strike had on the filibuster, but it seems to have encouraged senators to resolve the impasse over the civil rights bill. On May 6, 1964, one of the nation's most widely respected observers of organized labor devoted his nationally syndicated column to the work stoppage. Reporting that NALC members held leadership positions in AFL-CIO unions in thirty-one cities across the United States, Victor Riesel argued that black trade unionists were likely to gain support from local chapters of the NAACP, Urban League, SCLC, and SNCC. Some labor leaders predicted the effort would fail, but Riesel noted that they were "the same forces which shied from the capital demonstration until it became apparent in cities across the nation that the big unions would support it and that scores of thousands would pour into Washington." It was significant, "especially in this election year," that black trade unionists were most influential in "the vast northern and far western industrial areas," the columnist predicted, noting that if the strike won support from the same unions that had endorsed the March on Washington it "could roll and keep workers from huge factories and service industries across the land—and set a precedent for a series of stay-aways." Senate staffers may have missed the articles in the *Amsterdam News* on May 30 and the *Chicago Defender* on June 8, both of which reported that 300 black trade unionists had endorsed Randolph's proposal at the NALC convention; but it is almost certain that Riesel's column made its way through the Senate office building at some point before June 10, when northern Republicans broke with the southern Democrats and voted to end the longest filibuster in U.S. history. After a series of fights over amendments and a second vote in the House, Lyndon Johnson signed the Civil Rights Act on July 2, 1964.[43]

Even before President Johnson signed the Civil Rights Act, the limitations of the law became clear. On June 21, two days after thousands of people gathered outside the Capitol to cheer the Senate's approval of the bill, three SNCC workers disappeared after going to investigate the burning of a black church in Philadelphia, Mississippi. Johnson authorized 200 Navy sailors to search for them, along with 150 FBI agents who were already in the state; but civil rights leaders pointed out that the unprecedented attention given to those three activists—two of whom were white—did nothing to protect others from violence or to change federal policies toward the broader problem of racist terrorism. SNCC workers reported that over twenty-five homes and churches were bombed, dozens of activists beaten, shot, or threatened, and 300 arrested on minor charges in the first two months of the Freedom Summer, often while FBI agents stood around taking notes and talking cordially with local police. They also noted that violence declined only in places where black citizens kept guns in their homes and made it clear they were willing to use them to defend themselves and civil rights workers. While SNCC maintained an official commitment to nonviolence, many in the organization began to question its effectiveness in the absence of federal protection. "It is a shame that national concern is aroused only after two white boys are missing,"

SNCC president John Lewis remarked, charging that if federal authorities did not do more to protect civil rights workers in Mississippi then "blood will be on their hands." A few days later the bodies of the three activists were found buried under a dam.[44]

The frustration of activists in Mississippi was amplified when Senator Barry Goldwater, one of six Republicans to vote against ending the filibuster on the Civil Rights Act, won his party's nomination to challenge Lyndon Johnson in the November election. Having dismissed the archconservative as a "minor-league extremist with a following of 'nuts and kooks,'" many in the press and the Republican establishment were slow to recognize that he was backed by a "greater army of the discontented and frustrated" than they had ever imagined. Goldwater was not a segregationist. He had supported the NAACP in his home state of Arizona and voted in favor of the far weaker Civil Rights Acts of 1957 and 1960. His opposition to the 1964 law was based on the claim that it violated the constitutional rights of states, employers, and private property owners. Most assumed that Goldwater would pick up support from white southerners who were furious at Johnson's defection on civil rights. The question was whether he could win votes from working-class whites in the urban North, who supported "big government" programs like social security and federal support for housing, education, and collective bargaining but not those that would force them to live, work, or send their children to schools with African Americans. "It seems hard to believe . . . that millions of them will desert their own party to cast pro-Goldwater votes in November," one observer wrote from the Republican national convention. "Yet what is happening here in San Francisco also seems hard to believe. One must wait and see."[45]

Goldwater's nomination ensured that the November election would be a referendum of sorts on the Civil Rights Act, but the Democrats' commitment to racial equality was challenged by a riot that broke out just a few days later in New York City, where Mayor Robert Wagner presided over one of the most liberal administrations in the United States. Sparked by the shooting of a fifteen-year-old black boy during an altercation with an off-duty white police officer in Harlem, the violence escalated after local residents marched to the police precinct demanding an explanation. A shouting match ensued and, after citizens started banging on cars, throwing bricks and bottles, and smashing windows in stores, police responded by storming into the crowd with clubs and firing their weapons into the air. "The police were hysterical," said CORE leader James Farmer, who described officers "charging into a grocery store indiscriminately swinging clubs" and "shooting into tenement windows" and into a nearby hotel. "People threw bottles and bricks, I'm not saying they were not partly to blame," Farmer told a reporter, "but it is the duty of police to arrest, not indiscriminately shoot and beat." The next morning Farmer attempted to contact Mayor Wagner, as well as Governor Rockefeller, but was told that both politicians were on vacation and unavailable for comment. Civil rights leaders joined the acting mayor in calling for "restraint and respect for law and order," but violence erupted anew when police charged into a crowd of mourners who had gathered for the funeral of the slain teenager, waving nightsticks and shooting into the air. When reporters asked how Lyndon Johnson would respond to what James Farmer had called "New York's night of Birmingham horror," a White House spokesman replied: "The President has made it clear that any time local authorities need help in keeping law and order we stand ready to help." Rioting continued for three days, spreading to Brooklyn and resulting in one death, 150 injuries, 500 arrests, and millions of dollars in damage.[46]

Combined with Goldwater's nomination, the Harlem riot presented a serious challenge to civil rights leaders who saw Johnson's reelection in November as essential for the realization of the agenda they had laid out a year earlier at the March on Washington. "The Civil Rights Act of 1964 could well be diminished or nullified and a decade of increasingly violent and futile disorder ushered in if we do not play our hand cooly and intelligently," A. Philip Randolph, Bayard Rustin, and Roy Wilkins wrote in a memorandum to other leaders of the Big Six organizations, asking them to attend a meeting in New York City on July 29. Fearing that tensions were running so high that even well-organized demonstrations might descend into violence, the three of them convinced James Farmer, Martin Luther King, Whitney Young, and John Lewis to join them at a press conference in which they asked all civil rights organizations "voluntarily to observe a broad curtailment, if not total moratorium, of all mass marches, mass picketing and mass demonstrations until after Election Day." The statement was extremely controversial. Farmer and Lewis refused to formally sign it before consulting the national leadership of CORE and SNCC, and Bayard Rustin admitted that demonstrations were called for when, a few days later, Mayor Wagner rejected demands for a civilian review board to monitor abuses by the New York Police Department. "If the moratorium on demonstrations causes any relaxation in the sense of urgency municipal officials now feel about searching for answers to the problems of jobs, education and housing and promoting better interracial cooperation," the New York Times reported in an article titled "Who Speaks for the Negro?," "the Negro leaders will find themselves helpless to bottle up the indignation of their people."[47]

For many SNCC activists, the answer to the question posed by the New York Times arrived at the Democratic national convention a few weeks later in Atlantic City, where Johnson and other party leaders refused to recognize the biracial Mississippi Freedom Democratic Party's demand to be seated instead of the white supremacist Democratic Party of Mississippi. Joseph Rauh, who as a young attorney had drafted the executive order that convinced A. Philip Randolph to call off the March on Washington in 1941, worked out a compromise in which the segregationists were given all but two at-large seats at the 1964 convention in exchange for an agreement that all future delegations would be selected without regard to race. Martin Luther King, Bayard Rustin, and Walter Reuther encouraged the Freedom Democrats to accept Rauh's compromise, but SNCC activists dismissed it as a "back-of-the-bus deal." Storming out of the meeting, they marched down the Atlantic City boardwalk and occupied the entire Mississippi section on the convention floor. Party leaders avoided a major conflict by removing them one by one and slowly turning the seats over to official delegates who pledged to support Johnson in November and, on March 31, 1964, the Credentials Committee imposed the compromise without any debate. Most civil rights leaders and much of the press, both black and white, celebrated the compromise as "A Major Victory" that laid the basis for a realignment of the Democratic Party around a coalition of civil rights, labor, and other liberal forces without the impediment of white supremacists in the South. John Lewis recalled that it "was a major letdown for hundreds and thousands of civil rights workers, both black and white, young and old people alike who had given everything they had to prove that you could work through the system."[48]

Lyndon Johnson won the November election with the largest landslide of any presidential candidate since the nineteenth century, but by that point many civil rights activists wondered how much his victory would help their cause. Malcolm X argued that African Americans would be better off with Goldwater in the White House, since, "they would at least know they were fighting an honestly growling wolf, rather than a fox who could have them in his stomach and have digested them before they even knew what [was] happening." Few black voters shared that cynicism; nearly 95 percent of them cast ballots for Johnson on November 3. More troubling was the solid support that Goldwater enjoyed among white voters in the South, who made him the first Republican in nearly a century to win South Carolina, Georgia, Alabama, Louisiana, and Mississippi. Without large numbers of African Americans casting votes in Virginia, North

Carolina, Tennessee, and Arkansas, he could have won those states as well. Johnson won his home state of Texas and every state outside the deep South except Goldwater's native Arizona, but white opposition to the civil rights movement was evident in those places as well. The most alarming sign came from California, where the same electorate that sided overwhelmingly with Johnson voted by a 65 percent majority for Proposition 14, which overturned a law passed by the state legislature a year earlier to prohibit racial discrimination in the rental or sale of housing. "If we believe in the American democratic system, we must acknowledge that it is a right of the people to tell the government what to do," said a prominent supporter of Proposition 14, demonstrating the degree to which conservatives had succeeded in framing the debate over civil rights as a contest between "big government" and individual freedom rather than between the rhetoric and reality of "self-evident" truths.[49]

EPILOGUE

*The Civil Rights Revolution has been caught up in
a crisis of victory; a crisis which may involve great
opportunity or great danger to its future fulfillment.*

—A. PHILIP RANDOLPH, 1965[1]

ON JANUARY 30, 1965, A. Philip Randolph finally opened the State of the Race Summit that the Negro American Labor Council had proposed to address the "internal conflicts and cross currents" that swept through the civil rights movement the previous May. Observing that divisions had expanded since the passage of the Civil Rights Act in July, Randolph warned that the movement was in danger not only of failing to realize its full agenda but also of losing ground on the tremendous victories that it had already achieved. He compared the current situation to that of the decade before his own birth, when a rising "counterrevolution" threatened to destroy "virtually every vestige of freedom and citizenship" that African Americans had secured since emancipation. He also saw similarities with the decade following the Second World War, when the conservative backlash against New Deal labor laws undermined organized labor's commitment to aiding "the battles of the unskilled workmen, neglected migrant farm laborers, and the Jim Crow, underclass black laboring masses." In each previous case, historic legal victories had "provoked a sense of relaxation" within a social movement, "weakened the will to struggle and resulted in the loss of much of its freedom." Pointing to the popularity of Barry Goldwater and the defeat of the open housing law in California, Randolph asserted that those challenges had exacerbated a "psychological and social gap" between the "Negro classes," who benefited from expanded opportunities in education and employment, and the "black masses," who still suffered from low wages and rising rates of unemployment. Arguing that the only solution was to unite around economic concerns that faced working-class Americans of all races, the seventy-six-year-old trade unionist urged his old friends and allies to "take the leadership" in forging a "national consensus" around the need for affordable housing, quality education, full employment, and economic security. "Negroes must move ahead with their fellow white poor and citizens of good will," he warned, "or history will again pass us by."2

Black trade unionists invited leaders from a broad range of "Negro civil rights organizations, churches, fraternal groups, women's groups, etc." to the State of the Race Summit, but they failed to unite them around a solution to Randolph's "crisis of victory." While the NALC's original proposal for the conference emphasized the need to include the Nation of Islam and black nationalists, Randolph sent invitations only to groups that were "committed to integration." Black trade unionists wanted to hold the conference in Washington but moved it to the Manhattan headquarters of the National Council of Churches, where Anna Arnold Hedgeman was employed, to facilitate participation by leaders of the NAACP, CORE, and the Urban League. Randolph attempted to create "an atmosphere of mutual confidence rather than suspicion" by excluding the press and asking participants to focus on practical solutions rather than "Grand Strategy." Nevertheless, a shouting match erupted soon after his opening remarks. The first presentation was a paper by Whitney Young, of the Urban League, who had an assistant read it because he had more pressing duties in Washington. Young's paper provided a detailed account of his efforts to expand President

Johnson's War on Poverty. When he claimed that his objective was to give African Americans the "foundation for a normal middle-class American life," however, SNCC activist James Foreman objected that Young was too focused on "middle-class values such as [the] drive for money, status and accumulation for himself and [his] children." SCLC leader Andrew Young agreed with Foreman, stating that the movement's goal was not to "assimilate into white society." Psychiatrist Kenneth Clark, who had helped formulate the NAACP's argument in the *Brown* decision, insisted that the goal was "upward mobility."[3]

Cleveland Robinson attempted to defuse the conflict by reminding the assembled that Johnson's War on Poverty was hardly sufficient to lift anyone into the middle class. Timuel Black, the NALC leader from Chicago, urged them to be less critical of each other and try to understand their respective views. Positions hardened, however, when Bayard Rustin read a nine-page paper attacking black nationalists and Communists—none of whom were present to defend themselves—as middle-class intellectuals and "confused" revolutionaries who had "little relevance to the plight of that 10% of America which is black." Pauli Murray chimed in that even if they did, such a small minority was unlikely to accomplish much without support from the remaining 90 percent. Randolph had hoped to close the conference with a presentation of resolutions and proposals that participants could bring to their respective groups for approval, but the weekend ended only with a vague statement of unity to the press.[4]

The failure of the State of the Race Summit set the scene for the continued fracturing of the civil rights movement in the late 1960s. Within two years, both SNCC and CORE had adopted the slogan "Black Power," which emphasized racial autonomy and defiance rather than interracial cooperation or compromise. That move sharpened conflicts with the Urban League and the NAACP, which continued efforts to strengthen civil rights and antipoverty programs while using lawsuits to enforce the *Brown* decision and the Civil Rights Act. The SCLC remained committed to interracial collaboration, but exacerbated competition with established civil rights groups by expanding its focus to include poverty and discrimination in the urban North. In March 1965 Randolph announced that he had received $50,000 from the AFL-CIO and other groups to form an institute to develop solutions to automation and other economic developments that threatened "not only the Negro but, in one way or another, all Americans." He recruited Bayard Rustin to lead the A. Philip Randolph Institute and gained support from Maida Springer and other leaders of the Garment Workers Union but resigned from leadership of the NALC because of failing health and continuing criticism of his close ties to George Meany. Cleveland Robinson succeeded Randolph as president of the NALC and launched an ambitious campaign to mobilize black workers in agriculture, public service, retail, and other sectors that had been neglected by the AFL-CIO. Targeting both union and nonunion workplaces, he and other black trade unionists aimed to "force the leadership of these unions to clean up their own houses and represent the Negroes as any other members, or we will find a new house to move into." Meanwhile NALC cofounder Dorothy L. Robinson grew so frustrated with male civil rights leaders' refusal to enforce the Civil Rights Act's prohibition on sex discrimination that she proposed the formation of "an NAACP for women." In 1966, Robinson, Pauli Murray, Anna Arnold Hedgeman, and a group of white women—many of them labor feminists from the 1940s—formed the National Organization for Women.[5]

Ironically, frustration with the failure to realize the more radical goals of the March on Washington led some to suggest that its agenda had never been so ambitious. The term "classical" was first applied to the decade between the *Brown* decision and the Civil Rights Act by Bayard Rustin, in an article that was designed to increase support from white liberals for the A. Philip Randolph Institute. Assuming that his audience already supported demands for integration and voting rights in the South, he wrote in 1965: "the Negro today finds himself stymied by obstacles of far greater magnitude than the legal barriers he was attacking before: automation, urban decay, *de facto* school segregation." A similar strategy was adopted by Stokely Carmichael, who succeeded John Lewis as the chairman of SNCC, as he sought to steer that organization into a more direct engagement with poverty and unemployment in black communities. "We must face the fact that, in the past, what we have called the movement has not really questioned the middle-class values and institutions of this country," he and Charles V. Hamilton wrote in their 1967 manifesto *Black Power*. Paraphrasing A. Philip Randolph's address to the March on Washington, without attribution, they urged young militants to reorient themselves toward "an emphasis on the dignity of man, not on the sanctity of property." By 1968, when Martin Luther King sought to highlight poverty and unemployment though his Poor People's Campaign, it was common sense that this represented "a transition to a second phase" of the civil rights movement.[6]

The assassination of Martin Luther King, as he attempted to launch the Poor People's Campaign by supporting a strike by black sanitation workers in Memphis, Tennessee, solidified the historical memory of a moderate and geographically restricted "classical" phase. While the murder pushed Carmichael and other Black Power activists further from their roots in nonviolence and interracial cooperation, it gave moderates a new appreciation for King's thoughtful and forgiving radicalism. The "I Have a Dream" speech, which had been largely forgotten since 1963, acquired new meaning as an artifact of a more hopeful era. "His dream sustains us yet," President Jimmy Carter stated as he awarded the Presidential Medal of Freedom to the slain minister in 1977. By the time A. Philip Randolph died in 1979 at the age of ninety, the *Amsterdam News* noted that his name was no longer "as recognizable" in black America as those of Martin Luther King, Malcolm X, or even Marcus Garvey. That simplification of the historical narrative was completed by 1983, when Congress passed a law creating a national holiday on Martin Luther King's birthday. Signed by President Ronald Reagan, who began his political career as a supporter of Barry Goldwater in 1964, the law established King as the nation's "preeminent nonviolent commander."[7]

While political leaders and the media reduced the memory of the movement to Martin Luther King's address to the March on Washington, however, some retained a more accurate view of the "civil rights revolution." The original bill for the King holiday was introduced to Congress by John Conyers, the son of a black trade unionist from Detroit, and promoted by the Negro American Labor Council. "We don't want anyone to believe we hope Congress will do this," Cleveland Robinson stated in 1969. "We're just sayin', us black people in America just ain't gonna work on that day anymore." The sanitation workers that King was supporting in Memphis belonged to the American Federation of State, County and Municipal Employees (AFSCME), one of the unions that helped A. Philip Randolph raise funds for the Montgomery Bus Boycott in 1956, and they institutionalized the holiday by writing it into collective-bargaining agreements with school boards, universities, and state and city governments across the country. In 1972 Cleveland Robinson, Charles Hayes, Addie Wyatt, and other leaders of the NALC joined with leaders of AFSCME to form the Coalition of Black Trade Unionists, which dedicated itself to the "unending effort to achieve economic, political and social justice for every American." A similar vision of social and economic citizenship also continued to animate the NAACP, the National Organization for Women, and countless unions and smaller organizations that have roots in the March on Washington. Together, they carry on the struggle "For Jobs and Freedom."[8]

NOTES

PREFACE

1. Martin Luther King, Jr., "I Have a Dream," in Washington, ed., *A Testament of Hope: The Essential Writings and Speeches of Martin Luther King, Jr.*, 217–220; "200,000 March for Civil Rights," *NYT*, August 29, 1963.
2. "Final Plans for the March on Washington for Jobs and Freedom," unlabeled folder, box 39, BMP.
3. "Excerpts from Addresses at Lincoln Memorial," *NYT*, August 29, 1963.
4. "Excerpts from Addresses at Lincoln Memorial"; "Text of Lewis' Speech at Washington," *Student Voice* 4, no. 3 (October 1963), 1, 3.
5. Williams, *Eyes on the Prize*, 287. The term "classical" is from Bayard Rustin, "From Protest to Politics: The Future of the Civil Rights Movement," in Rustin, *Down the Line*, 112; Thernstrom and Thernstrom, *America in Black and White*, 145; Marable, *Race, Reform, and Rebellion*, 76; Gilmore, *Defying Dixie*; Sugrue, *Sweet Land of Liberty*; Sugrue, *Origins of the Urban Crisis*; Hall, "The Long Civil Rights Movement"; Evelyn Brooks Higginbotham, "Foreword," in Theoharis and Woodard, eds., *Freedom North*, viii, ix; Dudziak, *Cold War Civil Rights*, 13. For important exceptions see Hamilton and Hamilton, *The Dual Agenda*; D'Emilio, *Lost Prophet*; Jackson, *From Civil Rights to Human Rights*; and MacLean, *Freedom Is Not Enough*. For a more detailed discussion of this literature see Jones, "Unknown Origins of the March on Washington."
6. Barack Obama, "A More Perfect Union," March 18, 2008, reprinted in Sharpley-Whiting, ed., *The Speech*, 237–251; "Clinton and Obama United in Pleas to Blacks," *NYT*, March 5, 2007; David Remnick, "The Joshua Generation: Race and the Campaign of Barack Obama," *The New Yorker*, November 17, 2008.
7. "Latino and Black Unemployment Rates Fall at Faster Clip, Boosting Obama's Election Chances," *Huffington Post*, October 5, 2012, http://www.huffingtonpost.com/2012/10/05/latino-black-unemployment-rates_n_1943676.html (accessed November 16, 2012); "Polls Show Widening Racial Gap in Presidential Contest," *WP*, October 5, 2012; Frederick C. Harris, "The Price of a Black President," *NYT*, October 27, 2012.
8. King, "I Have a Dream," 217.

9. Barber, *Marching on Washington*, 159.

10. Russell Baker, "Capital Is Occupied by a Gentle Army," *NYT*, August 29, 1963; Breitman, ed., *Malcolm X Speaks*, 17.

11. Thernstrom and Thernstrom, *America in Black and White*, 131; "Pushing Too Fast: Survey," *NAN*, September 7, 1963.

12. "Real Battle with Congress Shapes Up for JFK in '62," *CD*, January 2, 1962; "JFK Wants 'New Tools' to Halt Economic Drop," *ADW*, June 9, 1963; Murray Kempton, "The March on Washington," *New Republic*, September 14, 1963, 19.

13. Malcolm X, *The Autobiography*, 281; Barber, *Marching on Washington*, 175–176; Jackson, *From Civil Rights to Human Rights*, 183.

14. A. Philip Randolph, "Opening Remarks at Conference of Negro Leaders," folder 3, box 3, GWP.

CHAPTER ONE: THE MOST DANGEROUS NEGRO IN AMERICA

1. A. Philip Randolph, "March on Washington Movement Presents Program for the Negro," in Logan, ed., *What the Negro Wants*, 141.

2. Sitkoff, *A New Deal for Blacks*, 314; "Won't Serve in U.S. Army; Cites Bias" and "Balks Call to Arms," *CD*, January 11, 1941; " 'Defense Rotten'—Randolph: Let's March on Capital," *PC*, January 25, 1941.

3. Franklin D. Roosevelt, "1941 Annual Message to Congress," January 6, 1941, in Waldman, ed., *My Fellow Americans*, 415; Foner, *Story of American Freedom*, 196–207.

4. Taylor, *A. Philip Randolph*; Fink, *Progressive Intellectuals*, 184–213; "Negroes' Leader a Man of Dignity," *NYT*, August 29, 1963.

5. Pfeffer, *A. Philip Randolph*, 6–9; "A. Philip Randolph: Who Is This Man?" *NAN*, July 5, 1941; Chateauvert, *Marching Together*, 8.

6. Spero and Harris, *The Black Worker*, 385–401.

7. Wilson, ed., *The Messenger Reader*, 346, 319; Fink, *Progressive Intellectuals*, 192.

8. Wendell Wray, ed., "The Reminiscences of Dr. A. Philip Randolph," July 18, 1972, Oral History Collection of Columbia University; Pfeffer, *A. Philip Randolph*, 16; Stein, *The World of Marcus Garvey*.

9. Perry, *Hubert Harrison*, 1; Pfeffer, *A. Philip Randolph*, 6–9; Spero and Harris, *The Black Worker*, 385–401.

10. Pfeffer, *A. Philip Randolph*, 11; Jones, " 'Nothing Special to Offer the Negro,' " 215, 219.

11. Pfeffer, *A. Philip Randolph*, 21.

12. Arnesen, *Brotherhoods of Color*, 84–90. .

13. Harris, *Keeping the Faith*, 35–38; Spero and Harris, *The Black Worker*, 430–460.

14. Chateauvert, *Marching Together*, 9.

15. Arnesen, *Brotherhoods of Color*, 90–94; Spero and Harris, *The Black Worker*, 457, 460.

16. Sitkoff, *A New Deal for Blacks*, 34–35.

17. "The New Deal Begins," *PC*, March 4, 1933; "Kelly Miller Says," *ADW*, November 8, 1932; "Analysis of Cabinet," *NAN*, March 8, 1933.

18. Jones, *The Tribe of Black Ulysses*, 89–124; "Harlemites Demand Rights under Recovery Act," *CD*, August 5, 1933.

19. Jones, *The Tribe of Black Ulysses*, 122–124; "Harlemites Demand Rights under Recovery Act."

20. "Porters Demand Accommodations on 'New Deal Special,'" *PC*, February 17, 1934; Arnesen, *Brotherhoods of Color*, 84–115.

21. Lichtenstein, *State of the Union*, 20–53; Arnesen, *Brotherhoods of Color*, 93–94.

22. Cayton and Mitchell, *Black Workers and the New Unions*, 419; Gellman, *Death Blow to Jim Crow*, 19–62; John P. Davis, "Let Us Build a National Negro Congress," box 105, APC.

23. Jones, *The Tribe of Black Ulysses*, 139–141; Frazier, *Negro Family in the United States*, 355; Gellman, *Death Blow to Jim Crow*; Davis, "Let Us Build a National Negro Congress."

24. Cayton and Mitchell, *Black Workers and the New Unions*, 419; "The Official Proceedings of the National Negro Congress," February 14, 15, 16, 1936, box 242, NRR.

25. Miller quoted in Cayton and Mitchell, *Black Workers and the New Unions*, 421; Gilmore, *Defying Dixie*.

26. Cayton and Mitchell, *Black Workers and the New Unions*, 421; Myrdal, *An American Dilemma*, 817.

27. Gellman, *Death Blow to Jim Crow*, 47–58; Goodman, *The Committee*, 24–58.

28. "National Negro Congress Girds for Third Conference," *CD*, April 27, 1940; Gellman, *Death Blow to Jim Crow*, 149–156; Zieger, *The CIO*, 90–140.

29. J. Robert Smith, "A. Philip Randolph: Who Is This Man?" *NAN*, July 5, 1941, 4; Arnesen, "No 'Graver Danger,'" 14–15, 17; Gellman, *Death Blow to Jim Crow*.

30. Bates, *Pullman Porters*, 143–146.

31. Myrdal, *An American Dilemma*, 411–414; Foner, *Story of American Freedom*, 242; " 'Defense Rotten'—Randolph."

32. Myrdal, *An American Dilemma*, 420; "Urban League Hits Jim Crow in Defense Industries," *ADW*, July 9, 1940.

33. Sitkoff, *A New Deal for Blacks*, 75–77, 326–328.

34. Gilmore, *Defying Dixie*, 357; "Leaders Charge 'Trick' to President's Army Edict," *ADW*, October 15, 1940.

35. "Army Policy Was Misinterpreted," *NAN*, November 2, 1940; "B. O. Davis Becomes First Negro General," *CD*, November 2, 1940; "We've Just Begun to Fight," *PC*, December 7, 1940.

36. "Watchtower," *NAN*, December 7, 1941.

37. "Won't Serve in U.S. Army; Cites Bias" and "Balks Call to Arms"; "Red Cap Official Opposes Draft Service," *ADW*, June 6, 1941; "The Calloway Case," *PC*, January 18, 1941; "Calloway Protests against Jim Crowism in Army," *Workers Age*, January 1, 1941, folder 22, box 230, JLP.

38. " 'Defense Rotten'—Randolph."

39. "Chair-Car Porters in 3 Day Meet," *CD*, February 8, 1941; "C and N Porters Win Pay Increase," *CD*, February 15, 1941; "GMO Rail Porters Effect a Work-Wage Settlement," *CD*, March 29, 1941; "AFL and the Negro," *NAN*, February 8, 1941;

"VA Slayer Execution Held Again," *CD*, March 15, 1941; Gilmore, *Defying Dixie*, 329–367; "Seek Senate Probe of Defense Jim Crow," *CD*, March 1, 1941; "Chatter Chimes," *NAN*, March 8, 1941; "Foes of Defense Jim Crow Invade Washington," *CD*, March 29, 1941; "A. Philip Randolph," *CD*, February 8, 1941; "The Randolph Plan," *CD*, March 15, 1941.

40. Garfinkle, *When Negroes March*, 131; Dominic J. Capeci Jr., "The Harlem Bus Boycott on 1941," in Birnbaum and Taylor, eds., *Civil Rights since 1787*, 300; Hamilton, *Adam Clayton Powell, Jr.*, 102–104.

41. "Plan All-Out March to DC," *NAN*, April 12, 1941; Bates, *Pullman Porters*, 153–156; Self, *American Babylon*, 50–51; Randolph, "March on Washington Movement," 154; Garfinkle, *When Negroes March*, 131; White, "Nixon Was the One."

42. "Outline Plans for March on Capital," *ADW*, May 11, 1941; "Organization of Local 'March on Washington' Committee Is Announced," *NAN*, May 24, 1941; "Threat of Washington March Seen as Accomplishing Much," *ADW*, June 27, 1941; "100,000 to March to Capital," *NAN*, May 31, 1941; "Alpha Kappa Alpha Sorors Issue Call for June," *CD*, May 31, 1941; White, *Too Heavy a Load*, 142–175; "Jeanetta Welch NCNW Secretary," *ADW*, April 30, 1943; Garfinkle, *When Negroes March*, 39.

43. "100,000 in March to Capital," *NAN*, May 31, 1941; "A. Philip Randolph Explains Purpose of Pilgrimage," *NAN*, June 7, 1941; "March on Washington Drive Draws Nationwide Response," *NAN*, June 7, 1941; "Knox Summons Randolph to Capital about March," *NAN*, June 14, 1941.

44. "Knox Summons Randolph to Capital about March"; "Mitchell Flays Randolph in Commencement Address," *ADW*, June 19, 1941; "Administration Seeks to Curb D.C. March," *ADW*, June 18, 1941; "Most Dangerous Negro in America," *CD*, June 28, 1941.

45. "Knox Summons Randolph to Capital about March"; "At White House Conference," *NAN*, June 28, 1941; "Roosevelt Opposed to March on Washington," *PC*, June 28, 1941; Garfinkle, *When Negroes March*, 58.

46. "Pres. Roosevelt Opposes March," *ADW*, June 24, 1941; "At White House Conference"; "Roosevelt Opposed to March on Washington"; "Roosevelt Issues Order," *NAN*, June 28, 1941.

47. Terkel, *The Good War*, 337; "Pres. Roosevelt Opposes March"; "President Orders an Even Break for Minorities in Defense Jobs," *NYT*, June 26, 1941.

48. "FDR's Order Kills Defense Bias," *CD*, July 5, 1941; "Randolph in First Report Defends Action in Calling Off D.C. March," *ADW*, August 10, 1941; Lerone Bennett Jr., "Protest Threat Forced President Roosevelt's Hand," *Ebony*, February 1977, 136.

49. "FDR's Order Kills Defense Bias"; "Nation Has Varied Reactions to FDR Order and 'Jobless March,'" *CD*, July 5, 1941; "Hits Dictator Action in Calling Off March," *PC*, July 12, 1941; "Charges 'Sell-Out' on March Decision," *PC*, July 12, 1941, 7; "Grumbling Follows March Halt," *ADW*, July 3, 1941; "Roosevelt's Executive Order," *CD*, July 12, 1941; "Postponed," *PC*, July 5, 1941.

CHAPTER TWO: THE MARCH ON WASHINGTON MOVEMENT

1. "Hearing Delay Is Rapped by Leaders," *ADW*, July 2, 1941; "Leaders Flay Walter White," *PC*, July 5, 1941; "Act to 'Fool-Proof' FDR Ban on Jim Crow," *CD*, July 12, 1941; "National Grapevine," *CD*, July 12, 1941.

2. "Women Hold Defense Confab at Howard," *CD*, July 5, 1941; "Women Urged to Seek Jobs," *NAN*, October 4, 1941.

3. "Laud FDR at March Victory Meeting," *PC*, July 12, 1941; "Act to 'Fool-Proof' FDR Ban on Jim Crow."

4. "D.C. March Group Shapes Future Plans," *ADW*, July 9, 1941; "Atlantic City Welcomes Elks," *ADW*, August 23, 1941; Gellman, *Death Blow to Jim Crow*, 135–144.

5. Ruchames, *Race, Jobs and Politics*, 24.

6. Gellman, *Death Blow to Jim Crow*, 135–144; "Steel Workers Foresee CIO Election Victory," *CD*, September 27, 1941; "Women Urged to Seek Jobs," *NAN*, October 4, 1941.

7. White, *Too Heavy a Load*, 110–75; McCluskey and Smith, *Mary McLeod Bethune*, 3–19, 132; Mary McLeod Bethune, "Closed Doors," in Collier-Thomas and Franklin, eds., *Sisters in Struggle*, 19–20.

8. "Jeanetta Welch, NCNW Secretary," *ADW*, April 30, 1943; "Jeanetta Welch Brown," *Akron Beacon Journal*, August 27, 2006; Height, *Open Wide the Freedom Gates*, 156, 81–83.

9. Harvard Sitkoff, "African American Militancy in the World War II South: Another Perspective," in McMillen, ed., *Remaking Dixie*, 72; A. Philip Randolph, "What Are We Fighting For?" *PM*, April 9, 1942; "Shortage of Defense Bonds Ends," *NYT*, January 15, 1942; Gilmore, *Defying Dixie*, 376.

10. "Cite 'Traitors' before FEPC in Job Probe," *CD*, January 24, 1942; 1; Kersten, *Race, Jobs, and the War*, 21–33; Garfinkle, *When Negroes March*, 74; "Lehman Deplores 'Passive' Defense," *NYT*, July 13, 1941.

11. Robert C. Weaver, "Defense Industries and the Negro," *Annals of the American Academy of Political and Social Science* 223 (September 1942), 64; Weaver, "Racial Employment Trends in National Defense, Part II," *Phylon* 3, no. 1 (1942), 23, 30.

12. "FEP Sets New Date for B'ham," *PC*, May 16, 1942; "Birmingham Forms Group to Aid FEPC," *CD*, May 30, 1942; "5 FEPC Agents in Birmingham," *PC*, May 30, 1942; "Order Shipyard Courses Opened to Negroes," *ADW*, June 4, 1942; "FEPC Gets Results in Dixie," *PC*, June 27, 1942; "FEPC Made Part of WPB," *NAN*, August 8, 194; "Segregation on Trial," *PC*, August 1, 1942; "Postpone El Paso FEPC Hearings," *CD*, August 29, 1942; "U.S. Accused of Ruining South's Race Relations," *ADW*, July 27, 1942, 1; Reed, *Seedtime for the Modern Civil Rights Movement*, 74–87; Foley, *Quest for Equality*, 64.

13. "Proposes Protest Blackouts in 3 Cities; Advises Plan to Fight U.S. Discrimination," *CD*, June 6, 1942; Tarry, *The Third Door*, 192; Gilmore, *Defying Dixie*, 366–367; "25,000 Roar Approval as Speakers Define 'Real-Democracy,'" *PC*, June 27, 1942; "12,000 in Chicago Voice Demands for Democracy," *CD*, July 4, 1942; "White

Charges Roosevelt Acted Contrary to Promise," *PC*, August 15, 1942; "Randolph Urges Fight to Save FEPC Status," *CD*, August 15, 1942; "Protest to President," *NYT*, August 17, 1942; "Highlights, Footnotes on New York's Protest Rally," *PC*, June 27, 1942.

14. Garfinkle, *When Negroes March*, 107, 110; Tarry, *The Third Door*, 192.

15. Sitkoff, "African American Militancy in the World War II South," 83; "McNutt to Address Victory Mass Meet," *PC*, June 27, 1942; Horne, *Black Liberation/Red Scare*, 94; "6000 in Harlem Cheer War Pleas," *NYT*, June 29, 1942; "Randolph Stole Show," *PC*, July 25, 1942; ". . . Wags Dog," *PC*, July 25, 1942.

16. Gilmore, *Defying Dixie*, 366–370; Murray, *Song in a Weary Throat*, 175.

17. Kersten, *Race, Jobs, and the War*, 39; M. S. Stuart, "Southern Say-So," *PC*, August 29, 1942; "Over 10,000 Attend St. Louis 'March on Washington' Rally," *PC*, August 22, 1942; "FDR Refuses Audience to Negro Race Leaders," *CD*, September 5, 1942.

18. Murray, *Song in a Weary Throat*, 71–114; Gilmore, *Defying Dixie*, 247–290, 346–399; New Workers School, "Problems of American Workers," n.d., flyer, folder 21, box 230, JLP; Morgan, *A Covert Life*.

19. "Form Permanent Structure for March on Washington," *NAN*, October 24, 1942; Gilmore, *Defying Dixie*, 385; "Name New Secretary of 'March,' " *CD*, December 26, 1942; "Before the Dream: Pauline Myers, Foot Soldier in a Long-Ago March for Civil Rights," *WP*, August 26, 1993; "Social Activist E. Pauline Myers Dies," *WP*, September 3, 1998.

20. Horace Cayton, "NAACP-March," *PC*, October 10, 1942.

21. Anderson, *A. Philip Randolph*, 267.

22. Cayton, "NAACP-March"; "3 Agents of Japan, 142 Aliens Seized in Raids by F.B.I.," *NYT*, September 6, 1942; "Seize 84 Negroes in Sedition Raids," *NYT*, September 22, 1942; "Views and Reviews," *PC*, August 22, 1942, and July 17, 1943; "The Horizon," *PC*, July 24, 1943; "Randolph Tells Philosophy behind 'March' Movement," *CD*, June 19, 1943; "Timely Topics," *NAN*, September 29, 1945.

23. "Negroes Should Back India Says Randolph," *PC*, August 22, 1942; Kapur, *Raising Up a Prophet*.

24. Gilmore, *Defying Dixie*, 386–391; " 'March' Movement Adds New Units," *PC*, October 31, 1942; White, "Nixon Was the One," 45–63.

25. Dwight Macdonald and Nancy Macdonald, *The War's Greatest Scandal!: The Story of Jim Crow in Uniform*, March on Washington Movement pamphlet, n.d., box 29, PPP; Kluger, *Simple Justice*, 155–282.

26. Walker, *In Defense of American Liberties*, 165–166; "Says Lynn Case Caused by Bias," *NAN*, December 5, 1942; "Lynn Gets Court Writ to Test Draft Legality," *PC*, January 2, 1943; George Q. Flynn, "Selective Service and American Blacks during World War II," *Journal of Negro History* 69, no. 1 (Winter 1984), 21–23; D'Emilio, *Lost Prophet*, 38–63; Macdonald and Macdonald, *The War's Greatest Scandal!*

27. D'Emilio, *Lost Prophet*, 7–63; Farmer, *Lay Bare the Heart*, 67–116; Meier and Rudwick, *CORE*.

28. Ransby, *Ella Baker*, 105–131; Richard M. Dalfume, "The 'Forgotten Years' of the Negro Revolution," *Journal of American History* 55 (June 1968), 99.

29. Arnesen, *Brotherhoods of Color*, 167–175; "The Labor Front," *CD*, November 7, 1942.

30. Ransby, *Ella Baker*, 105–131; "Randolph Prepares for New 'March,'" *PC*, December 26, 1942; "Randolph Urges 'I Am an American, Too,'" *PC*, January 9, 1943; "Randolph to Adopt Gandhi Technique," *CD*, January 9, 1943.

31. "Randolph Plans 'Civil Disobedience' Campaign," *NAN*, January 9, 1943; "Randolph to Adopt Gandhi Technique"; "Civil Disobedience," *PC*, January 23, 1943; "On Mr. Randolph's Proposal for Negro Action," *ADW*, January 19, 1943; "Four Talk on Passive Resistance," *CD*, March 13, 1943; "As the Crow Flies," *NAN*, January 9, 1943.

32. "Capital Groups Back Drive to Get Jobs for Negroes on Buses," *NAN*, August 15, 1942; "Riot Rumors Keep D.C. on Edge for Entire Week," *CD*, May 15, 1943; "Democracy Wins a Round," *CD*, May 15, 1943, 15.

33. Nelson, "Organized Labor and the Struggle for Black Equality"; "Outward Calm at Mobile with New Shipyard Setup," *CD*, June 12, 1943.

34. Lichtenstein, *The Most Dangerous Man in Detroit*, 207–210; "Kelly Acts to Ease Detroit Riot Curb," *NYT*, June 24, 1943.

35. "Fear New Trouble in Mobile," *CD*, June 5, 1943; "John Brown's Spirit Needs a Compass," *CD*, May 29, 1943; "N.A.A.C.P-M.O.W.M.," *PC*, June 19, 1943; Jones, "'Simple Truths of Democracy,'" 253–254; "Decides against March on Capital," *NYT*, July 4, 1943.

36. "Ross Next Chairman of FEPC!" *PC*, October 16, 1943; "FEPC Head's Red Leaning Bared in House Probe," *CT*, December 30, 1943; Ruchames, *Race, Jobs and Politics*, 68–86.

37. "Prepare Now," *CD*, July 17, 1943.

38. "Federated Clubs," *CD*, July 17, 1943; "National Council of Negro Women Swings into Action," press release, September 10, 1943, folder 11, box 11, Series 5, NCNW; "WAKE UP!" 1943, folder 5, box 11, Series 5, NCNW.

39. "'Hold Your Job' Week to Place Emphasis on Necessity of Keeping Economic Gains," *ADW*, July 21, 1943; "Federated Clubs"; White, *Too Heavy a Load*, 161–162.

40. "CIO Conference Opens Political Action Campaign," *CD*, January 15, 1944; Sullivan, *Days of Hope*, 178–179; Horne, *Red Seas*.

41. "Women in the National Picture," *CD*, January 29, 1944; Cobble, *The Other Women's Movement*, 1–49.

42. "Protests Hit Warren Ruling against FEPC," *CD*, November 6, 1943; "Roosevelt Gives FEPC New Life—Debunks Warren's Bias Ruling," *NAN*, November 13, 1943; "To Plan 'Back FEPC' Parley," *PC*, January 1, 1944.

43. Hedgeman, *The Trumpet Sounds*, 7, 28–36, 62, 75–78, 85; Murray, *Song in a Weary Throat*, 73–76; Ransby, *Ella Baker*, 76–78; "Job Group Has Mass Meeting," *NAN*, November 23, 1940; "Job Problems Facing Race Women Discussed at Hampton," *ADW*, May 14, 1941.

44. "Attend Mass Rally!" *NAN*, January 29, 1944; "Anti-Bias Measure Urged by Dubinsky," *NYT*, February 2, 1944; Hedgeman, *The Trumpet Sounds*, 85–90;

"Anna Arnold Hedgeman Heads Fine Staff," *PC*, December 1, 1945; Kesselman, *The Social Politics of FEPC*, 46.

45. Hedgeman, *The Gift of Chaos*, 18; Anna Arnold Hedgeman to Mary McLeod Bethune, July 6, 1944, folder 9, box 12, Series 5, NCNW; Hedgeman, "The Role of the Negro Woman," 496, 470, 472.

46. Hedgeman, *The Gift of Chaos*; Anna Arnold Hedgeman, "News from Washington," August 29, 1945, FEPC, 1943–52 folder, 19, APR; Chen, *The Fifth Freedom*, 32–87.

47. "National Grapevine," *CD*, June 24, 1944; Kesselman, *The Social Politics of FEPC*, 40, 43; "Seven Volunteer for Free Office Work for FEPC," *ADW*, February 6, 1946.

48. "FEPC-Post Mortem," *PC*, February 16, 1946; Richards, *Maida Springer*, 89; "Bethune Group Announces Vote for 12 Women of Year," *CD*, March 9, 1946; Hedgeman, *The Trumpet Sounds*, 88; "Minutes of Meeting of National Board of Directors," August 2, 1946, NCPF folder, box 258, Group IIA, NAACP; "Why Do We Need a Permanent FEPC?" n.d., flyer, folder 9, box 12, Series 5, NCNW.

49. "Minutes of Meeting of National Board of Directors," August 2, 1946; Roy Wilkins to Walter White, October 18, 1946, and Allan Knight Chalmers to Administrative Committee of the NAACP, October 25, 1946, NCPF folder, box 258, Group IIA, NAACP; "Plan to Make Mobilization Permanent; Would Supplant Council for Permanent FEPC," *ADW*, February 1, 1950; "Permanent FEPC Council to Function with Nat'l Emergency Rights Mobilization," *ADW*, February 9, 1950; Boyle, *The UAW and the Heyday of American Liberalism*, 108–110.

50. "Plan to Make Mobilization Permanent"; "Permanent FEPC Council to Function with Nat'l Emergency Rights Mobilization"; Hedgeman, *The Trumpet Sounds*, 95–128; "Jeanetta Welch Brown, Activist," *Tribune Business News* (Washington), August 29, 2006; Sullivan, *Lift Every Voice*, 321; Ransby, *Ella Baker*, 145–147; "Fraternal Council's Bureau Growing in Social Action," *PC*, May 26, 1945; "Student Fights Ban on Women in Law at Harvard," *NAN*, August 19, 1944; Murray, *Song in a Weary Throat*, 246–282; Sidney Wilkinson to Allan Knight Chalmers, May 19, 1947, folder 5, box 258, Group IIA, NAACP.

CHAPTER THREE: ROCKING THE CRADLE

1. Chen, *The Fifth Freedom*, 131; "Civil Rights Campaign Bans 'Red' Groups," *ADW*, December 25, 1949; "Red Issue Rips NAACP," *NAN*, January 21, 1950; "Pursuit of Democracy," *PC*, January 28, 1950; "Who's Right—Whose Wrong," *WAA*, January 21, 1950.

2. "Who's Right—Whose Wrong"; Wilkins, *Standing Fast*, 152; Schultz, "The FEPC," 80–92; Kluger, *Simple Justice*, 540; Murray, *Song in a Weary Throat*, 289.

3. Young, "Eisenhower's Federal Judges and Civil Rights Policy," 557; Sitkoff, *The Struggle for Black Equality*, 24–26.

4. Crespino, *In Search of Another Country*, 18–20; Smith, " 'When Reason Collides with Prejudice,' " 43.

5. Morris, *Origins of the Civil Rights Movement*, 38; White, "Nixon Was the One"; Burks, "Trailblazers," 80; Sullivan, ed., *Freedom Writer*, 81.

6. McGuire, *At the Dark End of the Street*, 3–39; Ransby, *Ella Baker*, 142.

7. Burks, "Trailblazers."

8. Morris, *Origins of the Civil Rights Movement*, 18–25.

9. McGuire, *At the Dark End of the Street*, 68–78.

10. Ibid., 76; Jackson, *From Civil Rights to Human Rights*, 56; Thornton, "Challenge and Response," 333–339.

11. Morris, *Origins of the Civil Rights Movement*, 17–25, 146; Burns, ed., *Daybreak of Freedom*, 82; Edgerton, *Speak Now against the Day*, 158–162.

12. "100,000 across Nation Protest Till Lynching," *CD*, October 8, 1955; "10,000 Jam Till Mass Meet Here," *CD*, October 8, 1955; "National Grapevine," *CD*, October 8, 1955; "50,000 New Yorkers Urge 'Dixie March,' " *Jet*, October 6, 1955; "Boycott Is Urged in Youth's Killing," *NYT*, October 12, 1955; "Plan D.C. March to Protest Till," *CD*, October 22, 1955; Feldstein, " 'I Wanted the Whole World to See.' "

13. Garrow, *Bearing the Cross*, 13; Parks quoted in Houck and Grindy, *Emmett Till*; "Bitter, Anguished Mourners Week at Bier of Lynched Boy," *PC*, September 10, 1955; "10,000 Jam Till Mass Meet Here"; "100,000 across Nation Protest Till Lynching"; Thornton, "Challenge and Response," 343.

14. Garrow, *Bearing the Cross*, 15; Thornton, "Challenge and Response," 340.

15. Garrow, ed., *The Montgomery Bus Boycott*, 47.

16. Abernathy, *And the Walls Came Tumbling Down*; Garrow, *Bearing the Cross*, 17.

17. Garrow, *Bearing the Cross*, 37, Edgerton, *Speak Now against the Day*, 239–240; "Stand and Fight Randolph Tells Men of M'House," *ADW*, June 6, 1945.

18. Jackson, *From Civil Rights to Human Rights*, 36–38; Garrow, *Bearing the Cross*, 41.

19. Garrow, *Bearing the Cross*, 17–19, 48, 51; Jackson, *From Civil Rights to Human Rights*, 36–38.

20. Parks, *Rosa Parks*, 125; Robinson, *Montgomery Bus Boycott*, 48–51; Morris, *Origins of the Civil Rights Movement*, 54; Garrow, *Bearing the Cross*, 18–19.

21. Robinson, *Montgomery Bus Boycott*, 55–58; Garrow, *Bearing the Cross*, 19.

22. Martin Luther King, Jr., "Stride toward Freedom," in Washington, ed., *A Testament of Hope*, 430; Garrow, *Bearing the Cross*, 22–23.

23. Edgar N. French, "The Beginnings of a New Age," in Garrow, ed., *The Walking City*, 179; King, "Stride toward Freedom," 432–434.

24. Burns, ed., *Daybreak of Freedom*, 94.

25. King, "Stride toward Freedom," 436.

26. Robinson, *Montgomery Bus Boycott*, 65; King, "Stride toward Freedom," 439–440.

27. Thornton, "Challenge and Response," 347; Jackson, *From Civil Rights to Human Rights*, 57–58.

28. Thornton, "Challenge and Response," 353.

29. Ibid., 353–355.

30. King, "Stride toward Freedom," 442–444.

31. Garrow, *Bearing the Cross*, 55, 59.

32. Burns, ed., *Daybreak of Freedom*, 150; "$1000 Reward Offered," *NYT*, February 1, 1956; "Second Negro Home in Alabama Rocked by Mysterious Bomb," *CT*, Febru-

ary 2, 1956; "10,000 in Alabama Hail Segregation," *NYT*, February 11, 1956; "Jail 115 Boycotters," *PC*, February 25, 1956.

33. Abernathy, "Natural History of a Social Movement," 154.

34. Burns, ed., *Daybreak of Freedom*, 151.

35. Ibid., 126.

36. D'Emilio, *Lost Prophet*, 224; AFSCME District 37, "Tentative Agreement on Merger," December 2, 1956, folder 8, box 27, AFSCME ST; "Cleveland Robinson, 80, Civil Rights Advocate," *NYT*, August 26, 1994.

37. Abernathy, "Natural History of a Social Movement," 161–162; D'Emilio, *Lost Prophet*, 227; Burns, ed., *Daybreak of Freedom*, 164–165.

38. Fairclough, *To Redeem the Soul of America*, 28; Burns, ed., *Daybreak of Freedom*, 168–169.

39. Burns, ed., *Daybreak of Freedom*, 170, 169.

40. Garrow, *Bearing the Cross*, 66–70; D'Emilio, *Lost Prophet*, 231–235.

41. Garrow, *Bearing the Cross*, 68–72.

42. "Administration Will Submit Plan on Civil Rights Today," *NYT*, March 28, 1956; "Rights Bill Dead, Eisenhower Told," *NYT*, July 26, 1956; Garrow, *Bearing the Cross*, 74–77.

43. "New Group to Aid Negroes in South," *NYT*, March 1, 1956; "Fund Announced by Union VEEP Philip Randolph," *ADW*, May 15, 1956; Reed, *The Chicago NAACP*, 180; King, *"All Labor Has Dignity,"* 75; Richards, *Maida Springer*, 91.

44. Richards, *Maida Springer;* Murray, *Song in a Weary Throat*, 279; Cobble, *The Other Women's Movement*, 43–45.

45. Richards, *Maida Springer*, 91; "16000 Rally in N.Y.," *PC*, June 2, 1956; "Randolph Reports on Garden Rally," *NAN*, June 16, 1956; Raines, *My Soul Is Rested*, 39.

46. Morris, *Origins of the Civil Rights Movement*, 26–39, 67–71; Sullivan, *Lift Every Voice*, 425–426; Garrow, *Bearing the Cross*, 78.

47. Garrow, *Bearing the Cross*, 82–84; Fairclough, *To Redeem the Soul of America*, 31–32.

48. Garrow, *Bearing the Cross*, 81–85; Fairclough, *To Redeem the Soul of America*, 29–33; Rustin and Baker quoted in D'Emilio, *Lost Prophet*, 247–248, 245.

49. Garrow, *Bearing the Cross*, 83–92; "Rev. King Tells Aims of May 17 Pilgrimage," *CD*, May 11, 1957; "Randolph Compares '57 Pilgrimage to '41 March," *NYT*, May 4, 1957; "Ready to March on Washington," *PC*, April 6, 1957; "March on Washington Plans Ready," *NAN*, April 13, 1957; "Labor to Participate in Mass Protest Rally," *CD*, April 13, 1957.

50. Garrow, *Bearing the Cross*, 91; "King Emerges as Top Negro Leader," *NAN*, June 1, 1957; "Wilkins Raps Hicks on Pilgrimage Comment," *NAN*, June 8, 1957; "Why Was Thurgood Absent from the Prayer Pilgrimage?" *CD*, May 27, 1957; Sullivan, ed., *Freedom Writer*, 138, 152; "Gotham Women Set Pilgrimage Pace," *NAN*, May 25, 1957.

51. Dudziak, *Cold War Civil Rights*, 115–151; Wilkins, *Standing Fast*, 246.

52. Tyson, *Radio Free Dixie*, 148–149.

53. Ibid., 137–165.

54. Garrow, *Bearing the Cross*, 96–125; Ransby, *Ella Baker*, 170–238; McGuire, *At the*

Dark End of the Street, 131–158; Chafe, *Civilities and Civil Rights*, 71–79; Lewis, *Walking with the Wind*, 81–83.

55. Carson, *In Struggle*, 9–44; Lewis, *Walking with the Wind*, 45; Sale, *SDS*.

CHAPTER FOUR: JIM CROW UNIONS

1. "Garden Rally," *NAN*, June 2, 1956; Biondi, *To Stand and Fight*, 154–155.

2. Reed, *The Chicago NAACP*, 180; Richards, *Maida Springer*, 91.

3. Gregory, *The Southern Diaspora*, 237–282; Horowitz, *"Negro and White, Unite and Fight,"* 206–242; "Willoughby Abner Dead at 51," *NYT*, December 4, 1972; "Negro Labor Leaders," *CD*, September 4, 1954; "Chicago NAACP Hits Lily-White Federal Homes," *ADW*, April 1, 1954; "Packinghouse Workers Move against Bias in Employment," *ADW*, February 8, 1955.

4. "Negro Labor Leaders"; "Labor Unions Awaken," *CD*, September 4, 1954.

5. "Tells of Laundry Union's War Work," *NAN*, April 10, 1943; Richards, *Maida Springer*, 66–72; Cobble, *The Other Women's Movement*, 44–45; "D. Robinson Gets Labor Dept. Plum," *NAN*, May 21, 1955.

6. "Labor Unions Awaken"; Lichtenstein, *State of the Union*, 79; "Trade Unionists Appeal for Rights in Merger," *ADW*, November 16, 1955.

7. "250 Unionists Join Rep. Diggs in Appeal for Quick Civil Rights Laws," *CD*, November 26, 1955; "Undercurrent in Labor," *CD*, December 3, 1955; "Mich. Unionists Guard Race Gains," *CD*, December 3, 1955.

8. Richards, *Maida Springer*, 48–52; Freeman, *Working-Class New York*, 89; Halpern and Horowitz, *Meatpackers*, 54–55.

9. "Randolph Says AFL-CIO to Step Up Fight on Racism," *CD*, January 28, 1956; "Mich. Unionists Guard Race Gains," *CD*, December 3, 1955.

10. "Labor Rally," *NAN*, November 3, 1956; "3-Way Fight in NAACP Race for Presidency," *NAN*, December 1, 1956; "Joe Overton Will Oppose Crawford," *NAN*, October 18, 1958; Lang, *Grassroots at the Gateway*, 97–126; Labor and Industry Committee, New York NAACP, "Meeting Minutes," 1958–1960, folder 2, box 4, JHP.

11. Reed, *The Chicago NAACP*, 180; Horowitz, *"Negro and White, Unite and Fight,"* 225; Battle and Sheffield, "Trade Union Leadership Council," 34–40; "Raise Our Union Status That Whole Race May Be Improved," *PC*, August 29, 1959; Salvatore, *Singing in a Strange Land*, 179.

12. "In Friendship Club Formed to Aid South," *NAN*, March 17, 1956; "New Group to Aid Negroes in South," *NYT*, March 1, 1956; "Date with Destiny in DC—Rev. King," *NAN*, May 11, 1957; "World Watches Prayer Pilgrimage to Capital," *PC*, May 18, 1957; King, *"All Labor Has Dignity,"* 19; "District 65 Gives NAACP $10,000," *NAN*, November 1, 1958; Jones, *Selma of the North*, 42.

13. "Meeting Minutes," May 26, 1959, folder 2, box 4, JHP; "Labor's Side," *LAS*, August 6, 1959; "Reuther, Randolph to Address Labor Sessions of NAACP Meet," *ADW*, July 1, 1959; A. Philip Randolph Blasts Race Bias in NAACP Address," *ADW*, July 18, 1959.

14. "Meany, in a Fiery Debate, Denounces Negro Unionist," *NYT*, September 24, 1959;

"AFL-CIO Adopts 'Go Slow' Policy," *LAS*, October 1, 1959; "Defends NAACP's War on Union Bias," *CT*, June 25, 1960.

15. "200 New Yorkers Will Attend Labor Confab," *NAN*, May 21, 1960; "New Negro Labor Group Now Has 25 Councils," *NAN*, May 14, 1960; Negro American Labor Council (hereafter NALC), "Constitution," May 1960, folder 1, box 1, RPPM; "'Backing NALC All the Way,' Reuther Tells Labor Group," *PC*, June 4, 1960; Biography of Richard Parish, RPP; Freeman, *Working-Class New York*, 204.

16. A. Philip Randolph, "The Civil Rights Revolution and Negro Workers in the Labor Movement," Keynote Address to the Founding Convention of the NALC, Detroit, May 28, 1960, folder 13, box 2, JHP.

17. NALC, "Constitution"; Randolph, "Civil Rights Revolution and Negro Workers."

18. NALC, "Constitution"; Randolph, "Civil Rights Revolution and Negro Workers," 1; Kelley, "'But a Local Phase of a World Problem.'"

19. "NALC Faces 1st Dilemma; Should It Admit Whites?" June 7, 1960; Marable, *Malcolm X*, 160–162; Randolph, "Civil Rights Revolution and Negro Workers," 30.

20. "Story behind the Birth of Militant Labor Body," *CD*, June 8, 1960, 4.

21. "Martin King Says McCarthyism Up," *CD*, May 17, 1961; Garrow, *Bearing the Cross*, 194–196; Goodman, *The Committee*, 410.

22. "New Negro Labor Council Founded," *NAN*, June 4, 1960; "Negro Labor Unit Names 2 Women," *NYT*, May 30, 1960.

23. "Women Demand Positions on NALC Board," *CD*, June 9, 1960; "Negro Labor Unit Names 2 Women"; "The Women," *NAN*, June 4, 1960.

24. A. Philip Randolph, "Annual Report: Negro American Labor Council, 1960–1961," folder 3, box 3, JHP.

25. Herman Walker to A. Philip Randolph, January 23, 1961; and Ted Thomas to A. Philip Randolph, April 3, 1961, both in reel 5, RPPM; "Local NALC Unit Elects Officers," *PC*, July 16, 1960; "Longshoremen 'Break-through' on Bias Issue," *LAS*, September 8, 1960; Randolph, "Annual Report."

26. Dudziak, *Cold War Civil Rights*, 156–157; MacKenzie and Weisbrot, *The Liberal Hour*, 142–143.

27. "Negro Labor Group Meets in Capital," *NAN*, February 18, 1961; "President Wants All Americans Put Back to Work," *ADW*, February 22, 1961; Randolph, "Annual Report," 13; "Kennedy Bars Bias in Work Done for U.S.," *CT*, March 7, 1961; Kessler-Harris, *In Pursuit of Equity*, 212.

28. *New York NALC Newsletter*, May 1960 [*sic*], folder 8, box 3, JHP; *NALC Newsletter*, August 1961, ibid.; Randolph, "Annual Report."

29. *Newsletter, Chicago Area Chapter NALC*, April 1961; Leon Joy Jennings and Lola Belle Holmes to A. Philip Randolph, August 17, 1961; and A. Philip Randolph to Lola Belle Holmes, August 28, 1961, all in "Chicago Correspondence File," NALC Records, reel 5, RPPM; "NALC Women Plan Meet," *NAN*, March 18, 1961; "Call to Negro Women," *NY NALC Newsletter*, February–March 1962, folder 8, box 3, JHP.

30. *NALC Newsletter*, August 1961; Jones, *Selma of the North*, 44–45; "Negro Youths Picket Stores," *Milwaukee Star*, August 4, 1962; Turrini, "Phooie on Louie," 15; "Annual Report, NALC, 1960–1961."

31. "Drafted for Fred Small," folder 3, box 9, JHP; *NALC Newsletter*, August 1961.

32. "Mass Rally for Unity," Emergency Committee for Unity on Social and Economic Problems, folder 5, box 2, JHP; Marable, *Malcolm X*, 190–192.

33. "Negroes War on Top Labor Heads," *NAN*, May 6, 1961; "Annual Report, NALC, 1960–1961."

34. "Negroes War on Top Labor Heads"; James Haughton, "Minutes of Emergency Meeting of the National Executive Board, NALC," n.d., folder 1, box 2, JHP.

35. "Annual Report, NALC, 1960–1961"; Horace Sheffield, "Brief in Support of Proposed FEPC Legislation," NALC Records, reel 5, RPPM; "A Curb on Racism in Labor Opposed," *NYT*, August 22, 1961.

36. "Rights Unit Asks Congress to End Union Race Bars," *NYT*, October. 14, 1961, "'Jim Crow' Unions," *NYT*, October 15, 1961; Sheffield, "Brief in Support of Proposed FEPC Legislation."

37. Sheffield, "Brief in Support of Proposed FEPC Legislation."

38. Hill, "Racial Practices of Organized Labor," 288–289; "Negroes Gird for Support of Randolph," *CD*, November 13, 1961; "AFL-CIO Ends Halycon Days at Bal Harbour Site," *Toledo Blade*, February 19, 1996.

39. King, *"All Labor Has Dignity,"* 31–35; "Segregation Must Die If Democracy to Live—King," *LAS*, December 14, 1961; Anderson, *A. Philip Randolph*, 309.

40. King, *"All Labor Has Dignity,"* 35.

41. Ibid.

42. "Labor Leader George Meany to Address NALC," *NAN*, October 27, 1962.

43. NALC, "Gala Benefit Show," January 26, 1962, folder 17, box 2, JHP; Malcolm X to Cleveland Robinson, July 1962, General Correspondence, 1959–1966 file, box 10, CRP; "2500 at Moslem Rally," *NAN*, July 28, 1962.

44. James Haughton, "NALC Local Council Officers," 1962, folder 1, box 2, JHP; Horace Sheffield to Messrs. Wiley A. Branton and George Barrett, February 16, 1962, NALC–Detroit, 1961–62, NALC Records, reel 5, RPPM; Self, *American Babylon*, 181; Clarence D. Horton and Clarence Pace to "Friend," June 20, 1962, NALC–Newark, 1961–62, NALC Records, reel 5, RPPM; "Negro Youths Picket Stores," August 4, 1961, and "NAACP State Conference Supports NALC," *Milwaukee Star*, 1963, unidentified newspaper clippings, NALC–Milwaukee, 1962–66, NALC Records, reel 5, RPPM.

45. "Negro Labor Group Dwindles; Leftist Activity Is Blamed," *Buffalo Evening News*, September 28, 1961; A. Philip Randolph to John H. Coston, September 7, 1961; and "Randolph Bans Communist Infiltration and Domination of NALC," April 11, 1962, both in folder 12, box 4, RPPM; Charles Chavers to NALC National Executive Committee, June 27, 1962, "Cleveland Correspondence," Series II, reel 5, RPPM; Garrow, *Bearing the Cross*, 195.

46. Randolph to Chavers, July 25, 1962; Randolph to Frank Evans, July 6, 1962; Evans to Randolph, June 24, 1963, all in Cleveland Correspondence, Series II, reel 5, RPPM; Timuel Black to A. Philip Randolph, September 1, 1962, Chicago Correspondence, folder 15, box 4, RPP.

47. "SCHR Finds ILGWU Guilty of Racial Discrimination," *NAN*, July 7, 1962.

48. Richards, *Maida Springer*, 270; Lichtenstein, *State of the Union*, 162–166; "Union Chief Randolph Defends Dress Workers' Union," *CD*, August 27, 1962.

49. "Labor Leader George Meany to Address NALC," *NAN*, October 27, 1962; "NAACP Hits Back at George Meany," *NAN*, November 17, 1962.

50. "Meany Blasts NAACP for Union Attack," *CT*, November 10, 1962; "NAACP Hits Back at George Meany."

51. Timuel Black to A. Philip Randolph, September 1, 1962, Chicago Dispute File, folder 15, box 4, RPP; "Timuel Black a Historian—and Part of Civil Rights History," *CST*, February 1, 2012.

52. "Statement by the Chicago Delegation," 1962; Willoughby Abner to A. Philip Randolph, January 25, 1963; Leon Joy Jennings to A. Philip Randolph, February 23, 1963; "Woman Tells of Spying on Lightfoot for the FBI," *CT*, January 25, 1963; Timuel Black to A. Philip Randolph, April 15, 1963, all in Chicago Dispute File, folder 15, box 4, RPP; James Haughton, "Third Annual NALC Convention Exposes Fearful Leadership," folder 15, box 2, JHP.

53. Anderson, *A. Philip Randolph*, 323–325; Garrow, *Bearing the Cross*, 266.

CHAPTER FIVE: FOR JOBS AND FREEDOM

1. Hedgeman, *The Gift of Chaos*, 63–66; Hedgeman, *The Trumpet Sounds*, 168–170; Garrow, *Bearing the Cross*, 266.

2. Eskew, *But for Birmingham*, 193–216; Carson, *In Struggle*, 86; Lewis, *Walking with the Wind*, 188.

3. "A. Philip Randolph's Wife Is Dead at 79," *NAN*, April 20, 1963; Hedgeman, *The Gift of Chaos*, 168–171; Garrow, *Bearing the Cross*, 266; D'Emilio, *Lost Prophet*, 330; Barber, *Marching on Washington*, 145–146.

4. Hedgeman, *The Trumpet Sounds*, 168–169; "Problems of Negro Women Discussed at Meeting Sponsored by U.S. Group," *CD*, April 30, 1963; "JFK Commission Notes Needs of Negro Women," *NAN*, August 17, 1963; "Report Cites Burdens on U.S. Negro Women," *LAT*, October 15, 1963; Kessler-Harris, *In Pursuit of Equity*, 226–230; Murray, *Song in a Weary Throat*, 347; Barber, *Marching on Washington*, 159; Swados, "Revolution on the March"; Hedgeman, *The Gift of Chaos*, 67–70.

5. "Dr. King Denounces President on Rights," *NYT*, June 10, 1963; Hedgeman, *The Trumpet Sounds*, 168–169; Hedgeman, *The Gift of Chaos*, 67–70; Garrow, *Bearing the Cross*, 268–270.

6. Garrow, *Bearing the Cross*, 268–270.

7. Anderson, *A. Philip Randolph*, 326; Garrow, *Bearing the Cross*, 272; Murray Kempton, "A. Philip Randolph," *New Republic*, July 6, 1963, 17.

8. Salvatore, *Singing in a Strange Land*, 251–253; King, *"All Labor Has Dignity,"* 83–84.

9. "Proposed Plans for March," March on Washington folder, box 26, APR; D'Emilio, *Lost Prophet*, 340–345; Swados, "Revolution on the March."

10. D'Emilio, *Lost Prophet*, 340–345; Swados, "Revolution on the March."

11. "Labor Is Divided on Capital March," *NYT*, August 13, 1963; "Labor-Negro Rift Expected to Last," *NYT*, August 17, 1963; Anderson, *A. Philip Randolph*, 327.

12. D'Emilio, *Lost Prophet*, 343–344; Pfeffer, *A. Philip Randolph*, 261.

13. Nadle, "View from the Front of the Bus;" "Muslim Leader Plans to Join Washington March," *CD*, August 10, 1963; "'No Muslims in D.C. March': Malcolm X," *CD*, August 26, 1963; Marable, *Malcolm X*, 255.

14. Pfeffer, *A. Philip Randolph*, 258; Reese Cleghorn, "The Angels Are White," *New Republic*, August 17, 1963, 14.

15. Pfeffer, *A. Philip Randolph*, 258; Swados, "Revolution on the March," 106–107.

16. Swados, "Revolution on the March," 106–107; "Organizing Manual No. 2," Signs for Buses folder, box 39, BMP.

17. Hedgeman, *The Trumpet Sounds*, 173–180.

18. Ibid.; Richards, *Maida Springer*, 262–264; Height quoted in Juan Williams, "A Great Day in Washington," *The Crisis*, 110, no. 4, July/August 2003, 29; Collier-Thomas, *Sisters in the Struggle*, 91.

19. "Randolph Says Rights Revolution Underway," *ADW*, August 27, 1963; "Capital Ready for Big Rights March Today," *CT*, August 28, 1963; "Alert Troops for Rights March," *CT*, August 22, 1963; "Civil Rights," *Time*, September 6, 1963, 14; "Capital Is Ready for March Today," *NYT*, August 28, 1963; "Washington Gets Jittery over March," *LAT*, August 28, 1963.

20. "Most Whites in North, West Say They Oppose Rights Demonstrations," *WSJ*, August 28, 1963; "A Right and a Responsibility," *LAT*, August 27, 1963; "Republican Pessimistic," *NYT*, August 21, 1963; "Powder Keg," *CST*, August 24, 1963.

21. "Most Whites in North, West Say They Oppose Rights Demonstrations"; "A Right and a Responsibility"; "Beware of Marching Techniques," *LAT*, September 5, 1963; "The March," *The Nation*, 197, no. 7, September 14, 1963, 121; "Capital Ready for Big Rights March Today."

22. Russell Baker, "Capital Is Occupied by a Gentle Army," *NYT*, August 29, 1963; "Most of Capital Deserted for Day," *NYT*, August 29, 1963.

23. "Newsletter 2" and "Organizing Manual No. 2," Signs for Buses folder, box 39, BMP.

24. "Unions to Send Marchers," *NYT*, August 27, 1963; Nadle, "View from the Front of the Bus"; "The March," *The New Yorker*, September 7, 1963, 30.

25. "Brando Joins Rights March, 47 Arrested," *LAT*, July 28, 1963; "Hollywood March Committee," press release; and unsigned letter of dissent, n.d., both in folder 468, box 39, CHP; "Midnight Benefit Show," poster, August 23, 1963, RLG; "March on LA City Hall Slated for Wednesday," *LAT*, August 27, 1963.

26. "Unions to Send Marchers"; "80,000 Box Lunches Were Set Up by Nat. Churches," *PC*, August 31, 1963; Euchner, *Nobody Turn Me Around*, 8–9; William H. Johnson to Delegates, August 19, 1963; and March on Washington, press release, "Signs for Buses" folder, both in box 39, BMP.

27. Nadle, "View from the Front of the Bus," *Village Voice*, September 5, 1963, 5.

28. "March Sidelights," *CD*, August 29, 1963; "14000 Return by Train," *NYT*, August 29, 1963; "'Freedom Day' Will Live Forever," *CD*, August 29, 1963; "Local Groups

Prepare for Washington Trip," *ADW*, August 27, 1963; "2500 Jam Station Enroute to March," *CD*, August 28, 1963; "Capital Jammed," *CD*, August 28, 1963; "1686 Chicagoans En Route to Washington," *CT*, August 28, 1963; Euchner, *Nobody Turn Me Around*, 35; "Civil Rights," 14; "Trains Rolled in Every 11½ minutes," *BAA*, September 7, 1963.

29. "On to D.C.," *LAS*, August 22, 1963; Nadle, "View from the Front of the Bus"; Euchner, *Nobody Turn Me Around*, 66–67; "Hollywood March Committee," press release, August 7, 1963, folder 468, box 39, CHP; "Film Stars Await Flight to D.C. for Big Rights Rally," *LAS*, August 22, 1963.

30. "Congress Cordial but Not Swayed," *NYT*, August 29, 1963; "Senate Passes Rail Bill," *NYT*, August 28, 1963.

31. Baker, "Capital Is Occupied by Gentle Army"; "The March," *The New Yorker*, September 7, 1963, 30.

32. Baker, "Capital Is Occupied by Gentle Army"; Carson, *In Struggle*, 56–65.

33. Nadle, "View from the Front of the Bus"; Sugrue, *Sweet Land of Liberty*, 309; "March 'Impressed' Malcolm X," *NAN*, September 7, 1963.

34. Lerone Bennett, "Masses Were March Heroes," *Ebony*, November 1963, 119; "Big Day—End and a Beginning," *Newsweek*, September 9, 1963, 20; "Civil Rights," 14.

35. "Big Day—End and a Beginning," 20; "200,000 Demand Full Rights Now," *AC*, August 29, 1963; "The March," *The New Yorker*, September 7, 1963, 31; "Civil Rights," 14.

36. "Big Day—End and a Beginning," 20; "200,000 Demand Full Rights Now"; Haskins, *The March on Washington*, 85; "The March," *The New Yorker*, September 7, 1963, 31; "Civil Rights," 14; Bennett, "Masses Were March Heroes"; "Before the Dream: Pauline Myers, Foot Soldier in a Long-Ago March for Civil Rights," *WP*, August 26, 1993.

37. "King's Address a Fitting Climax," *PC*, September 7, 1963; Baker, "Capital Is Occupied by Gentle Army"; Educational Radio Network, "Celebrity Participation in the March on Washington," http://openvault.wgbh.org/catalog/march-bc109d-celebrity-participation-in-the-march-on-washington (accessed April 7, 2012).

38. Educational Radio Network, "The March Begins," http://openvault.wgbh.org/catalog/march-592217-the-march-begins (accessed April 7, 2012).

39. "King's Address a Fitting Climax"; Educational Radio Network, "The March Begins."

40. Educational Radio Network, "The March Begins."

41. Ibid.

42. "Congress Cordial but Not Swayed"; "King's Address a Fitting Climax"; Educational Radio Network, "The March Begins."

43. "King's Address a Fitting Climax"; Educational Radio Network, "The March Begins." For the original text of Lewis' speech see John Lewis, "Which Side Is the Federal Government On?" in Birnbaum and Taylor, eds., *Civil Rights since 1787*, 501–503. The speech as delivered is "Text of Lewis' Speech at Washington," *Student Voice* 4, no. 3 (October 1963), 1, 3–4.

44. Lewis, *Walking with the Wind*, 22–226; "Prelate Objects to Rights Speech," *NYT*, August 29, 1963; "Civil Rights," 15.

45. Educational Radio Network, "The March Begins."

46. "Excerpts from Addresses at Lincoln Memorial during Capital Civil Rights March," *NYT*, August 29, 1963.

47. "King's Address a Fitting Climax"; Martin Luther King Jr., "I Have a Dream," in Birnbaum and Taylor, eds., *Civil Rights since 1787*, 504–507.

48. Hansen, *The Dream*, 51–63.

49. E. W. Kenworthy, "200,000 March for Civil Rights in Orderly Washington Rally," *NYT*, August 29, 1963; Jackson, *From Civil Rights to Human Rights*, 181; Hansen, *The Dream*, 51–63.

50. "King's Address a Fitting Climax"; Murray Kempton, "The March on Washington," *New Republic*, September 14, 1963, 19.

51. "Civil Rights: A Message from 200,000 Marchers," *LAT*, September 1, 1963; "Marchers Award 'Today Is History,' " *NYT*, August 29, 1963; Nadle, "View from the Front of the Bus"; Euchner, *Nobody Turn Me Around*, 207; "Views Differ on Effect of Rights March," *CT*, August 30, 1963.

52. "Big Day—End, and a Beginning," 22; "President Meets March Leaders," *NYT*, August 29, 1963.

CHAPTER SIX: BATTLE LINES DRAWN

1. "Southern Press Plays Up March," *NYT*, September 2, 1963; "TV: Coverage of March," *NYT*, August 29, 1963; "Europeans View the March on TV," *NYT*, August 29, 1963; "Europe Shows Restraint in March Views," *NYT*, August 29, 1963.

2. "They Came Marching up Conscience Road," *Life*, September 6, 1963, 21; "3¹/₂-Year-Old Protest Movement Comes of Age in Capital Rally," *NYT*, August 29, 1963; "I Have a Dream," *AC*, August 30, 1963.

3. "Shots, Rocks Hit 'Freedom' Bus" and "Nightriders Raid Home," *BAA*, September 7, 1963; "3 Rights Buses Are Stoned," *NYT*, August 29, 1963; "DC Marchers Enroute Home Beaten in Miss.," *ADW*, September 11, 1963.

4. "Big Day—End and a Beginning," *Newsweek*, September 9, 1963, 22; "Angry Crowd Runs Police Barricades; Damage Home Purchased by Negro Couple," *ADW*, August 31, 1963; "Outsiders Blamed for Disorders," *NYT*, September 8, 1963; "Folcroft, PA, Peaceful after Anti-Negro Disorders," *NYT*, September 1, 1963; "Driven Crazy by Race Hate, Negro Pioneer Hospitalized," *CD*, December 3, 1963; "Harassed Negroes Find Another Home," *NYT*, April 3, 1963.

5. James Reston, "The First Significant Test of the Freedom March," *NYT*, August 30, 1963.

6. "Women Close Meeting: Emphasize Civil Rights," *ADW*, September 6, 1963; "NCNW Sponsors Leadership Conference," *PC*, September 13, 1963; Collier-Thomas and Franklin, eds., *Sisters in the Struggle*, 88–89.

7. D'Emilio, *Lost Prophet*, 360; Garrow, *Bearing the Cross*, 288, "Leaders of March Pledge Widening of Rights Drive," *NYT*, August 30, 1963.

8. "Building Unions Shunning Parade," *NYT*, August 30, 1963; "103,000 in Parade, Salute Labor Day," *NYT*, September 3, 1963.

9. "Labor's Meany Urges FEP Law in Civil Rights Act," *ADW*, September 1, 1963;

"Meany Presses for More Jobs and Equality," *NAN*, September 7, 1963; "Meany Urges Spur for Economy," *CT*, September 1, 1963.

10. D'Emilio, *Lost Prophet*, 358–361; Garrow, *Bearing the Cross*, 287–289.

11. "Racist Open Housing Foes Plan to March," *CD*, September 10, 1963; "Open Housing Would Lose at Polls: Berry," *CT*, September 16, 1963; "Halt Open Housing Referendum," *CD*, September 17, 1963; "Rights Hurting Kennedy Hopes," *LAT*, October 13, 1963; "Pushing Too Fast: Survey," *NAN*, September 7, 1963. Stewart Alsop and Oliver Quayle, "What Northerners Really Think of Negroes," *Saturday Evening Post* 236, no. 30 (September 7, 1963), 17.

12. "Rights Hurting Kennedy Hopes"; "Rights Drive Seen Harmful to Kennedy," *LAT*, September 10, 1963; "Goldwater Slicing into Kennedy's Lead," *LAT*, October 16, 1963; "Integration Pushed 'Too Fast,' Say 50%," *LAT*, September 11, 1963.

13. "Wallace Ends Resistance as Guard Is Federalized," *NYT*, September 11, 1963; Eskew, *But for Birmingham*, 321–324.

14. Eskew, *But for Birmingham*, 320–322; Garrow, *Bearing the Cross*, 292.

15. "Crisis of Tactics Is Facing Negroes," *NYT*, September 29, 1963; "Dr. King Calls Birmingham a Blow to Nonviolence," *NYT*, September 25, 1963; "Negroes 'Duped,' Aide of King Says," *NYT*, September 26, 1963; "Disillusionment and Disappointment," *PC*, October 5, 1963, Garrow, *Bearing the Cross*, 295–297.

16. "Urban League Drafts New 10-Point Integration Plan," *CD*, June 12, 1963; Whitney Young, "'Domestic Marshall Plan': 'Compensation—Yes,'" *NYT*, October 6, 1963; Kyle Haselden, "'Parity, Not Preference': Compensation—No," *NYT*, October 6, 1963; Brauer, "Kennedy, Johnson, and the War on Poverty," 105.

17. "JFK, Demos Try to Work Out Compromise on Civil Rights Bill," *CD*, October 29, 1963; "Wilkins Says Government Playing with Human Lives," *CD*, October 26, 1963.

18. Dittmer, *Local People*, 194–207; Carson, *In Struggle*, 97–100.

19. "March 'Impressed' Malcolm X," *NAN*, September 7, 1963; "Black Muslims Join New Militant Northern Negro Organization," *CD*, November 21, 1963; Salvatore, *Singing in a Strange Land*, 259–262.

20. George Brietman, ed., *Malcolm X Speaks*, 3–17.

21. "NCNW Convention Tribute to Women," *LAS*, November 28, 1963; "Negro Women's Council Holds Nat'l Convention," *ADW*, December 1, 1963; Pauli Murray, "The Negro Woman in the Quest for Equality," *The Acorn*, June 1964, reprinted in Lerner, ed., *Black Women in White America*; Dorothy Height, "We Wanted the Voice of a Woman to Be Heard," in Collier-Thomas and Franklin, eds., *Sisters in the Struggle*, 83–91.

22. Caro, *The Passage of Power*, 8–9, 173–175; "King Believes New President OK on Rights," *CD*, November 26, 1963; "Negroes Ponder Next Rights Step," *NYT*, November 25, 1963.

23. Johnson, *Public Papers*; Wilkins and Mathews, *Standing Fast*, 296; Caro, *The Passage of Power*, 257.

24. Wilkins, *Standing Fast*, 296; "Civil Righters Speculate over Johnson's Meeting with Wilkins," *CD*, December 5, 1963; "See High Hopes for Johnson," *LAS*, December 5, 1963; D'Emilio, *Lost Prophet*, 362.

25. "Force U.S. to Act, Rights Unit Told," *NYT*, November 30, 1963; "Student Group Vows No Lag in Rights Fight," *LAT*, November 30, 1963; Carson, *In Struggle*, 97–100.

26. "Rustin Sees Losses," *NYT*, December 2, 1963; D'Emilio, *Lost Prophet*, 363.

27. "Confetti," *CD*, December 4, 1963; "President Spurs Drive for House to Act on Rights," *NYT*, December 4, 1963; "CORE Leader Asks for Federal School Fund," *CD*, December 5, 1963; "Nobody Secure in Rights Until Everybody Is Secure—Randolph," *ADW*, December 11, 1963; "Threatens Church Sit-in If Senate Filibusters on Rights: Randolph," *CD*, December 14, 1963; "CORE Salutes One of Its Own," *NAN*, December 14, 1963.

28. "President Spurs Drive for House to Act on Rights"; "Leadership Conference on Civil Rights Slates Washington Meeting," *NYT*, December 4, 1963; "Pres. Johnson Throws Weight of Administration behind All Out Campaign for Civil Rights Bill," *ADW*, December 4, 1963; "Labor Pledges Support to Johnson on Rights," *CD*, December 5, 1963.

29. Johnson, *Public Papers*, 112–118; Brauer, "Kennedy, Johnson, and the War on Poverty," 114.

30. Caro, *Passage of Power*, 547; "Johnson Asks Negroes to Help Battle Poverty," *LAT*, January 19, 1964; "Negro Rights Leaders Talk with Johnson," *CT*, January 19, 1964.

31. Carson, *In Struggle*, 107–110; "Freedom Push in Mississippi," *LAT*, June 14, 1964; John Herbers, "In the South: Battle Lines Are Drawn for Summer Offensive," *NYT*, April 19, 1964.

32. "Negroes Ponder Malcolm's Move," *NYT*, March 15, 1964; "Malcolm X Ignores Brother," *NAN*, April 4, 1964; Marable, *Malcolm X*, 269–320.

33. "Will LBJ Name Woman to Top Federal Role?" *PC*, December 7, 1963; "Is LBJ Overlooking Negro Women in Filling Top-Paying Gov't Posts?" *PC*, April 4, 1964.

34. "The Committee for the Defense of Working Women," January 14, 1964, folder 4, box 4, JHP; "A Call to Civil Rights Organizations, Trade Unions, Churches . . . for an Action Workshop," June 13, 1964, folder 1, box 5, JHP; "For Better Working Conditions, Higher Wages and Job Security for Negro and Puerto Rican Women Workers," undated flyer, folder 3, box 4, JHP.

35. Murray, *Song in a Weary Throat*, 358; MacLean, *Freedom Is Not Enough*, 121.

36. "The South's Strategy," *NYT*, March 28, 1964; "Wisconsin Vote Hailed in South by Rights Foes," *NYT*, April 9, 1964; "Alabama Governor's Strong Showing in Wisconsin Primary Is Gratifying to the Segregationists," *NYT*, April 12, 1964.

37. "If Filibuster Lasts until May Civil Disobedience May Result," *LAS*, April 2, 1964; "Negroes Plan Pressure on Senators in Rights Fight," *LAT*, April 2, 1964; "Negroes Told to Pressure President," *LAT*, April 5, 1964.

38. "Malcolm X Ignores Brother," *NAN*, April 4, 1964; "NY NAACP Adopts Militant Stand," *CD*, April 4, 1964; "Civil Rights Groups to March on Fair in Its Opening Days," *NYT*, April 9, 1964; "CORE Maps Tie-up on Roads to Fair," *NYT*, April 10, 1964; "CORE Again Pickets Fair," *NAN*, May 2, 1964; "'CORE Is Going Back to the Fair!' Says Jim Farmer," *NAN*, May 2, 1964.

39. Herbers, "In the South."

40. "Declaration of War on Poverty with a One-Day Work Stoppage and Prayer Vigil," resolution submitted to the Fourth Annual Convention of the NALC, Cleveland, May 29–31, 1964, folder 16, box 2, JHP; "NAACP Maps One Day Work Stoppage," *NAN*, May 2, 1964.

41. A. Philip Randolph, "Crossroads of the Civil Rights Revolution," Keynote Address to the Fourth Annual Convention of the NALC, May 29, 1964, folder 16, box 2, JHP.

42. Resolutions adopted at NALC Convention, May 29–31, 1964, folder 16, box 2, JHP; "Work Halt, Prayer Next Big Civil Rights Move," *CD*, June 8, 1964; Randolph, "Crossroads of the Civil Rights Revolution."

43. "Labor Leaders Propose Rights Summit to Review Aims, Means," *NAN*, June 13, 1964; Victor Riesel, "One-Day Work Stoppage Planned," *LAT*, May 6, 1964; "Labor Convention Opens Friday in Cleveland with Many Demands," *NAN*, May 30, 1964; "Work Halt, Prayer Next Big Civil Rights Move"; "Dirksen the Real Hero in Battle for Cloture," *LAT*, June 22, 1964; Caro, *Passage of Power*, 568–569.

44. Carson, *In Struggle*, 114–115, 122–124; "Chairman Requests Federal Marshals," *Student Voice*, June 30, 1964, 2, in Carson, ed., *The Student Voice*, 164.

45. "Goldwater Appeal: Not Only 'Nuts and Kooks,' " *NYT*, June 21, 1964; "Appeal to the 'White Backlash' Appears to Be Goldwater Strategy," *LAT*, July 16, 1964; Perlstein, *Before the Storm*, 357–405.

46. "Harlem Riots over Death of 15 Yr. Old Boy," *CD*, July 20, 1964; "Violence Flares Again in Harlem," *NYT*, July 20, 1964; D'Emilio, *Lost Prophet*, 382–383.

47. "Texts of Statements by Negro Leaders," *NYT*, July 30, 1964; "Negro Leaders Split Again," *CD*, August 1, 1964; "Who Speaks for the Negro?" *NYT*, July 30, 1964; D'Emilio, *Lost Prophet*, 383–385.

48. "Some Refuse to Yield in Seating Fight," *LAT*, August 26, 1964; "Democrats' Fast 'Paste-up' Job Kept Convention from Blowing Up," *CD*, August 27, 1964; "Mississippi Seating Marks New Era for Negroes," *NAN*, August 29, 1964; "Johnson Criticized by Freedom Party," *NYT*, August 30, 1964; "A Major Victory," *NAN*, September 5, 1964; Lewis, *Walking with the Wind*, 291–292; D'Emilio, *Lost Prophet*, 388–392.

49. "Malcolm X Article Favors Goldwater," *NYT*, September 8, 1964; MacKensie and Weisbrot, *The Liberal Hour*, 170–172; Self, *American Babylon*, 260–262.

EPILOGUE

1. A. Philip Randolph, "Opening Remarks at Conference of Negro Leaders," folder 3, box 3, GWP.

2. Ibid.

3. A. Philip Randolph to Whitney Young, January 11, 1965, NALC file, box 39, part III, series A, NUL; "Randolph to Keynote Conference," *NAN*, January 23, 1965; Whitney Young, "Help Wanted: New Jobs for Negroes," January 30, 1965, folder 6, box 3, GWP.

4. George Wiley, "Notes on Conference of Negro Leaders," January 30–31, 1965, folder 6, box 3, GWP; Conference of Negro Leaders, "Statement to the Press," January 31, 1965, box 5, AAH.

5. Joseph, *Waiting 'Till the Midnight Hour*, 132–173; Jackson, *From Civil Rights to Human Rights*, 276–307; D'Emilio, *Lost Prophet*, 393–416; Cobble, *The Other Women's Movement*, 185; Murray, *Song in a Weary Throat*, 359–368; MacLean, *Freedom Is Not Enough*, 76–113; "Negroes Launch a Rival Union for Low Paid Workers," *WP*, May 28, 1967; Cleveland Robinson to Martin Luther King, July 14, 1967, folder 3, box 17, CRP.

6. Rustin, *Down the Line*, 111; Carmichael and Hamilton, *Black Power*, 41; "New Rights Phase Is Seen by King," *NYT*, June 11, 1967; King, "Where Do We Go From Here?" (1967), reprinted in Washington, ed., *A Testament of Hope*, 557; Honey, *Going Down Jericho Road*.

7. Hansen, *The Dream*, 212; "A. Philip Randolph, 1889–1979," *NAN*, May 26, 1979; Jones, "Working-Class Hero."

8. Jones, "Working-Class Hero"; Coalition of Black Trade Unionists, "Mission Statement," http://www.cbtu.org/mission.html; MacLean, *Freedom Is Not Enough*, 300–335.

BIBLIOGRAPHY

NEWSPAPERS

AC	*Atlanta Constitution*
ADW	*Atlanta Daily World*
BAA	*Baltimore Afro-American*
CD	*Chicago Defender*
CST	*Chicago Sun-Times*
CT	*Chicago Tribune*
LAS	*Los Angeles Sentinel*
LAT	*Los Angeles Times*
NAN	*New York Amsterdam News*
NYT	*New York Times*
PC	*Pittsburgh Courier*
WAA	*Washington Afro-American*
WP	*Washington Post*
WSJ	*Wall Street Journal*

ARCHIVES

AAH	Merritt and Anna Arnold Hedgeman Collection, Schomburg Center for Research in Black Culture and History, New York Public Library
AFSCME ST	AFSCME Office of the Secretary-Treasurer: Government and Civic Employees Organizing Committee Records, Walter P. Reuther Library of Labor and Urban Affairs, Wayne State University
AFSCME PD	AFSCME Program Development Department Files, Series 1, Women's Files, Walter P. Reuther Library of Labor and Urban Affairs, Wayne State University
APC	Allderdice Pamplet Collection, Hoover Institution of War, Revolution and Peace, Stanford, Calif.
APR	A. Philip Randolph Papers, Manuscript Division, Library of Congress
BMP	B. F. McLaurin Papers, Schomburg Center for Research in Black Culture, New York Public Library

CHP	Charlton Heston Papers, Margaret Herrick Library, Los Angeles
CLUW	Papers of Betsy Wade on the Coalition of Labor Union Women, Robert F. Wagner Labor Archives, New York University
CRP	UAW District 65, Cleveland Robinson Papers, Robert F. Wagner Labor Archives, New York University
GWP	George Wiley Papers, Wisconsin State Historical Society, Madison
JHP	James Haughton Papers, Schomburg Center for Research in Black Culture, New York Public Library
JLP	Jay Lovestone Papers, Hoover Institution of War, Revolution and Peace, Stanford, Calif.
NAACP	National Association for the Advancement of Colored People Papers, Manuscript Division, Library of Congress
NCNW	National Council of Negro Women Records, National Archives of Black Women's History, Washington, D.C.
NRR	National Republic Records, Hoover Institution of War, Revolution and Peace, Stanford, Calif.
NUL	Records of the National Urban League, Manuscript Division, Library of Congress
PPP	Pathfinder Press Papers, Hoover Institution of War, Revolution and Peace, Stanford, Calif.
RLG	RLG Photo Collection, Robert F. Wagner Labor Archives, New York University
RPP	Richard Parish Papers, Schomburg Center for Research in Black Culture, New York Public Library
RPPM	Richard Parish Papers [Additions], Microfilm Edition, published in cooperation with the Schomburg Center for Research in Black Culture, Manuscripts, Archives and Rare Books Division, The New York Public Library, Astor, Lenox, and Tilden Foundations
WHSP	Wisconsin State Historical Society Pamphlet Collection, Madison

BOOKS AND ARTICLES

Abernathy, Ralph David. *And the Walls Came Tumbling Down: An Autobiography*. New York: Harper and Row, 1989.

———. "Natural History of a Social Movement: The Montgomery Improvement Association." In David J. Garrow, ed., *The Walking City: The Montgomery Bus Boycott, 1955–1956*. Brooklyn: Carlson Publishing, 1989.

Anderson, Jervis. *A. Philip Randolph: A Biographical Portrait*. New York: Harcourt Brace Jovanovich, 1972.

Arnesen, Eric. *Brotherhoods of Color: Black Railroad Workers and the Struggle for Equality*. Cambridge: Harvard University Press, 2001.

———. "No 'Graver Danger': Black Anticommunism, the Communist Party, and the Race Question." *Labor: Studies in Working Class History of the Americas* 3, no. 4 (2006), 13–57.

Azaransky, Sarah. *The Dream Is Freedom: Pauli Murray and American Democratic Faith.* New York: Oxford University Press, 2011.

Barber, Lucy G. *Marching on Washington: The Forging of an American Political Tradition.* Berkeley: University of California Press, 2002.

Bates, Beth Tomkins. *Pullman Porters and the Rise of Protest Politics in Black America, 1925–1945.* Chapel Hill: University of North Carolina Press, 2001.

Battle, Robert, III, and Horace Sheffield, "Trade Union Leadership Council: Experiment in Community Action." *New University Thought* 3 (September/October 1963), 34–40.

Bennett, Lerone, Jr. "Protest Threat Forced President Roosevelt's Hand." *Ebony* 32, no. 4 (February 1977), 128–136.

Biondi, Martha. *To Stand and Fight: The Struggle for Civil Rights in Postwar New York City.* Cambridge: Harvard University Press, 2003.

Birnbaum, Jonathan, and Clarence Taylor, eds. *Civil Rights since 1787: A Reader in the Black Struggle.* New York: New York University Press, 2000.

Boyle, Kevin. *The UAW and the Heyday of American Liberalism, 1945–1968.* Ithaca: Cornell University Press, 1998.

Brauer, Carl. "Kennedy, Johnson, and the War on Poverty." *Journal of American History* (June 1982), 98–119.

Breitman, George, ed. *Malcolm X Speaks: Selected Speeches and Statements.* New York: Merit Publishers, 1965.

Burks, Mary Fair. "Trailblazers: Women in the Montgomery Bus Boycott." In Vicki L. Crawford, Jacqueline Anne Rouse, and Barbara Woods, eds., *Women in the Civil Rights Movement: Trailblazers & Torchbearers, 1941–1965.* Bloomington: Indiana University Press, 1990, 71–83.

Burns, Stewart, ed. *Daybreak of Freedom: The Montgomery Bus Boycott.* Chapel Hill: University of North Carolina Press, 1997.

Carmichael, Stokely, and Charles Hamilton. *Black Power: The Politics of Liberation in America.* New York: Vintage Books, 1967.

Caro, Robert A. *The Passage of Power.* New York: Alfred A. Knopf, 2012.

Carson, Clayborne. *In Struggle: SNCC and the Black Awakening of the 1960s.* Cambridge: Harvard University Press, 1981.

Cayton, Horace R., and George S. Mitchell. *Black Workers and the New Unions.* Chapel Hill: University of North Carolina Press, 1939.

Chafe, William H. *Civilities and Civil Rights: Greensboro, North Carolina, and the Black Struggle for Freedom.* New York: Oxford University Press, 1980.

Chateauvert, Melinda. *Marching Together: Women of the Brotherhood of Sleeping Car Porters.* Urbana: University of Illinois Press, 1998.

Chen, Anthony S. *The Fifth Freedom: Jobs, Politics, and Civil Rights in the United States, 1941–1972.* Princeton: Princeton University Press, 2009.

Cobble, Dorothy Sue. *The Other Women's Movement: Workplace Justice and Social Rights in Modern America.* Princeton: Princeton University Press, 2004.

Cohen, Lizbeth. *Making a New Deal: Industrial Workers in Chicago, 1919–1939.* New York: Cambridge University Press, 2008.

Collier-Thomas, Bettye, and V. P. Franklin, eds. *Sisters in the Struggle: African American*

Women in the Civil Rights–Black Power Movements. New York: New York University Press, 2001.

Crespino, Joseph. *In Search of Another Country: Mississippi and the Conservative Counterrevolution.* Princeton: Princeton University Press, 2007.

D'Emilio, John. *Lost Prophet: The Life and Times of Bayard Rustin.* New York: Free Press, 2003.

Dittmer, John. *Local People: The Struggle for Civil Rights in Mississippi.* Champaign: University of Illinois Press, 1995.

Drake, St. Clair, and Horace Cayton. *Black Metropolis: A Study of Negro Life in a Northern City.* New York: Harcourt, Brace, 1945.

Dudziak, Mary L. *Cold War Civil Rights: Race and the Image of American Democracy.* Princeton: Princeton University Press, 2000.

Edgerton, John. *Speak Now against the Day: The Generation before the Civil Rights Movement in the South.* Chapel Hill: University of North Carolina Press, 1994.

Eskew, Glenn. *But for Birmingham: The Local and National Movements in the Civil Rights Struggle.* Chapel Hill: University of North Carolina Press, 1997.

Euchner, Charles. *Nobody Turn Me Around: A People's History of the 1963 March on Washington.* Boston: Beacon Press, 2010.

Fairclough, Adam. *To Redeem the Soul of America: The Southern Christian Leadership Conference and Martin Luther King, Jr.* Athens: University of Georgia Press, 1987.

Farmer, James. *Lay Bare the Heart: An Autobiography of the Civil Rights Movement.* New York: Penguin, 1986.

Feldstein, Ruth. "'I Wanted the Whole World to See'": Race, Gender, and the Construction of Motherhood in the Death of Emmett Till." In Joanne Meyerowitz, ed., *Not June Cleaver: Women and Gender in Postwar America, 1945–1960.* Philadelphia: Temple University Press, 1994, 263–303.

Fink, Leon. *Progressive Intellectuals and the Dilemmas of Democratic Commitment.* Cambridge: Harvard University Press, 1997.

Foley, Neil. *Quest for Equality: The Failed Promise of Black-Brown Solidarity.* Cambridge: Harvard University Press, 2010.

Foner, Eric. *The Story of American Freedom.* New York: W. W. Norton, 1998.

Foner, Philip S. *Organized Labor and the Black Worker.* New York: Prager, 1974.

Frazier, E. Franklin. *The Negro Family in the United States.* 1939. Revised and Abridged Edition with foreword by Nathan Glazer. Chicago: University of Chicago Press, 1966.

A Freedom Budget for All Americans: Budgeting Our Resources, 1966–1976, to Achieve "Freedom from Want." New York: A. Philip Randolph Institute, 1966.

Freeman, Joshua B. *Working-Class New York: Life and Labor since World War II.* New York: New Press, 2000.

Garfinkle, Herbert. *When Negroes March: The March on Washington Movement in the Organizational Politics for FEPC.* 1959. Reprint, with new preface by Lewis M. Killian. New York: Atheneum, 1969.

Garrow, David J. *Bearing the Cross: Martin Luther King, Jr., and the Southern Christian Leadership Conference.* New York: Vintage, 1986.

———, ed., *The Montgomery Bus Boycott and the Women Who Started It: The Memoir of Jo Anne Gibson Robinson*. Nashville: University of Tennessee Press, 1987.

———, ed. *The Walking City: The Montgomery Bus Boycott, 1955–1956*. Brooklyn: Carlson Publishers, 1989.

Gellman, Erik S. *Death Blow to Jim Crow: The National Negro Congress and the Rise of Militant Civil Rights*. Chapel Hill: University of North Carolina Press, 2012.

Gilmore, Glenda. *Defying Dixie: The Radical Roots of Civil Rights, 1919–1950*. New York: W. W. Norton, 2008.

Gilmore, Stephanie, ed. *Feminist Coalitions: Historical Perspectives on Second-Wave Feminism in the United States*. Champaign: University of Illinois Press, 2008.

Goodman, Walter. *The Committee: The Extraordinary Career of the House Committee on Un-American Activities*. New York: Farrar, Straus and Giroux, 1968.

Gregory, James N. *The Southern Diaspora: How the Great Migrations of Black and White Southerners Transformed America*. Chapel Hill: University of North Carolina Press, 2005.

Hall, Jacquelyn Dowd. "The Long Civil Rights Movement and the Political Uses of the Past." *Journal of American History* 91, no. 4 (2005), 1233–1263.

Halpern, Rick, and Roger Horowitz. *Meatpackers: An Oral History of Black Packinghouse Workers and Their Struggle for Racial and Economic Equality*. New York: Twayne Publishers, 1996.

Hamilton, Charles V. *Adam Clayton Powell, Jr.: The Political Biography of an American Dilemma*. New York: Atheneum, 1991.

Hamilton, Donna C., and Charles V. Hamilton. *The Dual Agenda: Race and Social Welfare Politics of Civil Rights Organizations*. New York: Columbia University Press, 1997.

Hansen, Drew. *The Dream: Martin Luther King, Jr. and the Speech that Inspired a Nation*. New York: HarperCollins, 2003.

Harris, William H. *Keeping the Faith: A. Philip Randolph, Milton P. Webster, and the Brotherhood of Sleeping Car Porters, 1925–37*. Urbana: University of Illinois Press, 1977.

Haskins, James. *The March on Washington*. New York: HarperCollins, 1993.

Hedgeman, Anna Arnold. *The Gift of Chaos: Decades of American Discontent*. New York: Oxford University Press, 1977.

———. "The Role of the Negro Woman." *Journal of Educational Sociology* 17, no. 8 (April 1944), 463–472.

———. *The Trumpet Sounds: A Memoir of Negro Leadership*. New York: Holt, Rinehart and Winston, 1964.

Hill, Herbert. "The Racial Practices of Organized Labor: The Contemporary Record." In Julius Jacobson, ed., *The Negro and the American Labor Movement*. New York: Anchor Books, 1968.

Honey, Michael K. *Going Down Jericho Road: The Memphis Strike, Martin Luther King's Last Campaign*. New York: W. W. Norton, 2007.

Horne, Gerald. *Black Liberation/Red Scare: Ben Davis and the Communist Party*. Newark: University of Delaware Press, 1994.

——. *Red Seas: Ferdinand Smith and Radical Black Sailors in the United States and Jamaica.* New York: New York University Press, 2005.

Horowitz, Roger. *"Negro and White, Unite and Fight!": A Social History of Industrial Unionism in Meatpacking, 1930–90.* Urbana: University of Illinois Press, 1997.

Houck, Davis W., and Matthew A. Grindy. *Emmett Till and the Mississippi Press.* Jackson: University Press of Mississippi, 2008.

Jackson, Thomas. *From Civil Rights to Human Rights: Martin Luther King, Jr., and the Struggle for Economic Justice.* Philadelphia: University of Pennsylvania Press, 2007.

Johnson, Lyndon. *Public Papers of the Presidents of the United States: Lyndon B. Johnson, 1965.* Vol. 2. Washington, D.C.: Government Printing Office, 1966.

Jones, Patrick. *Selma of the North: Civil Rights Insurgency in Milwaukee.* Cambridge: Harvard University Press, 2009.

Jones, William P. "'Nothing Special to Offer the Negro': Revisiting the 'Debsian View' of the Negro Question." *International Labor and Working-Class History*, no. 74 (2008), 212–224.

——. "'Simple Truths of Democracy': African Americans and Organized Labor in the Post-World War II South," in Eric Arnesen, ed., *The Black Worker: Race, Labor, and Civil Rights Since Emancipation* (Urbana: University of Illinois Press, 2007), 250–270.

——. *The Tribe of Black Ulysses: African American Lumber Workers in the Jim Crow South.* Urbana: University of Illinois Press, 2005.

——. "The Unknown Origins of the March on Washington: Civil Rights Politics and the Black Working Class." *Labor: Studies in Working Class History of the Americas* 7, no. 3 (2012), 33–52.

——. "Working Class Hero: The Forgotten Labor Roots of the Martin Luther King Holiday," *The Nation*, January 30, 2006, 23–24.

Joseph, Peniel E. *Waiting 'Till the Midnight Hour: A Narrative History of Black Power in America.* New York: Henry Holt, 2006.

Kapur, Suarshan. *Raising Up a Prophet: The African-American Encounter with Gandhi.* Boston: Beacon Press, 1992.

Katznelson, Ira. *When Affirmative Action Was White: An Untold History of Racial Inequality in Twentieth-Century America.* New York: W. W. Norton, 2005.

Kelley, Robin D. G. "'But a Local Phase of a World Problem': Black History's Global Vision, 1883–1950." *Journal of American History* 86, no. 3 (December 1999), 1045–1077.

Kersten, Andrew Edmund. *Race, Jobs, and the War: The FEPC in the Midwest, 1941–46.* Urbana: University of Illinois Press, 2000.

Kesselman, Louis Coleridge. *The Social Politics of FEPC: A Study in Reform Pressure Movements.* Chapel Hill: University of North Carolina Press, 1948.

Kessler-Harris, Alice. *In Pursuit of Equity: Women, Men, and the Quest for Economic Citizenship in Twentieth-Century America.* New York: Oxford University Press, 2001.

King, Martin Luther, Jr. *"All Labor Has Dignity."* Edited with introductions by Michael K. Honey. Boston: Beacon, 2011.

——. *The Papers of Martin Luther King, Jr.: Vol. 3: Birth of a New Age, December 1955–December 1956.* Edited by Clayborne Carson, Stewart Burns, Susan Carson, and Peter Holloran. Berkeley: University of California Press, 1997.

Kluger, Richard. *Simple Justice: The History of* Brown v. Board of Education *and Black America's Struggle for Equality.* New York: Vintage Books, 2004.

Lang, Clarence. *Grassroots at the Gateway: Class Politics and Black Freedom Struggle in St. Louis, 1936–75.* Ann Arbor: University of Michigan Press, 2009.

Lerner, Gerda, ed. *Black Women in White America: A Documentary History.* New York: Pantheon, 1972.

Lewis, John, with Michael D'Orso. *Walking with the Wind: A Memoir of the Movement.* New York: Harcourt, Brace, 1998.

Lichtenstein, Nelson. *The Most Dangerous Man in Detroit: Walter Reuther and the Fate of American Labor.* New York: Basic Books, 1995.

———. *State of the Union: A Century of American Labor.* Princeton: Princeton University Press, 2002.

Logan, Rayford W., ed. *What the Negro Wants.* Chapel Hill: University of North Carolina Press, 1944.

Lucas, Steven E., and Martin J. Medhurst. *Words of a Century: The Top 100 American Speeches, 1900–1999.* New York: Oxford University Press, 2008.

Mackenzie, G. Calvin, and Robert Weisbrot. *The Liberal Hour: Washington and the Politics of Change in the 1960s.* New York: Penguin, 2001.

MacLean, Nancy. *Freedom Is Not Enough: The Opening of the American Workplace.* Cambridge: Harvard University Press, 2006.

Marable, Manning. *Malcolm X: A Life of Reinvention.* New York: Viking, 2011.

———. *Race, Reform, and Rebellion: The Second Reconstruction in Black America, 1945–1980.* Jackson: University of Mississippi Press, 1991.

McCluskey, Audrey Thomas, and Elaine M. Smith. *Mary McLeod Bethune: Building a Better World: Essays and Selected Documents.* Bloomington: Indiana University Press, 1999.

McGuire, Danielle L. *At the Dark End of the Street: Black Women, Rape, and Resistance—A New History of the Civil Rights Movement from Rosa Parks to the Rise of Black Power.* New York: Alfred A. Knopf, 2010.

McMillen, Neil R. *Remaking Dixie: The Impact of World War II on the American South.* Jackson: University of Mississippi Press, 1997.

Meier, August, and Elliot Rudwick. *CORE: A Study in the Civil Rights Movement, 1942–1968.* Urbana: University of Illinois Press, 1975.

Morgan, Ted. *A Covert Life: Jay Lovestone: Communist, Anti-Communist, and Spymaster.* New York: Random House, 1999.

Morris, Aldon D. *The Origins of the Civil Rights Movement: Black Communities Organizing for Change.* New York: Free Press, 1984.

Murray, Pauli. *Song in a Weary Throat: An American Pilgrimage.* New York: HarperCollins, 1987.

Myrdal, Gunnar. *An American Dilemna: The Negro Problem and Modern Democracy.* New York: Harper & Brothers, 1944.

Nadle, Marlene. "The View from the Front of the Bus." *The Village Voice* 18, no. 46 (September 5, 1963), 5, 14.

Nelson, Bruce. "Organized Labor and the Struggle for Black Equality in Mobile during World War II." *Journal of American History* 80, no. 3 (December 1993), 952–988.

Ottley, Roi. *A New World A-Coming: Inside Black America*. Boston: Houghton Mifflin, 1943.

Parks, Rosa, with James Haskins. *Rosa Parks: My Story*. New York: Scholastic, 1992.

Perlstein, Rick. *Before the Storm: Barry Goldwater and the Unmaking of the American Consensus*. New York: Hill and Wang, 2001.

Perry, Jeffrey Babcock. *Hubert Harrison: The Voice of Harlem Radicalism, 1883–1918*. New York: Columbia University Press, 2009.

Pfeffer, Paula F. *A. Philip Randolph, Pioneer of the Civil Rights Movement*. Baton Rouge: Louisiana State University Press, 1990.

Raines, Howell. *My Soul Is Rested: Movement Days in the South Remembered*. New York: Penguin, 1988.

Ransby, Barbara. *Ella Baker and the Black Freedom Movement: A Radical Democratic Vision*. Chapel Hill: University of North Carolina Press, 2003.

Reed, Adolph, Jr. *Stirrings in the Jug: Black Politics in the Post-Segregation Era*. Minneapolis: University of Minnesota Press, 1999.

Reed, Christopher Robert. *The Chicago NAACP and the Rise of Black Professional Leadership, 1910–1966*. Bloomington: Indiana University Press, 1997.

Reed, Merl E. *Seedtime for the Modern Civil Rights Movement: The President's Committee on Fair Employment Practice, 1941–1946*. Baton Rouge: Louisiana State University Press, 1991.

Reed, Touré F. *Not Alms but Opportunity: The Urban League and the Politics of Racial Uplift, 1910–1950*. Chapel Hill: University of North Carolina Press, 2008.

Richards, Yevette. *Maida Springer: Pan-Africanist and International Labor Leader*. Pittsburgh: University of Pittsburgh Press, 2000.

Robinson, Jo Ann. *The Montgomery Bus Boycott and the Women Who Started It: The Memoir of Jo Ann Gibson Robinson*. Edited and with a foreword by David J. Garrow. Knoxville: University of Tennessee Press, 1987.

Ruchames, Louis. *Race, Jobs and Politics: The Story of FEPC*. New York: Columbia University Press, 1953.

Rustin, Bayard. *Down the Line: The Collected Works of Bayard Rustin*. Chicago: Quadrangle Books, 1971.

Sale, Kirkpatrick. *SDS: The Rise and Development of the Students for a Democratic Society*. New York: Random House, 1973.

Salvatore, Nick. *Singing in a Strange Land: C. L. Franklin, the Black Church, and the Transformation of America*. Urbana: University of Illinois Press, 2005.

Schraff, Anne. *Rosa Parks: Tired of Giving In*. Berkeley Heights, N.J.: Enslow Publishers, 2005.

Schultz, Kevin M. "The FEPC and the Legacy of the Labor-Based Civil Rights Movement of the 1940s." *Labor History* 49, no. 1 (February 2008), 71–92.

Self, Robert O. *American Babylon: Race and the Struggle for Postwar Oakland*. Princeton: Princeton University Press, 2003.

Sharpley-Whiting, T. Denean. *The Speech: Race and Barack Obama's "A More Perfect Union."* New York: Bloomsbury, 2009.

Sitkoff, Harvard. *A New Deal for Blacks: The Emergence of Civil Rights as a National Issue: The Depression Decade*. New York: Oxford University Press, 1978.

———. *The Struggle for Black Equality, 1954–1992.* New York: Hill and Wang, 1993.

Smith, J. Douglass. "'When Reason Collides with Prejudice': Armistead Lloyd Boothe and the Politics of Moderation." In Matthew Lassiter and Andrew B. Lewis., eds., *The Moderates' Dilemma: Massive Resistance to School Desegregation in Virginia.* Charlottesville: University of Virginia Press, 1998.

Spero, Sterling D., and Abram L. Harris. *The Black Worker: The Negro and the Labor Movement.* 1931. Reprint, New York: Atheneum, 1972.

Stein, Judith. *Running Steel, Running America: Race, Economic Policy, and the Decline of Liberalism.* Chapel Hill: University of North Carolina Press, 1998.

———. *The World of Marcus Garvey: Race and Class in Modern Society.* Baton Rouge: University of Louisiana Press, 1986.

Sugrue, Thomas J. *The Origins of the Urban Crisis: Race and Inequality in Postwar Detroit.* Princeton: Princeton University Press, 1996.

———. *Sweet Land of Liberty: The Forgotten Struggle for Civil Rights in the North.* New York: Random House, 2008.

Sullivan, Patricia. *Days of Hope: Race and Democracy in the New Deal Era.* Chapel Hill: University of North Carolina Press, 1996.

———. *Lift Every Voice: The NAACP and the Making of the Civil Rights Movement.* New York: New Press, 2009.

———. ed. *Freedom Writer: Virginia Foster Durr, Letters from the Civil Rights Years.* New York: Routledge, 2003.

Swados, Harvey. "Revolution on the March." *The Nation*, September 7, 1963, 104–107.

Taylor, Cynthia. *A. Philip Randolph: The Relgious Journey of an African American Labor Leader.* New York: New York University Press, 2005.

Terkel, Studs. *The Good War: An Oral History of World War II.* New York: New Press, 1984.

Terry, Ellen. *The Third Door: The Autobiography of an American Negro Woman.* New York: Negro Universities Press, 1971.

Theoharis, Jeanne F., and Komozi Woodard. *Freedom North: Black Freedom Struggles outside the South, 1940–1980.* New York: Palgrave Macmillan, 2003.

Thernstrom, Stephan, and Abigail Thernstrom. *America in Black and White: One Nation, Indivisible.* New York: Simon & Schuster, 1997.

Thornton, J. Mills, III. "Challenge and Response in the Montgomery Bus Boycott of 1955–1956." In David J. Garrow, ed., *The Walking City: The Montgomery Bus Boycott, 1955–1956.* Brooklyn: Carlson Publishing, 1989.

Turrini, Joseph. "Phooie on Louie: African American Detroit and the Election of Jerry Cavanagh." *Michigan History*, Nov./Dec. 1999, 11–17.

Tye, Larry. *Rising from the Rails: Pullman Porters and the Making of the Black Middle Class.* New York: Henry Holt, 2004.

Tyson, Timothy B. *Radio Free Dixie: Robert F. Williams and the Roots of Black Power.* Chapel Hill: University of North Carolina Press, 1999.

Van Deburg, William L. *New Day in Babylon: The Black Power Movement and American Culture, 1965–1975.* Chicago: University of Chicago Press, 1993.

Waldman, Michael, ed. *My Fellow Americans: The Most Important Speeches of America's Presidents.* Naperville, Ill: Sourcebooks, 2010.

Walker, Samuel. *In Defense of American Liberties: A History of the ACLU*. New York: Oxford University Press, 1990.

Ward, Brian, and Tony Badger, eds. *The Making of Martin Luther King and the Civil Rights Movement*. New York: New York University Press.

Washington, James M., ed. *A Testament of Hope: The Essential Writings and Speeches of Martin Luther King, Jr.* New York: HarperCollins, 1986.

White, Deborah Grey. *Too Heavy a Load: Black Women in Defense of Themselves, 1894–1994*. New York: W. W. Norton, 1999.

White, John. "Nixon Was the One: Edgar Daniel Nixon and the Montgomery Bus Boycott." In Ward and Badger, eds., *The Making of Martin Luther King and the Civil Rights Movement*. New York: New York University Press, 1996, 45–63.

Wilkins, Roy, with Tom Mathews. *Standing Fast: The Autobiography of Roy Wilkins*. New York: Penguin, 1982.

Williams, Juan. *Eyes on the Prize: America's Civil Rights Years, 1954–1965*. New York: Penguin, 1987.

Wilson, Sondra Kathryn, ed. *The Messenger Reader: Stories, Poetry, and Essays from The Messenger Magazine*. New York: Modern Library, 2000.

X, Malcolm. *The Autobiography of Malcolm X: As Told to Alex Haley*. New York: Ballantine Books, 1965.

Young, Jeffrey R. "Eisenhower's Federal Judges and Civil Rights Policy: A Republican 'Southern Strategy.'" *Georgia Historical Quarterly* 78, no. 3 (Fall 1994), 536–565.

Zieger, Robert H. *The CIO, 1935–1955*. Chapel Hill: University of North Carolina Press, 1995.

ACKNOWLEDGMENTS

Tis BOOK BEGAN as a presentation to the Scholars-in-Residence Seminar at the Schomburg Center for Research in Black Culture in 2005, and I'm tremendously grateful for the encouragement and insights of Colin Palmer and my fellows Valerie Babb, Daphne Brooks, Charles Nero, Sandhya Shukla, and Jacqueline Stewart. Over the years I have also benefited tremendously from the advice and criticism of hundreds of scholars and students. Among them are Eric Arnesen, Daniel Bender, Herman Bennett, Martha Biondi, Eileen Boris, Dorothy Sue Cobble, Jane Collins, Jefferson Cowie, Ajamu Dillahunt, Christina Ewig, Leon Fink, Bill Fletcher, Dana Frank, Erik Gellman, Jacquelyn Dowd Hall, Michael Honey, Jerma Jackson, Peniel Joseph, Steve Kantrowitz, Andrew Kersten, Clarence Lang, Nelson Lichtenstein, Nancy MacLean, Florencia Mallon, Steve McKay, Genna Rae McNeil, Jack Metzgar, Jennifer Morgan, Paul Ortiz, Adolph Reed, Touré Reed, Lou Roberts, Renee Romano, Steven Ross, Jennifer Scanlon, Judith Stein, Tom Sugrue, Tim Tyson, Deborah Grey White, and James Wolfinger. I also benefited from the comments of participants in the Wisconsin Jobs Now Coalition, the American History Workshop at New York University, the Newberry Library Labor History Seminar, the Long Civil Rights Movement Conference at the University of North Carolina at Chapel Hill, and the Labor Studies for the Twenty-First-Century Graduate Seminar at the University of Wisconsin, Madison; and anonymous readers at *Labor: Studies in Working-Class History of the Americas* and the *Journal of American History*.

I am deeply indebted to the staff at the Schomburg, particularly Diana Lachantere and Peter Hobbs, and to staff at the Robert F. Wagner Labor Archives (particularly Erika Gottfried), the Library of Congress, the Walter Reuther Library, the Wisconsin Historical Society, the Hoover Institution, and the Margaret Herrick Library. Visits to those archives were made possible by generous funding from the National Endowment for the Humanities, the American Council of Learned Societies, and the Graduate School, the College of Letters and Sciences, and the Institute for Research in the Humanities at the University of Wisconsin, Madison. I am also grateful to Sandra Dijkstra, Jill Marr, and Steve Forman, who saw promise in this project and helped bring it to print.

Finally, I could not have completed this book without the support and encouragement of my parents, brothers, and, particularly, the endlessly patient and supportive Ewigs: Gabriel, Sebastian, Marianne, and Christina. It was Christina who first encouraged me to write this book, commented on countless drafts, and listened patiently while I went on and on about my latest discoveries. After all that, she took over my domestic duties during the mad dash to meet my deadline. For that and so much more, this book is already hers.

INDEX